POETICA 35

From Russian with Love

Also by Daniel Weissbort

Poetry
IN AN EMERGENCY
SOUNDINGS
LEASEHOLDER
FATHERS
INSCRIPTION
NIETZSCHE'S ATTACHÉ CASE
WHAT WAS ALL THE FUSS ABOUT?
LETTERS TO TED

Translation
NIKOLAY ZABOLOTSKY: SELECTED POEMS

As Editor
POST-WAR RUSSIAN POETRY
THE POETRY OF SURVIVAL
TRANSLATING POETRY: THE DOUBLE LABYRINTH

DANIEL WEISSBORT

From Russian with Love

JOSEPH BRODSKY IN ENGLISH

Pages from a Journal
1996–97

ANVIL PRESS POETRY

Published in 2004
by Anvil Press Poetry Ltd
Neptune House 70 Royal Hill London SE10 8RF
www.anvilpresspoetry.com

ISBN 0 85646 342 6

This book is published
with financial assistance from
Arts Council England

A catalogue record for this book
is available from the British Library

Designed and set in Monotype Ehrhardt by Anvil
Printed at Alden Press Limited
Oxford and Northampton

Contents

Preface

JOSEPH BRODSKY DIED, in New York, on 28 January 1996. Asked by the editor of a Russian newspaper if I would write something about him, I continued writing, almost on a daily basis, mostly in my office at the University of Iowa. This lasted for a year or so. At first the writing was an attempt to comfort myself for the loss; then it turned into a kind of posthumous discussion with Joseph, in which I also examined our friendship, dating from the time of his expulsion from the Soviet Union. This friendship owed its existence, in the first place, to my interest in contemporary Russian poetry, as a translator, anthologist and editor, although we became closer, as the years in America went by.

The journal is also a kind of meditation on the poetics of translation, particularly of course of translation from Russian, with which I have been preoccupied since the mid-sixties. I concentrated on one particular poem, "May 24, 1980"; 1980 was an important year for me, as it was for Joseph. I returned to the poem repeatedly, not least because Joseph himself had commended it to me.

Excerpts from this hotchpotch, which was not in the first instance intended for publication, are presented here. In its original form it includes a number of exhaustive analyses of translations, as well as a great deal of self-interrogation and speculation. I am indebted to Tatiana Schenk for helping me to extract from this mass of verbiage what I hope is a readable text.

DANIEL WEISSBORT
London, March 2002

First Meeting: My Unreliable Memory

Monday, 29 January, 1996

A BOOK of poetry, in Russian, by "*Iosif Brodskii*", entitled Ostanovka v pustyne [A Halt in the Wilderness]; *publisher, the Chekhov Press, New York, 1970. An inscription, in Russian, "Danielu Vaisbortu", followed by, in English, "i.e. From Russian with Love, London 29–11–72". Then the author's ballooning signature. The occasion: Poetry International, a British Arts Council-funded event. Locale: the huge Festival Hall, where Brodsky was to give a reading. He was fresh from Russia – from "Russian", as he would put it. He had come here with W. H. Auden, travelling from Auden's home in Vienna, Brodsky's first "Halt in the Wilderness" of the West.*

"From Russia with Love." Joseph was boyishly tickled by this and used the formula quite often. Still, the irony, if one can call it that, is also rather melancholic, perhaps even nostalgic, although he was not nostalgic about the Soviet Union. As for the variant, "Russian" – if not simply a slip of the pen, it was perhaps attributable to my being a translator. The inscription, in that case, turned out to be apposite, since poetry translation was to remain a leitmotif of our friendship.

A glance at the actual dates, though, shows me that Brodsky became an involuntary exile in June 1972, so that by the end of November, when he and his mentor came to London, he had been in the West for at least five months and was scarcely "fresh" from Russia. In any case, Auden, who died the following year, on this occasion protected the young poet, bodily interposing himself between Brodsky and the curious, journalists, scholars or what have you.

Auden read at each of the annual Poetry Internationals, up to the time of his death, whether formally invited to or not. Brodsky, for his part, had been invited to the London Poetry International, as well as to the Spoleto Festival dei Due Mondi, in 1970, but at the time was not permitted to leave the Soviet Union. In any case Auden, evidently, did not ask anyone's permission, just informed the organizers that he was bringing Brodsky with him.

This must have been Joseph's first public reading in the West. Even the normally reserved British public was moved by the sight of the young poet and by his emotional if stentorian recitation. Joseph stood on the stage, textless, his hands hanging by his side, or thrust into his jacket pockets. His head thrown back, he declaimed the poems, staring into the air above his listeners, as if communing with himself rather than addressing an audience. From time to time, there was a catch in his voice, a gasp, a sob almost. It seemed as if only his being on stage, speaking the words he had written, held him together. He was his words, his poems. An English reader? There must have been. (There was: Robert Lowell.) *At one point, Joseph forgot a line. He stopped, looked down, screwed up his eyes in concentration, pounding his forehead, a gesture that became familiar to later audiences. The forgetting was palpable. Then the poem was found again. This, too, was palpable . . .*

Whether you understood Russian or not, you understood Brodsky that night. When he ended, his audience was as stunned as the poet on stage was now silent – inaccessible, emptied, a kind of simulacrum of himself. It was as if the air had been drained of sound. And the appropriate response would have been that – a soundlessness, in which you would hear only your own breathing, be aware only of your own physicality, your isolated self . . .

I strung these rather inchoate fragments together, only a few hours after learning of Joseph's death: he died on Sunday, 28 January, 1996. Irina Muravyov, a Russian fiction-writer living in Boston and editing *Bostonskoe vremya* [Boston Times], had phoned me with the news and asked me if I'd give her something for *Russkaya mysl* [Russian Thought]. I agreed, because it seemed better than refusing. And since I had to start somewhere, I started there, with my first memory of Joseph. Afterwards, I began reading or re-reading what he had written, *hearing* it, the poems in his own English, in the original Russian, the essays; and *Watermark*, his book about Venice, which I had not been able to get through before. Now, having read it once, I began it again without a pause . . . But then I stopped myself . . .

What of Auden, after all? With the exception of a few poems, his work had never appealed to me (Joseph's fierceness in his defence puzzled me at the time, although I didn't care to investigate). Even the splendour of "In Memory of W. B. Yeats". Why was this? At one time, I speculated that it might have something to do with my Jewishness and his Englishness, but being Jewish doesn't explain everything! I turned to Joseph's pieces on Auden, in his first essay collection *Less Than One* (1987): "On 'September 1, 1939' by W. H. Auden" and "To Please a Shadow". I wanted to learn more about this enthusiasm of his, his reverence for the man and the poet. Why? What?

Acute though its critical insights were, the first essay, a kind of *explication de texte*, did not hold my chronicler-with-a-bad-memory's attention. But "To Please a Shadow" did. Joseph tells of his arrival in Austria, his meeting with Auden, on 6 June, forty-eight hours after his departure from Leningrad, and his attendance at the Poetry International in London, a fortnight or so later (Poetry International '72 ran from 19–24 of June). It is not clear from this account whether he actually stayed with Auden in the village of Kirchstetten (not Vienna), though it *is* clear that Auden literally took him under his wing – like a "mother-hen", as Charles Osborne, Director of Poetry International, later (1980) put it: "Wystan fussed about him like a mother-hen. An unusually knowing and understanding mother-hen."[1] Actually, Joseph was met in Austria by the late Carl Proffer, Professor of Russian at the University of Michigan, Ann Arbor. Proffer secured a university appointment for Joseph as poet-in-residence. What at once struck me was that my dates had been wrong.

In the same essay, Joseph remarks how he could scarcely credit it that, back in 1939, an English poet had said: "Time . . . worships language" (actually, in the unrevised version of

Auden's poem on the death of Yeats). Across the cultural and generational divide he recognized a fellow language-traveller . . .

So, an invitation ("c/o W.H. Auden") arrived for Joseph to participate in the Poetry International. Obviously it wasn't that Auden simply "brought him along". True, they booked on the same flight, but Joseph by then was already finding his feet. Evidently, an aristocratic connection of his (Olga Razumovsky) persuaded British European Airways to give the two poets the VIP treatment. And, finally, the reading was in the Queen Elizabeth Hall, a capacious enough place, but not on the scale of the Festival Hall. Arguably, I suppose, my hyperboles convey something of the excitement that surrounded Joseph's appearance. Joseph himself, on the other hand, is virtually silent about it, referring only to Auden's performance (Auden, too, recited his poetry by heart). Indeed, were it not that Joseph had already mentioned being invited to take part, one would hardly know, from his account, that he did read. He also alludes to himself and Auden reading together "again" and in the same place, presumably at Poetry International '73, a year later. Joseph remarks of Auden's earlier reading: "If I ever wished for time to stop, it was then, inside that large dark room, on the south bank of the Thames." The fact is that Auden had been an inspiration to him for some years before they met . . .

Joseph's death has sent me to his words, which is why what was intended simply as a record of what I remember has already turned into something even more problematical. Sadly, though perhaps understandably, it has taken his death to make me read him attentively, as though his living presence was as much as I could cope with before. This sounds improbable or plain silly, but perhaps I was trying to read him through *himself*, almost reluctantly referring to the actual words on the actual page. So, now I am doubly obsessed by these same words – confusingly, there being so many, or rather their being so imbued with Joseph's life, yes, the very sound of *him* . . .

I had assumed that it was either there – that is, in the Festival Hall, or rather Queen Elizabeth Hall – or at a reception (though I have no actual memory of a reception) that Joseph inscribed my copy of *A Halt in the Wilderness*. However, the significance of the date, 29 November 1972, has just dawned on me. So convinced was I that he had inscribed the book at Poetry International, that I mentally shifted the latter's date to accommodate this misapprehension. It is now clear that he inscribed the book on some other occasion, probably somewhere else, perhaps even in my home. What does it matter? All the same, I'd like to know. But in any case, book or no book, we did meet at the Festival.

It is possible that Joseph had come across my name because of my association with Ted Hughes, with whom, in 1964–5, I had started the magazine *Modern Poetry in Translation*, publishing translations of East European poetry and to a lesser extent of poetry from Russia itself. Ted Hughes was one of the originators of Poetry International. I myself was trying to translate contemporary Russian poetry, concentrating on work that had appeared after Stalin's death in 1953, especially of the so-called "thaw" period. So, Joseph gave me the impression of being familiar with what I had done.

His trial, in Leningrad, in February 1964, and the sentence of five years' hard labour for "social parasitism", meaning not so much political dissent, as an unorthodox or unconventional style of life – in a totalitarian state, the distinction in any case was academic – had attracted international attention. The trial itself included some memorable exchanges between the accused and the court, which were bravely noted down at the time and widely reported in the West. Perhaps the most notorious example:

JUDGE: Who recognized you as a poet? Who enrolled you in the ranks of poets?
BRODSKY: No one. And who enrolled me in the ranks of humanity?
JUDGE: And did you study this?
BRODSKY: This?

JUDGE: To become a poet. You have not tried to enter the university where they give instruction . . . where they study . . .

BRODSKY: I did not think . . . I did not think that this was a matter of instruction.

JUDGE: What is it then?

BRODSKY: I think that it is . . . from God.[2]

This still takes my breath away! God? His seriousness, sincerity is unmistakeable. No irony, not at that time. Or was he simply at a loss for words? Did he fall back in defiance – although the tone here suggests confusion rather than defiance – on the concept of God, anathema to the atheistic state, even in its milder post-Stalinist form? There is a certain helplessness, as though he'd no alternative but to plainly state what he believed . . .

Do what he might to deflect questions about the trial, Joseph could not prevent its becoming an ingredient in the legend constructed around him. ("Legend", I hear him exclaim, as he did once when questioned about Solzhenitsyn, "what legend?")[3] For me, to read was to translate; that is, I could not absorb what was on the page, without actually drafting a translation (as a child who is learning to read might have to mouth the words). In this manner, I had translated some poems of Brodsky, although he was not among *my* Russian poets. To some extent, this was due to my not having discovered him for myself, discovery being more than half the game for the talent-spotter in me. I would read poems that appealed to me as I tried to make sense of the texts; then I'd scribble rough translations of the marked texts, this process serving either to confirm my initial response or not. Brodsky was already celebrated, already being translated by a number of people, even if the American George Kline (Professor of Philosophy at Bryn Mawr) was still his principal translator. But it was not so much that I was reluctant to jump onto what might already be construed as a bandwagon, as that it did not interest me enough to do so. Brodsky's verse appeared in *Modern Poetry in Translation* only some years later, in 1977, when "Lagoon", a poem I had translated at the author's prompting, was reprinted in a feature on Russian émigré poetry.

I had also published a translation of "The Jewish Cemetery in Leningrad", the only one of his poems relating specifically to his Jewishness, and I was translating some early poems, sketches of boyhood friends: "From a School Anthology". In addition, I began a translation of a strange narrative poem, "Kholmy" (Hills), from *Ostanovka v pustyne*, the first (unauthorized) Russian-language collection of his work, published abroad. (My copy of this book has now vanished, and I fantasize that all this writing has dematerialized it!)

In general, though, my Russian was not up to the task of translating Brodsky's poetry and, apart from several arguably atypical autobiographical pieces, I was not particularly drawn to it either. It was too intellectual for me, too formal. What engaged me at the time was poetry that eschewed the Poetic, that unadornedly conveyed a determination to survive, what it took to remain human in a mass age and against the background of World War, Holocaust, and the violently repressive post-War régimes of the Soviet Bloc countries. But although the difference between Brodsky and the admired East European poets loomed large for me, it apparently did not for others, Roger Garfitt, for instance, who observed that the Russian poet perhaps benefited from the current interest in Eastern Europe.[4]

"Would you want to be judged by these?"

AT ANY RATE, I am fairly sure that it was at our first meeting, in June 1972, that Joseph referred to some translations I had made of the poetry of Natalya Gorbanevskaya. Since 1975, living in Paris, she had, astonishingly enough, been a civil rights activist in the Soviet Union and was the founder-editor of the underground journal *A Chronicle of Current Events*, which reported cases of persecution or abuse. In 1968, Gorbanevskaya took part in a protest demonstration in Red Square, against the Warsaw Pact invasion of Czechoslovakia, which put an end to the reform movement, known later as the Prague Spring. She refused to renounce or compromise her beliefs and was committed to a prison psychiatric hospital, with a diagnosis of schizophrenia. The book I had compiled, published by Carcanet Press in 1972, included poems translated by myself, a transcript of her trial, papers relating to her detention in the hospital, and an assessment by a British psychiatrist of her mental condition, based on the evidence available to us.

Gorbanevskaya's *poetry*, however, was not overtly political. In my introduction I called it "a poetry of pain, of separation, of isolation, of despair . . .". As with Brodsky's, this may not have been poetry that immediately appealed to me, but Gorbanevskaya's imagery, much of which I found mystifying, seemed closer to a core of passion or suffering, so that I was more able to identify with it, in spite of its strongly Christian flavour. (It is perhaps worth noting that Brodsky, too, was seen by many as a "deeply religious poet" (Garfitt again). Stephen Spender, in the first review of Brodsky's poetry in English translation[5] talks of Brodsky's "note" being "even in its irony, [. . .] pre-eminently that of the Old Testament, forced with a kind of ruthlessness upon the spectacle of Soviet planning." But, while I appreciated the opportunity of working with a poetry so different from my own and indeed from the Russian poetry to which I had previously been drawn, I also suspected that I did not have the language adequately to express the agony, even if as a reader I was responsive.

Anyway, as far as I can remember, we were lingering at the front of the Queen Elizabeth Hall auditorium, just below the stage, perhaps during an interval or at the end of that day's readings, when Brodsky said to me, apropos of the Gorbanevskaya versions (it surprised me that he was aware of them): "If you were to die tomorrow, would you want to be judged by these translations?"

It seems unlikely that this was a simple inquiry! I must have been somewhat shocked. Not only because we had just met, but also because his remark echoed, if more forcefully than I would have put it myself, my own doubts and anxieties about the whole business of poetry translation, as well as about my Gorbanevskaya versions. Although I had read the account of her trial and, in addition to translating the poetry, had also written about her "ordeal", I doubt whether I had much grasp of its significance. I imagine that Joseph was trying to get across the gravity of a situation when art, in a way, was all you had; that is, he was not merely suggesting that my translations left much to be desired. Though I took what he said as a comment on the translations, I may have received the other message too, since I did not respond as defensively as might have been expected.

In any case, he was probably right! Even if a practical purpose had been served by the Gorbanevskaya book's drawing attention to Soviet abuses of psychiatric procedures, my translations were largely the product of a kind of optimism. That they had their moments was perhaps the best that could be said of them. Still, I realized that, though possibly wrong-headed, Joseph was not being unkind or malicious. Certainly he was not mealy-mouthed, but this helped me begin to see that the context was larger than one simply of translation, the translation of words. My first exchange with Brodsky, thus, took the form of a kind of summons to greater personal commitment. What such a commitment might entail, in his view, was not immediately clear to me, although I already suspected that, prosodically at least, it had to do with formal imitation, the point being that this had a moral dimension.

At the time, I did not know about his friendship with Gorbanevskaya. Since Gorbanevskaya and Brodsky, as artists, were separately compartmented in *my* mind, it did not occur to me that *they* might have an actual connection with one another.

So, this is how I came briefly to question the strength of my own dedication. As a translator, I was more of an editor, a talent-scout, than a painstaking re-writer. Thus, although I now believe that I *heard* what he was saying, I was not able to take action. I dare say that the investment in myself, as a translator of Russian poetry, already precluded that.

Reading in Iowa City, Iowa

SOME YEARS ago, Joseph came to Iowa City, the University of Iowa where I directed the Translation Workshop, to give a reading; I was to read the English translation. At the end, he was asked a number of (mostly loaded) questions, including one (alluded to earlier) about Solzhenitsyn. "And the legend which had been built around him?" His answer managed to be both artfully diplomatic and truthful: "Well, let's put it this way. I'm awfully proud that I'm writing in the same language as he does." (Note, again, how he expresses this sentiment in terms of language.) He continued, in his eccentrically pedagogical manner, forceful, even acerbic, but at the same time disarming, without any personal animus: "As for legend . . . you shouldn't worry or care about legend, you should read the work. And what kind of legend? He has his biography . . . and he has his words."[6] For Joseph a writer's words *were* his biography, literally!

On another visit to Iowa, in 1987, Joseph flew in at around noon and at once asked me what I was doing that day. I told him that I was scheduled to talk to an obligatory comparative literature class about translation. "Let's do it together", he said. Consequently I entered the classroom, with its small contingent of graduate students, accompanied by that year's Nobel Laureate.

Joseph indicated that he would just listen, but soon he was engaging me in a dialogue, except it was more monologue than dialogue. Finally, he was directly answering questions put to him by the energized students. I wish I could remember what was said, but, alas, even the gist of it escapes me now. I did not debate with him, even though our views on the translation of verse form differed radically. Instead, I believe that I nudged him a little, trying – not very sincerely or hopefully, though perhaps in a spirit of hospitality and camaraderie – to find common ground. After the class, I walked back with him to his hotel, as he said he wanted to rest before the reading. On the way, the conversation, at my instigation, turned to Zbigniew Herbert, the Polish poet so greatly admired by Milosz and, I presumed, by Brodsky, and indeed translated by the former into English and by the latter into Russian. Arguably, Herbert was the pre-eminent European poet of his remarkable generation. He was living in Paris and apparently was not in good health. "Why hasn't Zbigniew been awarded the Nobel Prize? Can't something be done about it", I blurted out – recklessly, tactlessly, presumptuously. The subtext was: Surely you, Joseph Brodsky, could use your influence, etc. Joseph came to a standstill: "Of course, he should have it. But nobody knows how that happens. It's a kind of accident." He locked eyes with me. "You're looking at an accident right now!" This was not false modesty on his part, but doubtless he was being more than a little disingenuous. Nevertheless, I believe that, at a certain level, he did think of his laureateship as a kind of accident. Paradoxically, while he aimed as high as may be, he was not in the *business* of rivalling or challenging the great. They remained, in a sense, beyond him, this perception of destiny and of a hierarchy surely being among his saving graces.

In a far deeper sense, though, they were not in the least beyond him, nor was he uncompetitive, but it did not (nor could it) suit his public or even private persona to display this.

Brodsky certainly considered himself to be – and it is increasingly clear that he was – in the grand line that included Anna Akhmatova, Boris Pasternak, Osip Mandelstam and Marina Tsvetayeva. Even I sensed this, despite my ambivalence about his poetry. Indeed, the continuity embodied in his work accounts, in part, for my uncertainty: I have tended to rebel against *grand* traditions. But perhaps this is to exaggerate. At times I hear the music, at other times the man, even if, as a rule, I do not hear them both together . . .

But take, for instance, this (the last three stanzas of "Nature Morte" in George Kline's splendid version in the Penguin *Selected Poems*):

Mary now speaks to Christ:
"Are you my son? – or God?
You are nailed to the cross.
Where lies my homeward road?

How can I close my eyes,
uncertain and afraid?
Are you dead? – or alive?
Are you my son? – or God?

Christ speaks to her in turn:
"Whether dead or alive,
Woman, it's all the same –
son or God, I am thine."

It is true that, as I listen to or read the English, I hear the Russian too, in Joseph's rendition. I even *see* Joseph, his hands straining the pockets of his jacket, his jaw jutting, as though his eye had just been caught by something and he were staring at it, scrutinizing it, while continuing to mouth the poem, almost absent-mindedly, that is, while the poem continues to be mouthed by him. His voice rises symphonically: *Syn ili Bog* (Son or God), "God" already (oddly?) on the turn towards an abrupt descent; and then the pause and a resonant drop, a full octave: *Ya tvoi* (I am thine). And the poet, with an almost embarrassed or reluctant nod, and a quick, pained smile, departs his poem.

Cats

IT'S THE DAY after Joseph's death, 29 January, 1996. Jill, my ex-wife, phones from London. She has just heard and is desolate. "He was family", she almost wails. Yes, he visited us quite often, the red-brick Victorian mansion in West Hampstead (it must have been the early seventies). Anyway, the children were little at the time. I can summon up an image of Joseph and Véronique Schiltz standing in the garden. The words are gone, but I still see them there and I can imagine him smiling, almost apologetically, and chuckling or chortling, that sharp intake of breath, like a sob, or as if he were choking. Is he gazing at our white cat Osgood (a female, incidentally, inherited along with her name from a neighbour)?

Joseph talked to cats. The dust-jacket of his second essay collection *On Grief and Reason* shows him holding what looks like a grey and white cat, a fairly ordinary sort of cat really, except that no cat is ordinary. (No doubt the cat is Mississippi, who survived his master.) His hand rests tenderly, protectively on its ruff, while its paw rests proprietorially on his sleeve, as it peers myopically at the ground, over the ledge of his cradling arm. Joseph, for his part, is looking stolidly, almost defiantly at the camera, barely smiling, if he's smiling at all. There is a family resemblance between Joseph and the cat, their expression being alike . . .

If he suspected or feared that he had caused offence or hurt, Joseph would sometimes draw his fingernails down your arm and actually meow. There is a sketch by him,[7] dating from the 1960s, of a cat perched on what looks like an old-fashioned music stool, extending one paw towards a samovar that stands on the table. The paw again! Jill reminds me that Joseph sometimes ended his letters with a drawing of a cat, a sort of postscript. I have no memory of this and almost all the letters from Joseph that survived are in my archives in King's College London, while at this time of writing I am in the United States. But, in any case, I dare say that those very early letters did not survive.

How he took, for instance, to my friend Lucas Myers's fat old cat, Perdita. Joseph never failed to ask after her, even when Lucas had left New York City and moved to the West coast. The more "ordinary" the cat, the more he liked it, it seemed. But, then, I've already said, I think, that no cat is ordinary. So, was Osgood there with us? I think she must have been. Osgood was certainly not ordinary, but Joseph – I am convinced of this, although I still cannot actually picture him doing it – talked to her.

A mutual friend told me that, after Joseph's death, she was walking around in Venice, when a large ginger cat approached her and began to rub itself against her leg. She looked down and it looked up. She felt that it wanted to tell her something and recognized Joseph!

And here's a passage I just came across in *Watermark*, Joseph's essay about himself and / in Venice, a city to which he returned regularly at Christmas:

> *I walked a quarter of a mile along the Fondamente Nuove, a small moving dot in that gigantic watercolour, and then turned right by the hospital of Giovanni e Paolo. The day was warm, sunny, the sky blue, all lovely. And with my back to the Fondamente and San Michele, hugging the wall of the hospital, almost rubbing it with my left shoulder and squinting at the sun, I suddenly felt: I am a cat. A cat that has just had fish. Had anyone addressed me at that moment, I would have meowed. I was absolutely, animally happy. Twelve hours later, of course, having landed in New York, I hit the worst possible mess in my life – or the one that appeared that way at the time. Yet the cat in me lingered; had it not been for that cat, I'd be climbing the walls now in some expensive institution.*[8]

The cat in me lingered. As mentioned, he did meow, especially if he surmised that he had caused offence.

"A Part of Speech": Misunderstandings

IT WAS 1979 – I've extracted that date from my CV; it has its uses – and the occasion was the International Poetry Festival (not the Poetry International) in Cambridge, England. I was to read the English versions of Joseph's poems and was pleased to learn that the reading would include either the whole or a section of "A Part of Speech", as I had translated that sequence, published the translation in *Poetry* and even been awarded a prize for it. This was my one substantial Brodsky translation and it had been undertaken at his bidding – he said he thought the sequence would appeal to me, which it did, certainly far more than any of his other poems – and to some extent, in consultation with him. In short, my version was, I thought, virtually an "official" one. I welcomed the opportunity to read it, being more than a little proud of having preserved much of the form.

The readings took place in a rather ramshackle hall, and I was waiting, in the semi-darkness, by the makeshift rostrum, holding my translation – or perhaps I was actually holding the March 1978 issue of *Poetry*, with my translation in it. Joseph sidled up to me, and with an uncertain smile, stretched out his hand and slowly scratched my sleeve, meowing "Danny, don't be angry" and simultaneously handing me a wad of sheets with a new version of "A Part of Speech". My response may not have been very gracious, but at the same time, the following despairing words formed in my head, my fingertips twitching, as I typed rather than spoke them: "Wait a moment! I've no right to feel this way. It's his poem. After all, I'm *just* a translator . . ." So, not only did I *feel* martyred; I also played the martyr. I suppose Joseph tried to explain. If so, it only made matters worse, because in so doing he informed me that my versions were metrically weak. Or, to be more precise, that my line was too short. It is true that my line was shorter than his, but I had convinced myself that this was because I would not resort to padding. What was being imparted now was that actually I lacked the craft or resourcefulness to lengthen the line *without* padding. Of course, I still clung to the belief that I was right and he was wrong. But, in any case, I was powerless. Imagining, I suppose, that he was being tactful – or simply being truthful – Joseph then explained that he was now putting the book together and that all he wanted to achieve was a certain consistency in the metre, even though nobody – a despairing note was sounded here – would notice!

A Part of Speech was published in 1980. I didn't know whether the title had already been decided upon at the time of the Cambridge Festival. (He had simply preserved the Russian title of a collection, published in 1977.) I had assumed that when he proposed I try my hand at the sequence, it was because these poems were untypical of his work, more personal, more likely to appeal to me, given the nature of my own work. I treated quite casually his suggestion that I try my hand at the poem, although, as stated, I also made a considerable effort to achieve some formal mimesis, at least as regards rhyme. I did not make commensurate efforts to preserve the metre or rhythm of the poem. Anyway, Joseph told me that he had reworked or re-translated the poems with the help in particular of Derek Walcott. Furthermore, I did not even have the opportunity of glancing at the new version, before being asked to read it to the large audience in Cambridge, whereas I had doubtless rehearsed my own version. It angered and humiliated me to hear echoes of my own work, this being about all I did hear. Did I speak to Joseph (or anyone else) afterwards? I was demoralized. And I also despised myself for not refusing to read this bowdlerized text.

There followed a number of accusatory letters from me, some of which Joseph attempted to answer, humbling himself, while not admitting fault. And this was precisely what I was trying to get him to admit. Even if he had decided, as was his right, not to use my translation, he ought to have consulted me before cannibalizing it. It is hard to say what satisfaction such an admission might have afforded me, but in any case I never received it.

I had been hasty. In my confusion, I had not examined the translation closely, but had simply formed a general impression.

It became clear to me later that he had, in fact, cannibalized it less than I had supposed, when I noted some resemblances between old and new. After a flurry of letters, silence descended for quite a while. This was finally broken by Joseph, and the dispute, if such a one-sided affair can be called a dispute, came to an end. There was a Joseph-card, possibly from Rome, of an ancient mosaic of fighting cocks. Life's too short, he wrote – or words to that effect. But I think it was the rooster that did it. I had forgiven him anyway, I realized then, but the postcard made it possible for me to forgive myself too. Still, scars remained.

It is true that I was the one with the wounded ego. Joseph, however, had to (or at least did) put up with my tantrums, recriminations, general offensiveness. I would say that he did this almost tenderly, although he was unshaken in his beliefs.

"Tenderly Yours"

IT IS HIS *tenderness*, in particular, that I recall. He verbalized it, without embarrassment, making frequent use of the word itself, which, *to say the least* (also a favourite Brodskyan expression), is not much employed in Anglo-Saxon male society. And it is tenderness I feel for him now. He ended his letters with a "kisses, kisses" or "tenderly yours", and even on the phone, instead of good-bye, there'd be a brisk yet, yes, tender: "kisses, kisses!" And then he'd wait, never in a hurry to break off. (This may sound sentimental, but maybe he was for ever saying goodbye for the last time.) Although by many whose paths he crossed he is remembered as abrasive, pugnacious, he displayed an unostentatious strength, a *tender* strength.

Here was something I had not noted: his strength or courage. Reading recently about his time in the Arkhangelsk Region (he was sentenced to five years, in 1964, but released after twenty months of exile), I at first found it hard to reconcile the modest, rumpled, even somewhat disreputable if cocky figure with the man of principle, of valour. But then I understood that it was this courage that *informed* his personality. It was so much a part of him that one took it for granted. At least, I had so taken it. As if I were too close to see what was evident to others, even if fate had been immeasurably kinder to me than to him. It was something of a mystery to me that I could not love the poems as I did the man. Indeed, the poetry almost got in the way, as if I was jealous of his art, as of a rival for his affection! The poetry, even if he identified fully with it, represented his mission rather than himself, having as much to do with the language or with history . . .

I suppose I should make a distinction between the two. His preoccupation with language – Russian, of course, but also English, which he was in the process of idiosyncratically making his own – I shared. It was the glare of the power-and-the-glory, from which I shielded myself.

Yes, I have begun to realize, after his death, that courage was the catalyst . . .

Clichés are knocking at the door! It is rather that there was a sudden awareness of the whole man, whereas I'd seen only pieces before. The loss was overwhelming! I suppose that is why I am writing now, trying to keep the awareness intact, not allowing it to fade prematurely. As if it would? Still, I want my quotidian self, which has no option but to negotiate with the world, to absorb it. It? Joseph.

Our paths crossed at festivals and conferences. For instance, in 1979, at the University of Maryland, a "Symposium of Literary Translation and Ethnic Community" [*sic*!], we were on a panel. The panellists sat in a row, on the platform, at a long table. A "dialogue" between translators and translatees was supposed to take place . . .

Joseph and I meet by chance at breakfast. A vast self-service canteen. Joseph asks the woman behind the counter if she has any stronger coffee. She doesn't understand. He capitulates: "OK, make it regular." We go to a table, and he talks briefly about so-called "regular" American coffee. (I've come rather to like this innocuous beverage, which looks but doesn't really taste like coffee.) He lights a cigarette – you could still smoke on campuses then – and presses his hand to his chest, grimacing. A few moments later he lights up again . . .

He underwent his first heart surgery in December 1978. I felt the closeness of his death, certainly. He lived with it every day. So, why didn't he stop smoking? When I was diagnosed with cancer of the mouth, in 1982, I at once quit smoking, far too frightened not to. For Joseph, not quitting was even more suicidal. Was it his courage, paradoxically, that allowed him to continue smoking? Or perhaps, he did not love himself enough, did not value his own life enough. More precisely, his *individual* life? Or perhaps he just *enjoyed* living dangerously? To live meant to live dangerously.

Having it All: His Own Idiolect

JOSEPH, EVER the good host, is waiting, not inside but outside the restaurant. It's a Chinese dumpling house. Joseph adores dumplings, which are surely extremely bad for him. They reminded him, I'm told, of *pelmeni*, a Russian version of the same thing. It is late, due to the delayed arrival of Irina Muravyov and myself, and the cavernous restaurant is almost empty. The three of us sit at a table for eight. Joseph, at home, makes the selection from the passing trollies. I quite like dumplings, but they are not among my favourite delicacies. Irina politely tries those chosen for her by Joseph, who is discoursing on various, mostly literary, topics. Do I remember? Of course not! Except that the question of the Yevtushenko anthology of twentieth-century Russian poetry, soon to be published by Doubleday, comes up.[9]

Incidentally, since Joseph had dictated what poems went into the Doubleday anthology, and since he also marked some of the same poems for me in *To Urania* (1988) – the last of his non-posthumous collections in English – it would be reasonable to assume that the Doubleday selection represents the "essential" Brodsky in English, at least as he saw it: "Six Years Later", translated by Richard Wilbur; "Nature Morte", translated by George Kline; "Eclogue IV: Winter", translated by the author; "The Hawk's Cry in Autumn", translated by Alan Myers and the author; "Sextet", translated by the author; "May 24, 1980", translated by the author; "Letters from the Ming Dynasty", translated by Derek Walcott. Both Wilbur and Walcott presumably worked from literal versions, collaborating with the author himself. Walcott actually said that the translation attributed to him was as much Joseph's.[10]

What of "May 24, 1980"? It is the first poem in *To Urania*. Joseph ticked it in my copy of the book. He seemed particularly proud of it, proud as well of what he had managed to achieve as a translator. Presumably he believed he'd successfully demonstrated that rhetorically mimetic translation between Russian and English *was* possible. He must have been convinced that I would see this, when he urged me to read the poem. It was not his intention to crow over me or to humiliate me, but simply to set me on the right path.

I can visualize him marking the contents list of my copy of *To Urania,* even if I have no actual memory of the occasion, let alone of the time. But he seemed not to be alluding to his own work, his own success, as he saw it.

Does this make sense? Or does it, rather, smack of special pleading? As must be apparent, I am now inclined to think that he was probably more right than wrong about translation. I say this, in spite, for instance, of Yves Bonnefoy's magisterial essay, criticizing (rather late in the day) Brodsky's 1974 attack on the free-verse translation by Clarence Brown and W. S. Merwin of Mandelstam's poetry.[11] In this splenetically eloquent review, Brodsky asserted that regular or classical prosody could not, or rather should not be translated into *vers libre*. His actual words were: "Russian poetry has set an example of moral purity and firmness which to no small degree has been reflected in the preservation of so-called classical forms."[12] He further made the accusation that: "What was done to Mandelstam by Merwin is a product of profound moral and cultural ignorance". In view of the paramount importance of form for him, one can see why he might talk about "cultural" ignorance. But why "moral" ignorance? Joseph revered language, lived by it. In fact, this was no over-reaction, although it was less diplomatically put than it might have been.

Even if his essay was published in a specialist journal of limited circulation, not so visible as the *New York Review of Books*, Bonnefoy is after all a premier French poet. In any case, the article cheered me and I was disposed to agree with most of it. Brodsky simply could not appreciate what was entailed in translating verse form into English. For one thing, as I was fond of repeating, he could not really *hear* the sounds. Furthermore, rhyme and assonance were more abundant in Russian, largely due to the inflectedness of the language and the strong accent or stress, never more than one beat per multisyllabic word. Actually, I thought it unreasonable of him to accept slant-rhyme in Russian, but to be so reluctant (at least at that time) to countenance it in English. Rhymes being more plentiful in Russian, they did not call as much attention to themselves, and so were more readily assimilable. When an English translator sought faithfully to reproduce rhyme and metre, he was obliged to make extensive semantic and syntactical adjustments. Granted, formal mimesis *was* possible, but, while I did not much care for Robert Lowell's radically individualistic approach to translation, I concurred with what he had to say in the introduction to his *Imitations* (1962), when he called translators who followed the path of formal mimesis, "taxidermists not poets [whose] poems are likely to be stuffed birds". The trouble with Brodsky was that he simply wouldn't understand that he was asking for the impossible, for the Russian text to be *imported* into English wholesale, English having to be Russianized to accommodate it. It followed that English then ceased to be English. That this was to be avoided at all costs seems obvious.

Now I am not so sure! What did I understand by "English"? Was I so certain about my own English? It is perhaps partly because I myself was uncertain that I so adamantly opposed Brodsky. Had I followed my deeper (as I now think) inclinations, I might have offered him some encouragement and support; at the very least, I'd have given him a hearing.

The poet Lachlan Mackinnon, in his *Independent* obituary of Brodsky[13], refers to Joseph's English poems or translations of his own work: "Those who complained about apparent technical deficiencies too easily forgot [. . .] that Brodsky was engaged in creating a new idiolect, precisely the half-English of a deracinated man. From his mentor Auden he learnt to rummage in the more arcane areas of English vocabulary, and the resulting style is, while sometimes disconcerting, usually self consistent and achieved." My only objection here is to Mackinnon's characterization of this "idiolect" as "half-English", since it is neither half, nor quarter, but simply itself. But is this just more special pleading from another person who has fallen under Brodsky's spell? I might have thought so earlier, though I no longer do. Nevertheless, it still has to be said that many of Brodsky's early attempts to impose Russian on English, or at least, since he'd not have put it that way, to bring the two closer together, in effect to create "a new idiolect", might have worked phonetically, but were shaky from a syntactical and semantic point of view. Unless it is just that they took more getting used to than readers were willing to allow them.

But it's not just Mackinnon. Michael Hofmann writes, in his review of *So Forth* and *On Grief and Reason*:[14]

> *The reluctance to accept Brodsky in English – in particular, in his own English – always seemed rather churlish to me: the successive books [. . .] each have their distinct quality of language, moving from quite smooth to pretty rough [. . .]*
>
> *I think Brodsky was good enough to play by two sets of rules. Even in English, his poems have irresistible verbal authority, [. . .] because I think he wrote in such a way as to draw on American and Russian at the same time. There is something binaral or bipolar about the writing, an uncomplicated and perfectly natural contract with the reader, whereby on the one hand Brodsky can write [. . .] the most arrant and wilfully provocative translationese, and yet the reader continues to endow it with the status of an original, fully intended and supervised in every detail [. . .] We read it, as it were, both with the English and Russian parts of our English minds [. . .]*
>
> *Undoubtedly Brodsky's tolerance for eccentric English grew with time, as his desire to conform, perhaps, grew less, but even that I think has less to do with translation than authorship.*

I quote at length because, to my knowledge, there is very little in the commentaries on Brodsky that addresses this crucial question in so open-minded a way. I'd be tempted to say that Hofmann is able to do so, because as a translator himself, with dual linguistic roots, he is also inevitably working in the borderland between languages, but Yugoslav-born Pulitzer

Prize-winner Charles Simic, also an experienced translator, in an otherwise sympathetic review of the *Collected Poems in English*,[15] takes a less positive view of Brodsky's Englishing of his own work.

George Steiner, whose *After Babel* (1975), preceded by his translator-emphasizing anthology *The Penguin Book of Modern Verse Translation* (1966), inaugurated the boom (if one can call it that) in the general area of what has come to be called Translation Studies, also illuminatingly raised the question of Brodsky's auto-translations, in a short review of *To Urania*.[16] He asks several questions that are extraordinarily difficult (perhaps impossible?) to answer:

> *In what way are these poems translations? [. . .] The composition of major verse via self-translation [. . .] is rare. To circumscribe the integral status of* To Urania *one would need to compare the Anglo-American with the Russian. How much has been lost and how salient are the differences in the music of meanings? Above all, are there points at which even a metamorphic craftsman of Brodsky's genius has to yield to "translationese", to uses of American English which are closer to the Russian source than they are to themselves?*
>
> *At those moments in Brodsky's poetry [. . .] there is in the lyric prodigality of invention more than an edge of strangeness, a flicker of the forced. How could it be otherwise for a great poet who [has had] to survive first political despotism and second the shadow-zone between tongues [. . .]*

Steiner is not the only one to note that Brodsky writes in American- rather than Anglo-English. In a letter to me, the British poet Alan Jenkins, for instance, remarked that, in his view, "the whole issue is distorted by talk of [Brodsky's] 'English', correct or otherwise – he wrote what for the most part he heard and spoke, which was American." As a fellow immigrant (in my case, part-immigrant) to America, I'd agree with this by and large. American informality (paradoxically, in view of his insistence on formal mimesis in translation) was probably more accommodating when it came to finding room for himself in English. The somewhat less distinct American pronunciation also may have helped Joseph in his search for English rhymes . . .

It is a question, I suppose, of where you begin or, as used to be said, where you are coming from. Hofmann, Steiner, Mark Strand, Walcott, Jenkins, and a few others come from one place (although it's hardly fair to lump them together); Craig Raine, Christopher Reid – both criticized Brodsky's English severely and I'll discuss these reviews in due course – and Michael Schmidt, for instance come from another. Schmidt's views (more circumspect than either Raine's or Reid's), as expressed in his piece on *A Part of Speech*, represent, I would say, what might be called the standard dismissive British approach, at least on the linguistic level (he is not dismissive of Brodsky the poet and thinker): "Exile has filled his ear with English. All the same he is his worst translator . . . Kline, in the 1973 selection, declared 'A Song to No Music' to be important but untranslatable. Brodsky and David Rigsbee expend much energy in the new book and prove Kline conclusively right." [17]

Interlude

I HAVE ARRIVED *in Moscow. I leave the station square and find myself in a picturesque, bustling quarter – at the same time, gemütlich. I understand that I am now in the "old city". This pleases me, even though I am also conscious of the fact that this quarter, the original city, is surrounded by huge buildings of the far larger new city. The crowd is mixed, locals and tourists. I am with Joseph. "Nice", I say. "It is, isn't it", he responds, with pride and enthusiasm. I ask: "This is in the vicinity of the station?" He looks at me enigmatically.*

Moscow! His city. He is back. But Moscow! Moscow. Still, the classical architecture is Petersburgian. And the drabness has vanished. Yes, tourism has certainly improved matters. Back. I am with Brodsky, back in Russia. Incognito, but how long before he is recognized. For the time being, though, and in this crowd, he can enjoy the anonymity, can experience the simple pleasure of Being Back. I want to ask him about it, but wonder how I myself happen to be here. Much must surely have happened for this to be possible. I have forgotten, whereas Joseph takes it for granted. I would like an explanation, but it would be indiscrete to ask for one. Perhaps we have only temporarily shaken off his entourage, his escort.

Such a large and confusing crowd! Now he is walking in front of me, outdistancing me, but apparently confident I'll catch up. Or he doesn't care one way or the other. Perhaps he has already forgotten me? How did he get so far ahead? Suddenly the crowd is not just a mass of people, but a barrier between us. I'm losing him! Then I see his balding head again. Relieved, I steer towards it. He's not there!

I find myself revisiting the places where we were before. Small likelihood that I'll find him. I don't. Now it's certain I'm alone. Alone in Moscow.

Is Russian Translatable?

WHEN I NOW say that perhaps he was right about translation, do I really mean it? He believed (naively, many thought) that the reason for there being so much free-verse translation of texts that were formal in the original was that translators, for the most part, were not up to the task, not dedicated or skilled enough. As Alan Myers, one of Joseph's earlier translators, reminded me, Joseph once claimed, in an interview, that translating poetry was like doing a crossword puzzle. In other words, I suppose, that it was a matter of verbal dexterity and patience (read dedication). There is surely more than a little truth in this, at least as regards the neophyte translator. Before he has exhaustively explored all possibilities, his obligations cannot be said to have been fully carried out. Joseph's standards may have been absolute – and translation is not an absolute or scientific business – but even if they seem unreasonable or simplistic, they are at least salutary.

Well, *was* he right? And did his own translations into English constitute, as he evidently thought or hoped, a kind of proof of his rightness? For me, the question is now an open one. Possibly the problem lay as much in Joseph's combativeness, which was understandable, given his dependence on translation. Under normal circumstances (i.e. had he not been coerced into leaving his native land), translation surely would have played a less important part in his life and artistic development. He would not have been obliged to stake out territory for himself between languages, a kind of medial marginality.

I didn't know that a new collection of Brodsky's own poetry was due from Farrar, Straus & Giroux, Joseph himself having read the proofs shortly before his death. I wonder whether the distinction between poems written in English and poems translated by the author into English will be clear. Increasingly it has not been clear to me, although he still uses the formula:

36

"Translated by the Author". I suspect, though, that having for so long entrusted the translation of his poetry to others, even if under close supervision, he was engaged on a long-term (alas, short term, as it turned out) experiment – that may be putting it too circumspectly – in applying his own ideas about translation, bypassing the often recalcitrant translators. Thus, he was bringing his poems, in translation, syntactically and acoustically (metrically, rhythmically, above all), closer to his own Russian. I wonder if he was, at the same time, bringing his Russian closer to their *potential* English translation. After all, he had inhabited an English-speaking world for twenty-six of his fifty-five years. Russian was still the mother tongue, but English, given his reverence for its literary tradition and for some of its writers, was far more than just a second language.*

In a review-essay on a new translation of the celebrated elegies on the death of his daughter by the Renaissance Polish poet Jan Kochanowski (*New York Review of Books*, 15 February, 1996), Czeslaw Milosz, whom Joseph regarded as one of the preeminent poets of our time, re-iterated his belief that Russian poetry was "hardly translatable because of its particular features – strongly rhymed singsong verses among them". He added: "Modern Polish poetry does a little better because, in contrast to Russian, the Polish language benefits from abandoning both meter and rhyme, so that equivalents in English can more easily be found." He also believed, however, that the situation had improved somewhat, as a result of the increasing collaboration between poets in English and poets in the source language. The review in question is of a collaborative translation by Stanislaw Baranczak (Polish poet, essayist and Shakespeare translator, also the translator of Brodsky into Polish) and Seamus Heaney, the 1995 Nobel Laureate.

While I may have some doubts, in general, about "tandem translations", it would be foolish to argue with Milosz, when he speaks from experience, the experience of co-translating his own poetry with the American poets Robert Hass and Robert Pinsky. I wonder whether Joseph, who quite often collaborated with American poet friends, and who had hoped that Richard Wilbur,

* Brodsky's actual "second" language, learned in school, was Polish. 37

certainly a master of formal verse translation, would commit himself to translating more than one or two poems, was convinced of the efficacy of this method. When Wilbur turned out an impeccably crafted version of a Brodsky poem, however flattering this may be, was it Brodsky? No doubt partly due to his being so productive – he could not expect his illustrious poet friends to keep pace or to translate more than the occasional poem – he continued to work with lesser known, more malleable translators; under the circumstances, it is hardly surprising that he increasingly resorted to translation of his own poetry, while continuing to consult his poet friends. After George Kline, Joseph never again had his personal translator. He may not have wanted one. The purpose of the operation was to get the poems into English with minimal loss, not to be loyal to translators. Since Joseph took over more and more, it became less important to work through a single translator in order to achieve consistency. Indeed, it was perhaps preferable for him to collaborate with Russianists, who produced, as Alan Myers put it to me, *polufabrikaty* or half-finished products, working drafts in English for Joseph to revise and complete. When a Walcott had a hand in things, however, it was presumably a matter of bringing an auto-translation into contact (or conflict?) with another's poetic sensibility. Granted, this is a form of collaboration, but I imagine that Milosz, in commending collaborations between poets from the source and target languages, had something different in mind.

And what of the Polish poet's observation about the quasi-untranslatability of Russian? Milosz is quite matter-of-fact about it, but is he right? "Strong rhymed singsong verses." Joseph maintained that least of all could these be represented by free-verse. I wonder, therefore, how he reacted to Milosz's contention that "the Polish language *benefits* [my italics] from abandoning both rhyme and meter." As far as I know, he never commented on it. Given his interest both in Milosz and in Polish poetry, it is hard to believe that he never saw the review.

Nabokov at once springs to mind. Of course, he goes much further. Recently, a Russian graduate student, a philologist by training, consulted me about her proposed thesis, which was an inquiry into the celebrated inadequacy of English translations of Pushkin's masterpiece "Eugene Onegin". I dug out my copy of Nabokov's *Partisan Review* essay, "Problems of Translation: 'Onegin' in English" – it had been one of the hand-outs I used in a translation-history class, as well as in the translation workshop – which preceded the publication, in 1964, of his four-volume magnum opus on Onegin, which of course includes his own polemically literalistic rendering. "The clumsiest literal translation", Nabokov fulminates, taking issue with the Ciceronian tradition of sense-for-sense as against word-for-word, "is a thousand times more useful than the prettiest paraphrase . . . The person who desires to turn a literary masterpiece into another language, has only one duty to perform, and this is to reproduce with absolute exactitude the whole text, and nothing but the text. The term 'literal translation' is tautological since anything but that is not truly a translation but an imitation, an adaptation or a parody."[18] He seeks to show that this is particularly true of Russian, listing no fewer than six characteristics (to Milosz's one) of Russian language and prosody that cannot be rendered in English: (1) There are far more rhymes, both masculine and feminine, in Russian. "If in Russian and French", he remarks jocularly, "the feminine rhyme (e.g.) is a glamorous lady friend, her English counterpart is either an old maid or a drunken hussy from Limerick." Joseph vigorously rejected such notions. I put it to him once, and he reprimanded me mildly, though had I cited Nabokov – I cannot recall ever doing so – I suspect that he would have been less kind to the latter's shade than he was to me. Brodsky, as we have seen, held that the alleged paucity of full rhymes in English was simply an excuse, a cover-up for inferior skills or workmanship. Rhyming might require greater ingenuity in English, but that precisely was the challenge. He did not accept that the greater ingenuity required would tend to make the rhyme intrusive in English, and that it was not unreasonable to try to modify the impact by using slant-rhymes. But to continue . . . (2) Russian words, no matter how long, have only one stress, whereas polysyllabic English words often have secondary stresses or two stresses; (3) Russian is considerably more polysyllabic than English; (4) in Russian, all syllables are pronounced, without the elisions and slurs that occur in English verse; (5) inversion of trochaic words, common in English iambics, is rare in Russian verse; (6) as against that, Russian iambic tetrameters contain more modulated lines than regular ones, the reverse being true in English poetry. This, in the latter case, may lead to monotony, not unknown for instance with such a poet as Byron. Nabokov concludes that, "shorn of its primary verbal existence, the original text will not be able to soar and to sing; but it can be very nicely dissected and mounted, and scientifically studied in all its organic details." By which he meant that "the absolutely literal sense, with no emasculation and no padding" could be conveyed, with the help of exhaustive commentary. He does grant that, "in regard to mere meter", the characteristic English iambic is perfectly able to accommodate the Russian without loss of literal accuracy. Nabokov's recommendations are cogent. And after all, he is not some hack, but unquestionably a master (even if, actually, a minor poet) of the Russian language, as well as of the (or of his) English . . .

"May 24, 1980" and Reading Aloud

BUT IT WOULD be more profitable, I think, to look at a poem, translated by the man himself, and to try to see what he was up to or thought he was up to. So, how about "May 24, 1980"? This is the title in English; the Russian text is untitled, the date appearing at the end of the poem, as is quite usual with Brodsky. May 24, the day of his birth. 1980, his fortieth year to heaven . . .

Here is the poem itself, in rough transliteration, with an interlinear, literalistic English version. Note: "kh" is pronounced like the "ch" in the Scottish *loch*, and "zh" like the "j" in the French *jeu*. The vowels as accented by Joseph Brodsky in his reading are underlined.

1   Ya vkhodil vmesto dikovo zverya v kletku,
      It was I, no wild beast, that entered the cage,
2   vyzhigal svoi srok i klikukhu gvozdyom v barake,
      with a nail scorched his (my?) prison term and nickname
      in the wooden barrack,
3   zhil u morya, igral v ruletku,
      lived by the sea, played roulette,
4   obedal chort znaet s kem vo frake.
      dined in coat-tails with the devil-knows-who.
5   S vysoty lednika ya oziral polmira,
      From the top of a glacier, I surveyed half the world,
6   trizhdy tonul, dvazhdy byval rasporot
      thrice drowned, twice was unpicked (unstitched).
7   Brosil stranu, shto menya vskormila.
      I left (abandoned) the country that raised me.
8   Iz zabyvshikh menya mozhno sostavit' gorod.
      You could people a city with those who have forgotten me.

9   Ya slonyalsa v stepyakh, pomnyashchikh, vopli gunna,

I wandered aimlessly about in the steppes, recalling the howl
of the Hun,

10   nadeval na sebya shto syznova vkhodit v modu,

clothed myself in what again has become fashionable,

11   seyal rozh, pokryval chornoi tolyu gumna

sowed rye, tarred barn roofs,

12   i ne pil tol'ko sukhuyu vodu.

and drank not only dry water.

13   Ya vpustil v svoi sny voronyonyi zrachok konvoya,

I admitted into my dreams the sentry's burnished pupil,

14   zhral khleb izgnanya, ne ostavlyaya korok.

guzzled the bread of exile, leaving not even a crust.

15   Pozvolyal svoim svyazkam vse zvuki, pomimo voya;

I've permitted my vocal cords to utter all manner of sounds,
except for a howl;

16   pereshel na shopot. Teper' mne sorok.

I went over to a whisper. Now I am forty.

17   Shto skazat' mne o zhizni? Shto okazalas' dlinnoi.

What should I say about life? That it turned out to be long.

18   Tol'ko s gorem ya chustvuyu solidarnost'.

It is only with sorrow (grief) that I feel solidarity.

19   No poka mne rot ne zabili glinoi,

But until my mouth is crammed with clay,

20   iz nevo razdavatsa budet lish blagodarnost'.

only gratitude will resound (ring out) from it.

There are 10–15 syllables per line, giving an average of 12.2. The stresses are somewhat problematical, the above transcription being based on the reading Joseph gave at the University of Iowa. Line 17 is semantically and acoustically climactic. (In the reading, Brodsky's voice rises in semi-tones, until it reaches the plateau, as it were, of the last four lines.) The stress on *zhizni* (life) is particularly strong, since the caesura occurs here, and it is followed by a full-stop. Line 17 is unique in that it contains two complete sentences, in the form of question-and-answer. Brodsky, characteristically, rides over the full-stop in line 16, but then slows down, his voice dipping on the rhyme word, at the end of each hemistich of line 17. The harrowing "i" assonance is heightened by Joseph's nasal intonation: *zhizni . . . dlinnoi . . . zabili . . . glinoi . . .*

What of the metre? It seems now anapaestic, now trochaic. I feel that I am reading a performance score, rather sparsely marked – by the author, of course. But had I not heard him, would that be so? The pattern of accents and feminine rhymes throughout (this being less of a tour-de-force in Russian than in English) heightens the compactness of this poem. At the same time, the combination of a flexible metre and a regular (if opportunistic) rhyme scheme makes the poem eminently performable, the natural rhythms of Russian prevailing, at least as delivered by Brodsky, who recited the poem with great force and (mock?) pathos. He was deliberate, but at the same time brisk, as though he knew time was short.

Enjambment is a feature of Joseph's work on the page. In his readings, he often augmented this effect by not pausing at line ends and at rhymes, even when punctuation or sense seemed to require it. It was almost as though he were trying to transmit the poem in its entirety, irrespective of length, as perceived in a single moment.

Joseph's delivery has been likened to liturgical chanting, as in a synagogue. Not that he slurs the tones, but that he oscillates before settling onto individual notes.So far as I know, he generally denied that there was anything ancestrally Judaic about it. He disarmingly implied that it was simply the way he had been taught at school to recite! And yet there was a liturgical element also. After his 1978 reading in Iowa, he was asked whether the famous Russian declamatory style derived from Mayakovsky, whether there was a sort of "school of declamation".[19] His answer: "Well, actually, I never heard any recordings of Mayakovsky, but if his style is declamatory, it comes from something much further back in our history. The first literature which appeared in Russian was liturgical literature, psalms (translations, of course). So, they've been rendered in Russian in a kind of rhythmical form. And, in the Russian equivalent of high school, the children are made to memorize lines and lines of poetry. And, after that, they are compelled to deliver them with so-called expression. That is, if they deliver it they should underline by their intonation, by stress, whatever it is, their understanding of the text. OK? So, this comes in the schooling, the normal schooling." His response strikes me rather as an example of his deflationary tactics. What is the "kind of rhythmical form" in which this liturgical literature was rendered? And as for "so-called expression", Joseph's masterful renditions *are* expressive, but often more of form or structure than of content, even deliberately ignoring the latter. It is as though meaning now expressed form rather than the other way. Still, his answer is rather ingenuous.

The late Yefim Etkind, critic and translation scholar, describes quite differently a poetry reading in Leningrad.[20] "Brodsky astonished me by his unceasing flow of short and long poems which he recited as if in a trance, his eyes half shut, and in such a deafening guttural chant that the windows shook. His delivery was as unusual as his poetry; it showed a frantic energy, the monotony was only rarely broken by a raising or lowering of the voice, but the gaps between the stanzas were marked by an increasing urgency." Etkind's description seems rather negative. It is also somewhat contradictory. I am struck by the contrast between "frantic energy", "increasing urgency", on the one hand, and "monotony" on the other. And what of "frantic"? Not if he means out of control, surely, since Joseph was neither crushed nor lacerated by his poems; "frantic *energy*" possibly, because the energy was able to contain or channel the excitement.

Joseph usually downplayed, even if he did not deny, his Jewishness: perhaps because keeping a low profile was second nature; perhaps because Jewishness was associated with being a victim and he had no time for the culture of complaint. In a radio interview with Ian Hamilton (for BBC 2's *Bookmark*, 2 October, 1986), he said: "I don't really think that my experiences are so unique . . . First of all you don't want to be a hostage to any moment in your biography, in your life . . . You want to keep moving, keep going." In a review of *Watermark*[21] Hamilton, for his part, accused Brodsky of almost total ego-centrism: "His instinct is always to assimilate the object to the self . . . Most of the time, Brodsky's self-absorption makes for the abstract and sententious." Brodsky rejected the martyr rôle and refused to allow himself to be cast as a Great Man.[22] He was only too aware of the danger posed by journalists and others, as they cast about for a little drama, and did what he could to deflate or pre-empt them, not only in his responses to questions, but in his life, his conduct, his scrupulous informality.

Even so, as I listened to the tape again, I was reminded of my father's recitation of the Passover prayers. His chanting, too, was perfunctory and he would press on regardless, his concentration unwavering. As he mouthed the text, father's voice would sink to a whisper, as though he were taking a personal tally of the service prayers, while simultaneously leafing, in private contentment, through the pages of the prayer book. Joseph's voice, of course, never sank to a whisper. Indeed, even though his health deteriorated, his voice never lost its power, although occasionally, as he read or rather recited from memory, he would hesitate over a word or a line. Five years my junior, Joseph nevertheless reminded me of my father (my father as a young man, in his student photographs). There indeed seemed to be a family resemblance, as there also was with the young Osip Mandelstam (not the prematurely aged Mandelstam of the final years). On the other hand, there was nothing paternal in Joseph's treatment of me, nothing in the least *de haut en bas*; rather the reverse.

Joseph certainly gave value for money. But in any case, readings were not undertaken merely to supplement his income. One might say that he was a kind of language publicist, in the first place of Russian, but increasingly of English as well. The British poet Roy Fisher remarked: "It's a salutary and quite a noble sight, if a quixotic one, to see Brodsky coming into English and fighting, practically, to reverse its retreat as a matter of principle, and in gratitude for what it's given him."[23] At his third Iowa reading, he began by saying that "Mr Weissbort" would read the English first and that he would then read the Russian "version". He joked that he could, of course, read the English as well, but since the verse had already had to suffer the violence of translation, he did not wish to "add accent to injury!" Actually, because of the eccentric nature of his English diction, it was *his* voice that was needed, rather than that of some native speaker like myself, although it may also be that in trying to normalize Brodsky's versions, the native reader helped them on their way into the language, making them more acceptable.

If Joseph seemed to be in too much of a hurry, I do not think this showed poor judgement, since in reality he had little time and knew it. Besides, the way he learnt was by doing, by doing in public. In the process, he supplied his critics, native defenders of their turf, with much ammunition. Nor was he as thick-skinned as he may have seemed. But he held to his course. Towards the end of the Iowa reading, Joseph commented, as he had often done before: "You are probably puzzled why we are reading the same poem twice. I simply think that the best every country has is its language. To say the least, I am perfectly confident that the best thing Russia has ... had ... will have ... is its language. And I am simply trying to give you its maximum ... as much as I can do. I simply don't want to miss this opportunity." Obviously it was not just a question of writing. I sometimes wonder even whether the oral performance of his poetry wasn't, in a way, more important to him than the actual writing of it. Of Joseph's love of poetry, Derek Walcott remarks: "the man is excited, he's physically excited, the same as a footballer is excited about a football match, for example, or a soldier about war, a tennis player about tennis. That is physical excitement."[24] So, when Joseph, in a trancelike manner, declaimed, say, "May 24, 1980", probably he was indeed experiencing a kind of ecstasy, which inevitably he shared with his audience. The basis for it was physiological. Mandelstam, for instance, in his "Conversation about Dante", writes: "The inner form of the verse is inseparable from the countless changes of expression flitting across the face of the narrator who speaks and feels emotion."[25]

There is another side to this. In his quite unsentimental obituary of Nadezhda Mandelstam, Joseph describes her feat of memorizing Osip Mandelstam's poetry and thus saving it from oblivion: "repeating day and night the words of her dead husband was undoubtedly connected not only with comprehending them more and more but also with resurrecting his very voice, the intonations peculiar to him [. . .] To memorize [. . .] is to restore intimacy. Gradually the lines of those poets [*she memorized the poetry of others, too: Akhmatova, for instance*] became her mentality, became her identity [. . .] her linguistic norm."[26] To memorize is to make explicit the materiality of the poem, confirming the universality of that which has given such intimate pleasure. It is as if self-indulgence and altruism have become indistinguishable.

"May 24, 1980", the Brodsky Version

A NOT QUITE ad-verbum translation, Joseph's own version, in italic, alternating with it:

1   It was I, no wild beast, that entered the cage,
I have braved, for want of wild beasts, steel cages,
2   with a nail scorched his (my?) prison term and nickname
       in the wooden barrack,
carved my term and nickname on bunks and rafters,
3   lived by the sea, played roulette,
lived by the sea, flashed aces in an oasis,
4   dined in coat-tails with the devil-knows-who.
dined with the-devil-knows-whom, in tails, on truffles.
5   From the top of a glacier, I surveyed half the world,
From the height of a glacier I beheld half a world, the earthly
6   thrice drowned, twice was unpicked (unstitched).
width. Twice have drowned, thrice let knives rake my
       nitty-gritty.
7   I left (abandoned) the country that raised me.
Quit the country that bore and nursed me.
8   You could people a city with those who have forgotten me.
Those who forgot me would make a city.
9   I wandered aimlessly about in the steppes, recalling the
       howl of the Hun,
I have waded the steppes that saw yelling Huns in saddles,
10 clothed myself in what again has become fashionable,
worn the clothes nowadays back in fashion in every quarter,
11 sowed rye, tarred barn roofs,
planted rye, tarred the roofs of pigsties and stables,
12 and drank not only dry water.
guzzled everything save dry water.
13 I admitted into my dreams the sentry's burnished pupil,
I've admitted the sentries' third eye into my wet and foul

14   guzzled the bread of exile, leaving not even a crust.

        dreams. Munched the bread of exile: it's stale and warty.

15   I've permitted my vocal cords to utter all manner of sounds,
            except for a howl;

        Granted my lungs all sounds except the howl;

16   I went over to a whisper. Now I am forty.

        switched to a whisper. Now I am forty.

17   What should I say about life? That it turned out to be long.

        What should I say about life? That it's long and abhors
           transparence.

18   It is only with sorrow (grief) that I feel solidarity.

        Broken eggs make me grieve; the omelette, though, makes
           me vomit.

19   But until my mouth is crammed with clay,

        Yet until brown clay has been crammed down my larynx,

20   only gratitude will resound (ring out) from it.

        only gratitude will be gushing from it.

Line by line comparisons show, of course, that Joseph is not inhibited by any notion of Nabokov's "absolute literal sense, with no emasculation and no padding". It is certainly arguable that he does not emasculate, but that he elaborates (or pads) cannot be denied. Examples abound: line 3: played roulette / *flashed aces in an oasis*; line 4: dined / *dined on truffles*; lines 5–6: half the world / *half the world, the earthly* [enjambment] *width*; line 6: twice was unpicked / *thrice* [sic] *let knives rake my nitty-gritty*; line 10: became fashionable / *back in fashion in every quarter*; line 13: I admitted into my dreams / *I've admitted . . . into my wet and foul dreams*; line 14: bread of exile, leaving not even a crust / *bread of exile: it's stale and warty*; line 17: That it turned out to be long / *That it's long and abhors transparence.*

How about those last four lines? Joseph has, of course, rewritten them in English, substituting or adapting a rather too well-known political saw: You can't make an omelette without breaking eggs. Rewriting or revising tends to lead to expansion rather than the reverse. Dramatically effective these lines may be in performance, but "gushing" or "vomiting" gratitude is a kind of oxymoron, hyperbolical, whereas the original is both more subtle and more direct.

However, the liberty-taking translator, in this case, is at the same time the original author. As George Steiner remarked in his review of *To Urania*, it is unusual for poets, even bilingual ones, to translate their own poetry. In assuming responsibility for this, Joseph was doing double duty; he was writing the poem twice. This is a formidable proposition, not just technically, but emotionally, though perhaps there are hidden benefits as well (apart, presumably, from getting the translation you want, or at least having only yourself to blame for the translation you do get). The "liberties" taken – I dare say he would not have called them liberties – he also tried to insist that other translators take. But there was a catch. They were, in fact, prescribed by Joseph, specifically related to his own experiments with or under- standing of the English language, rather than to any potential collaborator's or translator's sense of linguistic propriety. But if one adopts the view that Joseph was developing a new "idiolect", his eagerness to get others, native-speakers of English, to try out what he proposed looks less like insistence on having his own way, than like the zealousness (over-zealousness perhaps) of a man with a mission, who needed the support or co-operation of others. Towards the end, he was, as I have suggested, in the process of himself assuming the entire burden of translation. To sum up, he was a stickler for metre and rhyme (while making increasingly bold forays across the conventional borders of English prosody and syntax), but probably, in his own way, as *rigorously* free with the "strict literal meaning" as were, say, Cowley, Dryden, or Pope.

Still, not to exaggerate: lines 7, 8, 15 and 16 in Joseph's English version are literally fairly accurate, and as (or even more) concise than the original. Though many of the changes seem dictated by the exigencies of rhyme and metre, the assonantal feminine rhymes are also ingenious. For example, lines 1 and 3: *cages/ oasis*; 5 and 7: *earthly / nursed me*; 17 and 19: *transparence / larynx*. Quite often though, their idiosyncrasy makes these rhymes barely acceptable even in a mock-heroic poem. Joseph may have been able to deploy them as freely as he did, because, as a non-native speaker, he was undeterred by a comic effect to which he was virtually deaf. But while this may initially have been so, I suspect that he came to appreciate the problem, believing or hoping, not without reason, that the self-consistency of his versions would be sufficient to annul any lingering sense of absurdity.

To speculate, while his mixing of registers – for instance his use of near-obsolete words in a contemporary context – may have offended critics, in time these "anachronisms" might not be so shocking. William Morris's archaicizing translations of Icelandic poetry, or Browning's Agamemnon, for instance, seemed "unreadable" not so long ago but are now being reconsidered. I know that opponents will maintain that a Morris or Browning start from a secure basis in English, whereas a Brodsky really does not, but the English language now is more open to "foreignizations" of one sort or another. Brodsky cannot so easily just be dismissed as a foreigner.

Still, occasionally things surely seem to have got out of hand. One such instance, is in line 6 (aside from the fact that the Russian has him drowning *thrice* and *twice* being unstitched, whereas the English reverses this): "Twice have drowned, thrice let knives rake my nitty-gritty"; "rake my nitty-gritty", instead of the characteristically ironical "twice was unpicked" (literal translation). "Nitty-gritty" rhymes with "city" in the succinct, if somewhat unidiomatic Brodsky rendering: "those who forgot me would make a city". But even with knives *raking* it, "nitty-gritty" is hardly acceptable as a stand-in for heart, the problem being compounded by the possessive pronoun "my". The Russian text, of course, is far more oblique: "twice was unstitched / unpicked". On the other hand, one might argue that this euphemistic periphrase is matched by Brodsky's awkwardly elaborate metaphor. Perhaps he also felt that the English reader was likely to need more clues than the Russian.

Just for the hell of it, I'll look up "nitty-gritty" in my desktop *Heritage Dictionary*. "The specific or practical details; the *heart* of a matter." Also, he gets a compound rhyme for the price of a single one ("nitty-gritty / city").

But what about lines 14 and 16? The addition of "stale and warty" is surely a problematical move? On the other hand, these adjectives are quite plausible. And, for dramatic as well as acoustical reasons, a strong rhyme is desirable, to balance "forty".

Lines 16 and 17, with their caesuras and end-stops, stand out from among the rest. This climactic moment is extended over the last five lines, before the defiant turn, with the final word *blagodarnost'* (gratitude), life validated in the face of death, the poem's and the poet's. Unfortunately, for syntactical reasons and also because the English words "solidarity" (*solidarnost'* in Russian) and "gratitude" (*blagodarnost'*) do not rhyme, the effect is not transferable. Joseph throws caution to the winds in his search for a striking feminine rhyme, coming up with the Gilbertish "vomit / from it", which he derives from the metaphor about broken eggs. Of course, what he is *saying* makes sense, that individual tragedies merely sadden him, whereas he is literally nauseated by the indifference to human suffering of the great system-makers. But the ironic dignity of the original ("Only with grief do I feel solidarity") seems poorly served by what, at the same time, pedantically fills in the blanks, even if the clichéd political dictum in a way echoes the fatuous term *solidarnost'* (not a reference to the Polish trade union movement of that name, but to Party jargon) so prominently placed here.

I am doubtful about the addition of "abhors transparence" in line 17, not redeemed, it seems to me, by the ingenious rhyme ("larynx"). Life turned out to be long. Given his life expectations, is he being ironical too? Still, "Life turned out to be long" is plain, very plain, whereas "abhors transparence" sounds stilted. Arguably it does extend the notion of life, as both opaque and long. On the other hand, it is also somewhat highfalutin, and therefore reductive.

A problem, though, is that I have been keeping one eye on the literal translation of the Russian original and the other on Joseph's idiosyncratic (idiolectic?) Englishing of it. No way to read a poem! Or at least, not the way a non-translator and non-Russianist might read this poem.

Recently, I came across Christopher Reid's iconoclastic review of *To Urania*.[27] He also tries to warn off would-be defenders: "it is also necessary at this stage to counter the notion that something fresh, healthy, rich in artistic potential and urgently needed is being introduced into the poetic repertoire through this exotic treatment of the language." He mentions a number of poet-innovators (including Hopkins) but insists that they "get their strength from a secure and organic understanding of English idiom".

The tone of all this is rather condescending, but as for the "exotic treatment of the language", it is not hard to agree with him (certainly from an Anglo-of-a-certain-generation point of view); nor is it easy to take issue. He appears as the defender of good or, at the very least, correct English. He is confident about his own sense of the language, grammar, syntax, usage, and finds Brodsky's English beyond the pale. He is courteous, mildly but firmly expressing his doubts as to Brodsky's "status as a literary idol". Presumably many felt cheered by Reid's pragmatic assault on an established reputation, a "world name". The media pundits with their inflationary tactics, their non-literary criteria were being taken to task. Order was being restored.

True, Brodsky dispenses, as Reid rather sourly puts it, with the privileges enjoyed by the "stateless poem [. . .] peculiar to the culture of our time, especially when it is attached to an interesting personal history", presenting self-translations "that demand to be judged purely on their own merits [as English poems]". But this is not from a desire to spend the probably short time at his disposal translating his own verse, either for reasons of vanity or out of a failure or refusal to recognize his own incompetence in English. As he saw it, there was no one else he could rely on or persuade to follow his radical procedures, in effect foregrounding the source language, or at least attempting to narrow the gap between the two languages. The results may often have appeared ludicrous. I dare say Joseph was unaware of this. Or perhaps he was indifferent to it: that is, the ludicrousness may not have struck him as too high a price to pay.

Translating Oneself

IN ANY CASE, it can be shown that his translations of his own work were becoming more self-sustained as "English" artefacts. Joseph learnt in the doing; and for various reasons (e.g. lack of time) the doing had to be public. He was bold, stubborn (foolhardy?), and objectively speaking he *was* presumptuous. He was often abrasive, but he was not, as some claimed, arrogant. He simply didn't want his poems in translation to sound smooth. Arguably, this is what happened in the versions made by his earlier "name" translators, like Anthony Hecht and Richard Wilbur. Peter Porter, in a mixed review of *A Part of Speech*, put it nicely: "Brodsky worked with a number of American poets who are natural dandies . . . This gave the volume an Ivy League slickness which was plainly wrong . . ."[28] As Joseph himself stated in a prefatory note to *A Part of Speech*: "I have taken the liberty of reworking some of the translations to bring them closer to the original, though perhaps at the expense of their smoothness." Alan Myers, in a letter to me, remarked: "My own versions were too smooth, light and regular ('cute') for his taste, and often prompted him to set about actually re-writing his verse, working back from a bolder, more jaggedly energetic English rhyme. The line-length, (my) rhythm, even the meaning might all undergo change. Indeed, on one occasion, he went so far as to say that everything should be sacrificed to the rhyme! For a sharp increase in energy level, 'smoothness' was well lost." From a public-relations point of view, Joseph's tactics may have been disastrous, enraging the cohorts. Nevertheless, I believe he was on to something.

Donald Davie digs a little deeper. He does not pause to reprimand Brodsky for grammatical errors, but suspects that he "has failed to notice how Russian metres can be strict in a way no English metre can." Russian is more strongly accented than English. Davie argues that "the pounding Russian line can master and carry along with itself a clutter of exuberant tropes and 'physical detail', under the weight of which the lighter English line stumbles and hesitates and is snarled."[29] If there is something in this, it is as if Joseph were hoping to fashion out of English a conveyance with enough pace, *élan*, onward movement to carry all that material. He was trying to energize the English he had acquired. I see a similarity here with Hopkins.[30]

Davie's observations draw our attention to differences between Russian and English prosody; his conclusions, though, are less certain. It is *because* Brodsky is less inward with English, less conditioned by it, that he dares to try out "non-English" patterns. As Alan Myers put it to me: "He felt his own rhymes were rather more enterprising than those of the natives, whose ear might be dulled by familiarity." Time of course will tell, and in any case Joseph *was* becoming more inward with English; hardly surprisingly, a convergence of sorts was taking place. In English, as well as Russian, Joseph displayed a genial capacity for change or growth. However, his refusal to hide behind others, his combative manner, made him appear more set in his ways than he really was. It is true that his poems in English sometimes carry an excessive load, and that the enjambments give the impression of arbitrariness, having less to do with semantics than with an acoustical pattern. Joseph brings the two languages closer together, as it were, enabling Russian to *speak* English, syntax, accent and all. We are not talking of literal, word for word, word order for word order translation. A more radical procedure is in play, which involves an experimental blending, the product at this point being so novel that it is almost bound to be misunderstood and to offend, to be rejected as an aberration, or as hubristic.

I don't think that I am simply being contrary. I have just glanced again at my own translation of "A Part of Speech" and at the version used by Joseph in the book of that name. In many places my version is closer to the literal meaning *and* "more English" than Joseph's. It seems to me that he often, perversely or needlessly, substitutes a tortuous and unidiomatic trope for some relatively elegant solution of mine, although, of course, it is hard for me to be objective about this! So, there are at least two possible approaches: I might seek to show how much "better" than the author's translation is my own; or I might speculate about the relationship between the source text and the author's rewriting of it in English. Perhaps the comparative analysis of my version and Joseph's was misguided, since like was not being compared with like. Even if it may be claimed that both versions are valid (whatever that means), that they complement one another, a synthesis of the two is scarcely viable.

When I began writing this journal, I somehow managed to convince myself that I had been wrong to censure Joseph's English, to disparage his versions of his own poems and the poems he had written directly in English. The notion that he was creating an "authentic" English idiolect appealed to me and seemed to confirm my own findings, in December, working with him on the translation of Nikolay Zabolotsky's long poem "Agriculture Triumphant" (I'll come to that). Now I am not so sure that I *was* wrong. I am asking the impossible of myself: simultaneously to read and not read the English version of "May 24, 1980" as though it had been written in English, as though there were no source text other than Joseph's English. I say "simultaneously to read and not read", because it is a *fact* that an earlier text or "version", if you like, exists. The two versions, by the same author, are parallel texts. But if I am to confront Joseph's English without prejudice, I must surely "forget" the Russian. On the other hand, practically speaking, I cannot do that. Inevitably, the Russian is a presence, even if only a shadowy one; although its rôle may now be uncertain, it has not made itself scarce, being a component of, or more precisely a key to this new deployment of terms. It is not so unusual for one language to influence, even transform another, but generally this takes place over the long term. That the process might be subsumed in the life and works of a single individual seems improbable. Could this altered language stand alone, unsupported, i.e. without the author's authority, or rather without his living voice to vocalize it? Or is Brodsky's English Brodsky-specific? Again, time will tell. And maybe I should give *myself* a little more time?

Brodsky Remembered

YESTERDAY I received a card with details of the memorial service for Joseph, to take place in New York City, in the Cathedral of St. John the Divine, on 8th March. I try to let myself feel what I am feeling. But I am cautious too. After a month, I *still* do not think of him as dead. That is, I do, but only when I oblige myself to imagine him among the other dead. Family members, a friend or two.

Yesterday, walking to the office, I overheard myself actually asking Joseph what he thought of all this, that is, my writing about him, us, his poetry, the translation thereof. I particularly wanted to discuss the latter with him, and it seemed to me – in my folly, arrogance or optimism – that I ought to be able to construct an *ersatz* Joseph. Not so! Besides, this *ersatz* Joseph would have been at a loss anyway, although he, the real Joseph, rarely was? At the same time, he is apologizing – that's to say I am, on his behalf, in this impersonation or entertainment. Apologizing for the public nature of his rôle, for setting himself up as the defender of culture, tradition, including (not least) that of formal verse. As for myself, whatever culture I somehow embody (by default, it often seems to me) is inaccessible. The Classical legacy leaves me cold, even if (because?) my father was a Classicist . . .

The Cathedral of St. John the Divine,
112th and Amsterdam, New York City,
Friday, March 8, 1996, 5.00 p.m.

Lucas Myers, one of my oldest friends, from Cambridge days, lived at 106th and Amsterdam. It was with him that I used to stay.

Fall 1972 was the first of my early visits to the city. I had flown from London, via Chicago, directly to Cedar Rapids,

Iowa, bypassing New York. So, I now approached New York from the West, rather than from the East, as I'd always expected I would. And not just expected. Despite my British background, I had written "nostalgic" poems about New York, had even cornily dreamt I was an immigrant from Eastern Europe sailing past the Statue of Liberty.

Anyway, Lucas threw a party for me. Did Joseph come? Luke thinks not, and yet I picture him (Luke) straight-backed, hands by his side, chin well tucked in, peering at Joseph: the Tennessee aristocrat and the gingery Russian Jew. Well, Joseph certainly came to Luke's cosy apartment, and probably more than once, because he remembered the cat Perdita. He would murmur her name tenderly. Perdita was a large cat, also ginger, with a sagging undercarriage and a pretty face. I can see Joseph scratching her head . . . and murmuring: "Purr . . . Purr . . . Deetah".

Joseph didn't want people to fuss over him and he'd no use for self-pity. But am I fussing? You can't actually fuss over the dead. Although there is, perhaps, an element of retrospective fussing, insofar as they then seem not quite so dead. As for self-pity, or rather the absence of it, this made a clean break possible. There was nothing death could hold over his head. He was not intimidated by it. His life, more than most lives, was a preparation for it. He was familiar with it, which is not to say he was a thanatologist. There was nothing actually morbid about his dialogue with death. Sometimes it was almost breezy.

"The Poem"

As STATED earlier, I'd been scrutinizing this poem, "May 24, 1980", partly at least because Joseph had invited me to. And it is, after all, short and therefore more discussable, both in detail and as a whole. I had thought, that its shortness was another reason for his recommending it to me, since he knew that I myself wrote only short poems. The poem in Russian is a feat of compression and yet so personal that he could not let just anyone translate it. Having translated it himself, he felt that his version was sufficiently successful for him to commend it to others. So that in pressing it on me, he was not only asking me to read the poem, but also hoping I would be able to take some hints from it, from this translation, or at least that I would begin to appreciate what he expected of a translation, what mimetic qualities he believed a translation might aspire to. Since these exceeded what most translators thought achievable or even desirable, Joseph had no option but to attempt to demonstrate that it could be done and then trust that its virtues would speak for themselves . . .

Here's the Brodsky version:

> I have braved, for want of wild beasts, steel cages,
> carved my term and nickname on bunks and rafters,
> lived by the sea, flashed aces in an oasis,
> dined with the-devil-knows-whom, in tails, on truffles.
> From the height of a glacier I beheld half a world, the
>   earthly
> width. Twice have drowned, thrice let knives rake my
>   nitty-gritty.
> Quit the country that bore and nursed me.
> Those who forgot me would make a city.
> I have waded the steppes that saw yelling Huns in saddles,
> worn the clothes nowadays back in fashion in every quarter,
> planted rye, tarred the roofs of pigsties and stables,

guzzled everything save dry water.
I've admitted the sentries' third eye into my wet and foul
dreams. Munched the bread of exile: it's stale and warty.
Granted my lungs all sounds except the howl;
switched to a whisper. Now I am forty.
What should I say about life? That it's long and abhors
   transparence.
Broken eggs make me grieve; the omelette, though, makes
   me vomit.
Yet until brown clay has been crammed down my larynx,
only gratitude will be gushing from it.

Perhaps because my own poetry is largely personal and always
seemed to me quite straightforward, "May 24, 1980" also struck
me as a *relatively* straightforward poem (admittedly, more so in
the Russian than in Joseph's English),[31] more openly personal
than much of his work. I knew that he regarded poetry about
oneself and/or about one's family, even if not strictly in the
confessional mode, as a dead-end. I did not and still do not
disagree, but for myself was stuck with precisely that sort of
material and tried to make the best of it. Occasionally our
conversation touched on this topic, but evidently he was disinclined to censure me, or perhaps he neither wanted to upset me
nor felt it was worth the effort, or perhaps he thought the time
was not yet ripe. Anyway, such differences as there were
appeared not to affect our friendship.

On the other hand, I also hoped that we *would* eventually find
some common literary ground. But in any case, he might have
thought that "May 24, 1980", being both autobiographical and a
grimly humorous affirmation of life, would appeal to me. It was
also educative, as it demonstrated what was gained by formal
restraints, pointing a way out of the cul-de-sac of self – i.e. a way
through and therefore out.

On the other hand, he knew that I had translated and
published, in my *Post-War Russian Poetry,* his cycle of portrait-
poems, "From a School Anthology". And in the same volume
I had included my translation of his harrowing short poem

"On Love". Some other poems that he recommended and even suggested I translate were also roughly of this kind, that is more descriptive or autobiographical than metaphysical. For instance, "Autumn in Norenskaya", a poem that evoked his home in exile, in the Arkhangelsk region, and the title sequence of his second book *A Part of Speech*. Perhaps, too, he sensed that we shared a predilection for cheerless landscapes and for solitude. "Lagoon" was another poem that I translated, probably on his suggestion: the protagonist is "a nobody in a raincoat, owned by nobody" (from my version, not Anthony Hecht's, which is the one Joseph included in *A Part of Speech*).

"The Jewish Cemetery in Leningrad"

VENICE. I have not been there, but Joseph's Venice and even his Petersburg are familiar urban landscapes. Even if Joseph made little of it, perhaps his Jewishness was also in evidence. A sense of doom, of endurable disaster; of self-depreciation as well, alienation, although he managed to combine this with a kind of assertiveness, so that it never turned into Jewish *selbsthass*. In a way, the Jewishness was a given. Indeed, it was better not stated, since it could so easily lead to identification with victimhood. That may be why he never, so far as I know, re-printed the early "The Jewish Cemetery in Leningrad", another poem that I translated, also because of its overtly Jewish content, unique in his work. The poem may not be written from the point of view of a victim, but the Jew as victim or scapegoat features in it. Oddly – or not so oddly – this somewhat juvenile work was mentioned in an article entitled "A Literary Drone" in *Vechernii Leningrad* (Evening Leningrad) in November 1963, a sort of prologue to the famous trial in February. Casting around for evidence in his writings of "Jewish nationalism", which even so late in the history of the Soviet Union was still a heinous sin, all his accusers could come up with was this poem (friends of Joseph were also named, Vladimir Shveigolts, Anatoly Geikhman, Leonid Aronzon, all typically Jewish names):

> The Jewish cemetery near Leningrad.
> A crooked fence of rotten plywood.
> And behind it, lying side by side,
> lawyers, merchants, musicians, revolutionaries.
>
> They sang for themselves.
> They accumulated money for themselves.
> They died for others.

But in the first place they paid their taxes, and
    respected the law,
and in this hopelessly material world,
they interpreted the Talmud, remaining idealists.

Perhaps they saw more.
Perhaps they believed blindly.
But they taught their children to be patient
and to stick to things.
And they did not plant any seeds.
They never planted seeds.
They simply lay themselves down
in the cold earth, like grain.
And they fell asleep forever.
And after, they were covered with earth,
candles were lit for them,
and on the Day of Atonement
hungry old men with piping voices,
gasping with cold, wailed about peace.

And they got it.
As dissolution of matter.

Remembering nothing.
Forgetting nothing.
Behind the crooked fence of rotting plywood,
four miles from the tramway terminus.

    "Cemetery", as this poem is called in the article, is uncharacteristic, not only on account of the subject but prosodically as well. The first stanza is rhymed, but thereafter the poem resolves itself into *vers libre*. I know of no other poem like it in Joseph's published oeuvre. Indeed, were it not that he never denied writing it, one might almost have thought it was by someone else. In a sense, perhaps it was.
    I never discussed it with Joseph, since we didn't talk about our Jewishness, or even Judaism as such, though I may have

mentioned my own ambivalence. While it is sometimes suggested or claimed that Joseph had rejected Judaism, as far as I know he neither embraced it nor denied it. I think that his attitude did not really change. He was a Jew of the assimilated, Russified kind, a "bad Jew", as he put it, and not much interested in adopting or reclaiming the tradition; in short, he was no "refusenik". On the other hand, for instance, Anthony Rudolf, co-editor of the international anthology *Voices Within the Ark: The Modern Jewish Poets* (1980) tells me that when asked if he would be willing to be included in the book, Joseph replied that he *wanted* to be in it. And when, for instance, he was asked at a press conference in Stockholm, in December 1987, at the Nobel ceremonies, how he would describe himself, he answered: "I feel myself a Jew, although I never learnt Jewish traditions." He added, however: "But as for my own language, I undoubtedly regard myself as Russian."

Being a Jew, like being an exile, has certain advantages, in that (anywhere other than in Israel, perhaps New York, or wherever Jewish ghettos survive) it situates one on the margins, rather than at the centre of society. Jews tend to take on the colour of their surroundings. Jewish history, as a whole – and even "bad" Jews are heirs to that history – gives the individual Jew a claim, however tenuous, on a variety of cultural or linguistic territories. This is a source of strength, but also of weakness, in that he may feel that he truly belongs to none. Of course, Joseph did live in New York, but he was frequently on the road, in the States or abroad, and had another home in New England. Furthermore, his exceptionally wide, international circle of friends and acquaintances far transcended the Jewish cultural world, assuming that there is such a thing.

"The Jewish Cemetery in Leningrad" is not a good poem; it may even be a bad poem. And my reasons for translating it may not have been praiseworthy either. The poem seemed to me even then somewhat jejune. Those interred in Leningrad's Jewish cemetery were cut off ("sang for themselves"), landless ("they never planted seeds, only themselves") and superstitious, imprisoned by tradition ("hungry old men with piping voices"). Their hopes or beliefs were illusory: the peace they prayed for came to them as "dissolution of matter". There is no light; there is not even a "nobody in a raincoat". And that's partly the trouble. The poem is programmatic, its theme too large, given the means at the young poet's disposal. It is as if he simply did not know what to do with the material. But this in itself interested me, particularly in view of the extraordinary sureness of his hand in all the other poems I'd looked at, even from that early period. It may have been the first of the few poems by Joseph that I translated. For me it was a place of meeting with him, this having nothing, I suppose, to do with its literary worth.

When I asked Joseph if I might reprint my version, his response was: "Do what you like, Danny!" So, either he didn't give a damn, or he was disposed to indulge me. Perhaps both. Might he have responded differently, had I put it differently, viz. "Would you rather I didn't use it, Joseph?" After all, he had not said anything about his inclusion in the original Yevtushenko anthology, until Max Hayward gave him the opportunity to refuse, whereupon he did refuse!

But Back to "May 24, 1980" and Tonic Verse

WANDERING again! Am I trying to put some distance between myself and this poem, hoping maybe to lose sight of the Russian text (and of my own "literal" rendering, which commemorates the latter)?

Well, I am first brought up short by "flashed aces in an oasis". What could it signify? As far as I know, he wasn't a gambler! Or perhaps he did like poker, or the idea of poker? The triple feminine rhyme, *cages . . . aces . . . oasis*, seems strained. However ingenious, isn't the *aces / oasis* rhyme rather sophomoric? Was he trying to put English through its paces (sorry!)? "From the height of a glacier I beheld half a world, the earthly / width . . ." Of course, *earthly* makes a feminine slant-rhyme with *nursed me*, but why *width* on the following line? If *width* is omitted, not only do we not have to put up with an apparently pointless enjambment – the word seems to add nothing at all to the sense and isn't it metrically redundant? – but the discrete nature of the line is restored, in a poem which uncharacteristically avoids enjambment . . . But didn't I promise not to look at or think about the Russian text?

Perhaps it is the assonance, *width / nitty-gritty / Quit* that prompted him? Perhaps he simply wanted to surprise the reader, when the first line seemed complete in itself? Whatever the case, *width* is surely intrusive here, as well as being somewhat unidiomatic. Another intrusion occurs in line 10: "in every quarter". Semantically, what does this contribute to "worn the clothes nowadays back in fashion"? But he badly needed a feminine rhyme for "[dry] water" and no doubt he also wanted the extra syllables, the additional accent. Had he been prepared to deviate from the abab rhyme, or possibly to alter the order of the lines, he might have exploited the assonance *saddles / fashion*. The point is that "in every quarter" *seems* to be redundant, particularly in so tight a poem. Further down, lines 13–14, the enjambment, not present in the Russian (I couldn't stop myself having a look!) seems to be there mainly for the sake of the *foul / howl* rhyme. Semantically the linking of "foul" with "wet" (the nature of these dreams is not specified in the source text) is puzzling. Hyperbole? Does he really wish to express self-disgust? Isn't this misleading? Furthermore, he has resorted to masculine rhymes. Perhaps, though, they provide a counter-weight, a reminder of more standard English practice, as against the assonantal build-up: *quarter . . . water . . . warty . . . forty . . .* Do these rhymes seem provisional, as though he were using them as markers, intending to return later? I have questioned line 14, "bread of exile: it's stale and warty". While the adjectives may be plausible enough, they also seem contrived, a little too ingenious, particularly coming at the end of the line, the rhyme with "forty" too obviously a prime *raison d'être*. Even on its own, I think, "warty" would have seemed eccentric, grotesque.

The problem is how to make a rhyme *look* natural. Ingenuity alone may be counter-productive. *Warty / water* is a smart slant-rhyme of the kind Joseph increasingly favoured and tried to naturalize. And one can see why he was tempted. The two full-stops, in the middle and at the end of line 16, signal a change of pace, drawing out the climax to the point of neurasthenic shrillness: "switched to a whisper. Now I am forty." And this is followed by another line, consisting of two sentences, question and answer: "What should I say about life? That it's long and abhors transparence". A sustained climax, then, "forty" harking back to "warty", and "transparence", in Joseph's version, looking forward to the penultimate line-ending "larynx". (He expected to die well before he was forty.) So, Joseph roughly replicates the drama of the source text. But stepping gingerly into the force field of those final lines, I still find "transparence" dubious. It may surprise, since it is so recondite, but at the same time I am uncomfortably aware that it surely owes its place primarily to the rhyme with "larynx", particularly since it is not authorized (I looked again!) by the Russian text. Impressive and enjoyable as this display of virtuosity is, I still find myself struggling to justify "abhors transparence" semantically. Even if I didn't already know it, I would suspect that the circumlocutory "abhors transparence" was not part of the original wording. What can it mean? That life is complex, does not accede to our yearning for plainness, for simplicity, for lucidity, and so forth? That life is long (surprisingly so, in Joseph's case), but also tedious and dense, confused and confusing? Joseph, on the lookout for an effective resonance, has set himself the near impossible task of finding a rhyme for the rather medical-sounding "larynx". But then I ask myself: why "crammed down my larynx"? Would you cram something down the larynx? You might "cram it down the throat", but that's a cliché. The larynx contains the gullet, alluded to earlier, so very likely he is referring to sound, to speech. But then he does not directly mention sound in the last line, even if it is metonymically implied in "gratitude" . . .

If one does what I have tried, rather unsuccessfully, not to do and compares Joseph's English version with the Russian, or with an *ad verbum* English translation of the Russian, some of these problems are further highlighted. Thus there is no "aces in an oasis" but simply "played roulette", *ruletku* rhyming with *kletku* (a cage; not *steel* cage). There seems to be some inflationary activity, more adjectives, metaphorically or metonymically heightened descriptions. Knives raking his "nitty-gritty" (as noted earlier) replaces "was unpicked (or unstitched)", the latter a quieter and more sinister metaphor. As for the "wet and foul" dreams, in the original, as we have seen, they are only "dreams" ("admitted into my dreams the sentry's burnished pupil"). "Bread of exile" is described as "stale and warty", the original being adjective-free: "Not leaving a crust". I have already spoken of "abhors transparence". The final lines again are hyperbolical, as compared with the Russian. First, there is the image of "broken eggs", which introduces the notion of vomiting, the metaphor being extended all the way to the end of the poem, when gratitude "gushes" from the larynx until stopped by the "brown clay [. . .] crammed down it". However, there is a possible inconsistency here: if gratitude is being thrown up, one might be tempted to equate it with what causes the subject to throw up, i.e. the omelette! In any case, the original is more restrained: "What should I say about life? That it turned out to be long. / It is only with sorrow (grief) that I feel solidarity. / But until my mouth is crammed with clay, / only gratitude will *sound* (not gush) from it." The idea itself is striking enough without any additional items; there is only the paradoxical determination to live, to exalt life, even as disaster or death threatens. Or perhaps there is only the *inability* to do otherwise. To obtain the necessary rhymes, the desired measure, the translator has had to pull out all the stops. In Russian, with its polysyllabic words, its plentiful feminine rhymes, ternary metres (dactylic, anapaestic, amphibrachic) are common enough. Compensating for the regularity of the iambic metre in English, Brodsky has produced a less plain, less immediate text.

What of his predilection for feminine rhymes, some of which (like *transparence / larynx*) were maybe unprecedented? He was not unaware – at least, he had been told often enough! – that polysyllabic rhyming in English was associated with light or humorous verse and that it was generally felt that it had to be used sparingly or with caution. He did not use it sparingly or with caution, and it must be said that he did not entirely avoid the unintentional comic effect either. On the other hand, he worked hard to extend the range of polysyllabic rhyming, combining it, for instance, with an uninhibited exploitation of elision (perhaps, as suggested earlier, aided by his exposure to American pronunciation). He was prepared to risk ridicule or whatever else was thrown at him, because for him the stakes were so high, and also because, as a foreign national, he had never been conscripted into the army of native prosodists. Much of his English verse is indeed light, but the lightness also makes it possible to handle often quite weighty material. And, of course, Joseph's ear for English kept improving. For instance, he added consonantal rhyming to his repertoire, often as astute as the flamboyant feminine rhymes and a good deal more subtle. As far as I know, he'd not have countenanced this earlier. But it is also possible that those who were following his progress, even if with alarm, learnt to hear *him*.

So, I read that poem again, trying to *hear* it. I call on my memory of Joseph reading it. Unfortunately, though I have a recording of him reading the original, I do not have one of him reading the translation. Still, I've often heard him read in English, mostly his own poems, but also poems by others, for instance Auden, the nasal inflection, modulations, crescendos and decrescendos, much the same as when he is reciting in Russian. And the phrasing too, words swallowed whole. Quite apart from Joseph's strong Russian accent, the general effect is of a different language, at best another English. The tone, in English, is sometimes tragic, or mock-tragic, even more so than in Russian. Or perhaps it's just more noticeable in English which, in the late twentieth-century, tends to be less than respectful of the tragic and more or less incapable of distinguishing between mock and real. But in any case, since the content is not always tragic, I find this disconcerting. Dry, prosaic, even legalistic or bureaucratic diction receives the same treatment as high-flown or metaphorically rich passages. And since Joseph, at least on the occasions that I heard him, was not quite able to get his tongue around the English words spoken at speed, the result was not altogether happy. And yet, I can appreciate what he was trying to do, what a native speaker, under his orders, or he himself, had he lived long enough, might have been able to achieve.

In the Russian, the accents or stresses average 3.85 per line, the largest number of lines having four accents and the smallest, five. With roughly equal numbers of ten- and fourteen-syllable lines, the average is 12.2 syllables. The English version, treated in a similarly syllabic-accentual fashion by the translator / reader, might go something like this, accented vowels underlined (give or take the odd accent):

I have braved, for want of wild beasts, steel cages,
carved my term and nickname on bunks and rafters,

lived by the sea, flashed aces in an oasis,
dined with the-devil-knows-whom, in tails, on truffles.
From the height of a glacier I beheld half a world, the
    earthly
width. Twice have drowned, thrice let knives rake my
    nitty-gritty. [. . .]

In this imagined performance of the author's translation, over
50% of the lines have 3 accents, the average being 3 accents per
line. There are between 10–16 syllables per line, or an average of
10.2 per line, as against 12.2 in the Russian. So, on the average,
there are fewer accents but also fewer syllables in English.
Already, in an interview with John Glad (College Park,
Maryland, April 1979), Joseph remarked: "Today I use a greater
percentage of tonic verse, a lot more intonational verse, which,
I believe, makes the language a bit more neutral, a bit more
subtle."[32]

So much, as he might have said, for counting. It does seem,
though, that while Joseph is often called a classical poet, he
frequently subverts the classical norms of syllabic-accentual
verse (Zabolotsky does the same, as Joseph himself pointed out
to me). The number of syllables can be quite uneven, to the
point of varying line by line. Often, a prose rhythm asserts itself
almost contrapuntally.

His liturgical reading style served to project the poems as
highly formalized artefacts, despite their irregularities. But to
what extent was this formality an illusion that depended on the
author's own vocal rendition? In the Russian, the metre often
approximates to natural speech rhythms, while in English it
seems to be superimposed. However, this may be due simply to
the iambic nature of English, leading one to expect more accents
even when there are fewer syllables, although the stress in
English tends to be lighter. Certainly the phrasing is more drawn
out, words being grouped rather than functioning as single units.
A long breath is required to manage Brodsky's English. Again,
I'm reminded of Hopkins. Of course, what is at stake here is the
way the language is handled, or manhandled, not the content or

manner. In any case, Joseph may be said to have expanded the metrical range as well as that of rhyme, or at least to have exploited the potential for an expanded range, if indeed one accepts that his experiments are not just eccentric or egocentric displays with no relevancy beyond their author's life and work. After a while, his redundancies, elaborate metaphors appear less disruptive. Musical considerations gain the upper hand, not subsuming meaning, but somehow resolving the provisional formulations and rhymes.

But what, in more general terms, does it take for such practices to be assimilated into general literary commerce? For one thing, they have to demonstrate their usefulness. If they work in Joseph Brodsky's poetry, then why should they not work elsewhere? And they do, if you let them. It may be a bumpy ride, but in the end, if one feels shaken up one also feels invigorated. (Or perhaps one feels like a traitor to one's natural language!)

Something New

I HAD HOPED to demonstrate that Joseph was up to something new, and not just exposing his deficiencies as a writer in English, showing how poor a judge he was of the acceptability of his own verbal contortionism. What we are talking about is metre and rhyme, since his determination to have done with the constraints of the iambic pentameter opens the way to more polysyllabic and feminine rhyming. Whereas the standard approach in English verse translation, after Cicero and St. Jerome, ("not word for word but sense for sense"), has been to put sense first, Brodsky seems to have moved in the opposite direction. Evidently he had less regard for the niceties of usage than for the movement of the verse, its physical dimension. He once said: "I couldn't permit the poem in English to be less tactile than the Russian." As a translator of Russian verse myself, I understand the impulse. But I have never been willing (or able?) to subordinate my concern for English *as she is spoken and written*. I have done what I can to accommodate the Russian, its resonances, its contours; but given the differences between Russian and English prosody, this sometimes seems to have been precious little . . .

Even as highly motivated as he was, Joseph was surely not unaware of what he was doing. He claimed that he wrote verse in English so as to feel close to Auden. I find this credible. He admired Auden above other contemporary English poets, but they met only a year before Auden died. Joseph didn't get enough of Auden, even if he was always grateful for what he did get. Furthermore, increasingly, Joseph's poems in English came to resemble Auden's, even replicating Auden's firm iambic tetrameters, with their trenchant masculine rhymes. Here is a recent example, chosen at random (from "Reveille", first published in *The Times Literary Supplement* (2 February, 1996); the poem is now in *So Forth*).

74

Birds acquaint themselves with leaves,
Hired hands roll up their sleeves.
In a brick malodorous dorm
boys awake awash in sperm.

Clouds of patently absurd
but endearing shapes assert
the resemblance of their lot
to a cumulative thought . . .

As the sun displays its badge
to the guilty world at large
scruffy masses have to rise,
unless ordered otherwise . . .

It's all there: the structured argument, assertive imagery, positive rhyming, irony. But also rather arbitrary, still reading like an
exercise. And there is still the occasional stumble, e.g. line 4 of
the first quatrain, "awake awash . . ."; though much more
assured than his earlier English attempts. In another poem,
"The Tale", in the same issue of the *TLS*, also in quatrains, but
alternating masculine and feminine rhymes, his adeptness at
polysyllabic rhyming (with a Russian-American accent), stands
him in good stead, viz: *enemy / enema*; *warships / worships*;
carnage / Carthage; *horizon / eyes on*; *argue / Are you*, etc. – unless
the reader is by now gritting his teeth! However, whereas
Joseph's original English verse is still quite conventional, his
self-translations, challenging as they do the primacy of sense,
tend to be more innovative. But that is hardly surprising. His
poetry in English was a sort of mimicry, apprentice work really.
At the same time, of course, this apprenticeship helped develop
skills that could be used in his English translations, just as the
translations, which took greater prosodic risks, were probably
making it possible for him to widen the scope of his original
English verse. He seems to have been moving simultaneously on
at least three fronts: as a writer of somewhat light, Audenesque
verse; as a radical translator of Russian verse into English; and,
of course, as a poet in Russian.

JOSEPH DID NOT surrender to nostalgia. He accepted his situation as an emigré Russian artist (and Jew?) and made the most of it. He was not the only one to acknowledge, also, certain gains: as his scholarly friend, the poet Lev Loseff, put it, being an emigré helps you to be free. And another friend, Natalya Gorbanevskaya, flatly declares that for a poet, living in an alien country is "a source of new potency". She continues: "I think that we poets are in general enriched by the experience of emigration or exile. Well, if we don't snivel [. . .] that is if we don't just start to describe the exotica or just start getting nostalgic – in so far as we are submissive to the language, we bring to it everything that we can beg, borrow or steal from other languages. And the language, in so far as it is grateful to us, has yet more to give us in return."[33] Brodsky, as we have seen, refused to be labelled an exile, with all its connotations of tragic loss. In the first place, as he pointed out, his circumstances had greatly improved as a result of his emigration. Furthermore, to be outside was really to be at the core of things. "Technically speaking", as he put it, exile is ideal for the artist, who is in any case always observing, always on the outside looking in. Of course, there are losses too: for instance, an inevitable distancing from the language as it is spoken by contemporaries. But in our time, perhaps the gains outweigh the losses. For Joseph, not to snivel was to enter wholly into the life, the language of the new country whose literary world and, arguably, even literary language he helped to shape. Milosz felt that Brodsky was the first Russian emigré to manage this. Perhaps he was the first emigré poet to even try. It is doubly remarkable, in that Russian verse, unlike Polish (according to Milosz), is so stubbornly resistant to translation. Joseph was one hell of a fighter.

A bright, clear day in Iowa City, snow on the ground. If the weather in New York ("freezing rain") permits, we'll be off this evening. The service takes place tomorrow . . .

Reading the account of Joseph's trial brings his voice vividly to mind. Frida Vigdorova's transcript of the trial shows that reality in the Soviet Union, a decade after Stalin's death, was still as absurd as any absurdist drama. Vigdorova, who organized the protest, died of cancer shortly before Joseph was allowed to return to Leningrad, after twenty months in the Far North, and three years before the end of his period of banishment. Her concern was that "the red-haired boy" should be released; she was not interested in making a martyr out of him. Like Auden, therefore, she acted, at a critical time, *in loco parentis*. Akhmatova, who had joined in the protests, also died shortly after Joseph's return.

In the dock Joseph was a kind of Candide, bewildered but truthful. From time to time, when it was possible to do so without compromising himself, he offered to comply with the "recommendations", for instance when he said that if he was unable to make a living as a poet and translator, he would indeed take a job. In general, he simply pointed out the obvious, or responded as best he could to the questions of the prosecutor and the judge (virtually interchangeable), which apart from their mordacity also showed total ignorance of literary matters, let alone of the practice of literary translation, very much at issue since translation was Joseph's principal source of what little income he had. In general, the impression given by this grizzly farce is of a very young man, trapped in a demeaning situation, who yet managed to remain quite composed, even given his bewilderment at the absurdity of it all. I can hear the Joseph I knew in London, Ann Arbor, New York, Amsterdam, almost as if I were inside that courtroom. But then I hear the poetry too, the poet and his poetry. That his life and his writing were one is not the sentimental rubbish it might seem to be: for Joseph, writing was literally indistinguishable from life, which perhaps is why, though he exalted poetry, he spoke of it in terms of such familiarity. A poet's biography, he was fond of saying, is in his vowels and consonants.

Language and life. His literary essays were often pedagogical, even pedantic, line-by-line, word-by-word textual commentaries; many were, in fact, drawn from his lectures to students. His imagination was often so lexical that there appeared to be no visual counterpart, or the visual was secondary to the linguistic or prosodic. Even his prose, for instance in *Watermark*, is not quite what it seems at first. Consider the following passage:

I was smitten by a feeling of utter happiness: my nostrils were hit by what to me has always been its synonym, the smell of freezing seaweed [. . .] – partly because of onomatopoeic aspects of the very conjunction (in Russian, seaweed is a wonderful vodorosli *) . . .*[34]

Sunday, 10 March, 1996

Back from New York! The Memorial Service in the Cathedral of St. John the Divine, an elephantine, still uncompleted gothic construction, not far from Columbia University, between Broadway and Central Park.

As I stood there in the large congregation, I wondered what Joseph would have thought of it. Three Nobel laureates, Milosz, Walcott and Heaney, were among the readers of poems, mostly by Joseph, but also by Milosz himself, by Frost, Akhmatova, Auden, Mandelstam. Other readers included Mikhail Baryshnikov, Anthony Hecht, Mark Strand, Rosanna Warren, as well as a number of Russian poets, friends of Joseph, Lev Loseff, Yevgeny Rein, Vladimir Uflyand, Tomas Venclova. No encomia, only poems.

And organ music, choir and choristers; a Haydn string quartet. Also, a Mozart rondo, a Purcell motet. Joseph loved Haydn. I remember his mentioning this. I knew that he loathed Tchaikovsky! What of Prokofiev? Stravinsky? He must have liked him. But Beethoven? Probably too much *Sturm und Drang* already. The Procession, however, was to the stirringly senti-mental strains of "When Johnny Comes Marching Home Again", played by the United States Military Academy Band.

The service lasted about two hours . . .

Joseph, what do you think? There was a light moving across the cathedral's ceiling, from left to right. Valentina Polukhina pointed this out to David Betthea, who remarked: "My God, he's smoking even there!" But I'm not going to try to imagine a conversation with him.

Afterwards, there was to be a party for friends and family. I spoke to George Kline, who had promised me an essay on Brodsky for the forthcoming Russian issue of *Modern Poetry in Translation*. It was he who mentioned the reception, assuming that I had been invited. Coming from the Midwest, I knew nothing about it, but Kline suggested we meet at the service and go there together. I didn't want to do this, and so we didn't meet. I asked George if he was reading. He had anticipated the question. "They decided to have only poets." So much for translators!

When I thought of Joseph's progress from homeless young man to Nobel laureate, American Poet Laureate, to his death as the occasion for such obsequies, I was moved. He belonged to all these people.

At the same time, listening to the voices of the different read-ers made the absence of *his* voice, this final silence, tangible. I was particularly disturbed by the lugubriously slow reading of his poetry. So unlike his own manner. But I realized that it would have been far worse to mimic him. And still I yearned for *his* voice, this one last time. But when, at the very end of the serv-ice, Joseph's voice did resound – the Russian original of "Taps", his own English version of the poem, published in the *TLS* on 12th January – people were already drifting away and that voice seemed to pass almost unnoticed.

In general, I found the service hard to take. For me, it was not cathartic, simply a magnification. Of course, its purpose was to remember collectively someone whom so many remembered individually.

As we filed out, my two Jewish friends voiced their dismay and indeed outrage at its Christian nature. I, too, had been puzzled. Joseph and I may not have discussed Judaism, Christianity, affinity for one or the other or a combination of both, and yet he never claimed to be other than a Jew. My companions were angry. Joseph's parents – he had never seen them again and they had died in the Soviet Union, permission for them to visit him having been denied – were remembered in a prayer, a *Christian* prayer, whereas there should surely have been a kaddish for them. *Is that what you wanted, Joseph?* A way of getting closer to Auden? Joseph was among those who organized a commemoration for Auden, in 1973, in this same church.

Perhaps his Jewish friends, myself included, should have held a service for him in a synagogue as well? The thought, though, makes me shudder. We'd have had to have consulted him.

Joseph's "Christianity", the poems on Christian themes, didn't bother me. But then, what did I know? Was I, at such a time, going to look for someone to "blame"? There had to be an explanation.

I remembered "Nature Morte", one of the poems that was read in Russian (by Tomas Venclova), but not in English. (Would it not have been appropriate for George Kline to have read his excellent translation?)

The last three stanzas, quoted earlier, came back to me:

> Mary now speaks to Christ:
> 'Are you my son? – or God?
> You are nailed to the cross.
> Where lies my homeward road?
>
> How can I close my eyes,
> uncertain and afraid?
> Are you dead? – or alive?
> Are you my son? – or God?'

Christ speaks to her in turn:
'Whether dead or alive,
woman, it's all the same –
son or God, I am thine.'

This did not seem to me to be a message of piety: Man is born of woman and I am born of thee. George Kline, however, also refers to these three stanzas in his introduction to the *Selected Poems* (1973). "Even Christ", he writes, "appears as a divine-human still-life, a *nature morte*." He is drawing attention to Brodsky's "concern with death, solitude, and salvation". Actually, much of the early poetry (the later as well?) is concerned with death and parting. So, Christ is not *denying* his divinity, but he *is* making little of it, or making *it* little. And she, Mary, seems to be beyond, even *above* divinity.

Is there a clear Christian message? However, the very next poem in the English collection is "Nunc Dimittis", based on the account in Luke ii: 22–36, of Simeon, a pious man who, on seeing the infant Jesus in the Temple, spoke the words later set to the canticle "Nunc Dimittis" ("Now lettest thou thy servant depart . . .") Joseph, according to a note by Kline, considered this story to be the transition point from Old Testament to New. The poem in the original is entitled *Sreten'e* (Candlemas Day; Feast of the Purification). It is dated 16 February, 1972 which evidently is the Feast Day of Saints Simeon and Anna, and hence also the Name Day of Anna Akhmatova. Stanzas 5–7 quote the "Nunc Dimittis". In George Kline's translation:

he said: "Now, o Lord, lettest thou thy poor servant,

according to thy holy word, leave in peace,
for mine eyes have witnessed thine offspring, this Child –
in him thy salvation, which thou hast made ready,
        a light to enlighten the face of all peoples

and carry thy truth to idolatrous tribes;
bring Israel, thy people, its Glory in time."[35]

In the end, "the form of the Child" is held "to light up the path that leads into death's realm, / where never before until this point in time / had any man managed to lighten his pathway . . ." The message here is unequivocally one of Christian hope.

On the other hand, it is not unusual for Jews to be interested in or even obsessed with the Jew, Christ. As a boy of fifteen or so, I tried to convince a friend of my parents, the son of a famous rabbi, of the divinity of Christ, professing a passionate belief in it. I used to carry around a pocket edition of the Psalms, the Douai version. Thomas à Kempis's *The Imitation of Christ*, Santa Teresa's *Life* and other famous works of Christian devotion, such as *The Confessions* of Saint Augustine, were bedtime reading, though I remember little else about this heretical period of my life. As a historian, I espoused the Catholic cause, reading the (I'm told) anti-Semitic William Cobbett and others, and ascribed all the evils and woes of capitalism to Protestantism (*vide* the moralist social historian R. H. Tawney, *Religion and the Rise of Capitalism*). It was only later that I reminded myself of the anti-Semitic tradition of Catholic Christianity, but even then the love affair continued.

This was not, I think, what Joseph was on about. It's hardly a question here of an adolescent crush. Evidently a woman who looked after the infant Joseph, during the evacuation to Cherepovets, at the time of the Blockade of Leningrad, baptized him in secret. What significance he attached to this, I simply do not know.

Returning to "Nunc Dimittis". It is about death, as well as about salvation. And certainly there is a greater number of poems that draw on Classical mythology: "Sonnet" (Great-hearted Hector has been speared to death); "To Lycomedes on Scyros"; "Aeneas and Dido" (Joseph adored Purcell's *Dido and Aeneas*); "Odysseus to Telemachus" . . . At any rate, neither Christianity, nor Classical Antiquity can be ignored. Not only would it be irreverent: it would be a sort of cultural suicide.

So, I could not agree with my two friends.

But I had not really thought about this before. For me, if he was *anything*, he was a Jew! Yesterday we visited the Metropolitan Museum. The tranquillity of the place reminded me how very untranquil the Cathedral of St. John the Divine had been. The outside world, the city, intruded, the sustained howl of its traffic. At times it was even hard to hear what was going on inside the Church. The columns soared, the organ and choir reverberated. But New York prevailed over it all.

On the other hand, doesn't it always?

When I first came to New York I stayed near here. All through my first night in the city, police sirens ululated. The next day, Lucas and I learnt that a Puerto Rican boy had been raped and murdered in the basement of a shop close by. I was reminded of that, as I sat in the congregation, glorifying my Jewish friend, the poet Joseph Brodsky. He had become a public man. Offprints of a forthcoming article in the *New York Review of Books*, "The Russian Academy: Preliminary Notes", were distributed in the Cathedral. In it Joseph describes the plan he had "put forward to found an Academy in Rome where Russian scholars and artists could resume a long-standing tradition of Russian study in Italy" . . .

Tuesday, 12 March, 1996

Still troubled! I have been looking at Joseph's poem "Isaak i Avraam" (Isaac and Abraham) and one or two others. And then there are the various Christmas poems. So, was he, after all, a Jew with me and other Jews and a Christian with *them*? How Jewish of him that would be! Perhaps, in his early days, he regarded himself as Christian ("Isaak i Avraam" dates from 1963, when Joseph was 23)? What happened afterwards? From my point of view, he *was* quite Jewish, whatever that may mean. Certainly, as he got older, he *looked* more Jewish, whatever *that* may mean. We – I use the word, because he sometimes referred, without specifying, to our common Jewishness – at least that's what I took the "we" as meaning – we were the same kind of Jew,

I supposed. That is, we were *still* Jews. Being a Jew was simply a given.

He clung to language . . . But should I really say "clung"? He wasn't desperate. Still, it is at least conceivable that his devotion to language, to the word, had something to do with being a Jew, a Jew in Russia, or in *Russian*. The Slavophil Khlebnikov was important to him, not because he was a greater poet or as great as the Four – Joseph told me that he regarded Khlebnikov as a genius but actually rather a bad poet! – but because he laboured at the very pit face of language. Different as he was, that was where Joseph, too, found himself much of the time. He was fond of the word "job", meaning the business of putting a poem together; he used the adverb "technically" in the Classical sense for "artfully" (art, as in "the arts of war"). On the other hand, he did not wish to return to his native land. Or he may have wished to, but saw no possibility of so doing. And that he changed the language – though, in contrast to Mayakovsky & Co, he took on board the tradition – is not such a paradox. Not only did he change Russian, but he may also have been changing English, though I dare say it takes other *cosmopolitans* to register this. Was it a kind of subversion? And am I offering a hostage to linguistic anti-Semitism? I prefer to think of it as a search for routes along which what at first appears to be immovable might, in fact, be moved. Joseph himself tried to act as a conduit; the Jewish intellectual or artist, when not safely ghettoized, often does so act. His business was language, and his themes (time, love, loss, death) provided sufficient latitude.

Another Look at "the Poem"

ANOTHER LOOK at "May 24, 1980". Joseph's fortieth birthday:
he was half the age of the century.[36] Here is the last part of an
assonantal version of my own:

> I wandered steppes that remembered the yelling Huns,
> put on clothes that were back in fashion again,
> sowed grain, tarred the roofs of barns,
> and it wasn't just dry water I put away.
> I admitted the guard's burnished eye into my private
>   dreams,
> munched the bread of exile, crust and all,
> put my vocal cords through their paces, but instead of
>   a scream
> switched to a whisper. Now I'm two score.
> What can I say about life? That day followed day.
> It's only grief I'm inclined to cosset.
> But until my mouth has been stopped with clay,
> gratitude's all that will issue from it.

There's the bedevilling search for resonances, particularly at the
end, where the pressure is really on. And does "day followed
day" imply that life seemed long? If one is to take Joseph's
expansion (". . . and abhors transparence") as a commentary,
then it would seem that by "long" he also wished to convey the
notion of life being opaque, uninterpretable; my "day followed
day" suggests rather that it is monotonous, a tedious business.
And to "cosset" grief is by no means synonymous with feeling
sympathy for grief, let alone "solidarity" with it. At this point,
however, Joseph's "interpretation" of his own poem, as we have
seen, becomes of necessity riskily free. He abandons the literal
meaning, in an attempt to match the force of the Russian. He
makes somewhat more explicit, or explicit in a different way,

what is implied in the Russian: that unlike *homo sovieticus*, the author feels solidarity not with the Party and its collective aims, but rather with the grief or suffering of individuals. The word "solidarity" not having these connotations in English, Joseph has had to stretch. My attempt to return to a simpler formulation ("It's only grief I'm inclined to cosset") does not preserve or expand the meaning. Instead, it alters and dilutes it, suggesting self-indulgence rather than sensitivity towards the sufferings of others. In other words, without reference to the source text, my version would be misleading, in conflict with the former's spirit and indeed with Joseph's philosophy of life. The search for rhyme has led me seriously astray. I've lost my grip on the semantics.

Also, my lines appear to be shorter than Joseph's. I calculate that 14 of them have 3 accents, 4 have 2, and 2 have 4. In Joseph's English version, 9 lines, the largest number, have 4 accents. Both versions average approximately 10 syllables per line. My version has a slightly larger range of syllables, 7–15 to Joseph's 9–15; and Joseph's has a larger range of accents, 3–6 to my 2–4. So some of my lines have fewer syllables and fewer accents than any of Joseph's. This may account for their appearing shorter on the whole. The Russian has 9–15 syllables per line, and 3–6 accents, but is basically quadri-accentual, averaging 4 accents per line and 12 syllables. Joseph's English is *palpably* more like the Russian original and also, with all its elaborations, closer at crucial points to the sense. It moves right along, while my version is more or less stationary, straining to add zestfulness to something that is really rather bland.

Recriminations

A FEW DAYS ago I came across a brief correspondence between us concerning "A Part of Speech". It consists mostly of carbons of my letters, bristling with recriminations, Joseph having "revised" my version without consulting or even informing me. Leafing through my disintegrating copy of the book itself, published in 1980, I notice among the credits an unobtrusive paragraph by "J.B." which, it occurs to me, I may in my indignation have overlooked at the time, although if I did notice it, it probably only fuelled that indignation. Joseph thanks his translators, but adds: "I have taken the liberty of reworking some of the translations to bring them closer to the original, though perhaps at the expense of their smoothness. I am doubly grateful to the translators for their indulgence." I am not sure that any of the translators were given much choice, but I was one who would have preferred not to indulge him. Quite possibly, the above disclaimer was even occasioned by my recriminations, or mine added to those of other indignant translators. Clearly, he felt that it was worth sacrificing some "smoothness" if the translations could be brought "closer to the original". Generally he does bring them closer prosodically, especially with regard to rhyme. The content he reworks as he sees fit. And being the author, he is at liberty to do so. These additions or inventions sometimes seem provisional. Joseph, I believe, simply heard *through* the semantic or stylistic lapses (as well, unfortunately, as occasional actual errors in grammar or idiom) to the movement of the whole, the acoustical structure.

Since he was working or attempting to work with translators whose native language was English, his efforts to broker the differences between Russian and English prosody by arranging a marriage between the two, in the expectation or hope that the

87

parties would grow to like one another, probably received little if any encouragement. Hence his rueful allusion to "smoothness" lost. No doubt he was often told as much, but he was able to resist, partly, one supposes, because he was not a native and so could more readily tolerate the lack of smoothness. "Smoothness", of course, has negative, as well as positive connotations. And I still feel that he did some of his translators an injustice by implying that their primary aim was to achieve a glossy finish, no matter how rebarbative the original might have been. However, as I now mouth these *unsmooth* Brodsky-fabricated translations, I am grateful (as was Derek Walcott) to him. I hear – in or through the English – Joseph's own voice, that is, his *Russian* voice. It should be borne in mind, though, that for those, unlike Walcott or myself, who had not heard Joseph, the lack of "smoothness" might be an impediment.

Still, I'm reminded of what Ted Hughes wrote (in an unattributed editorial to *Modern Poetry in Translation* 3, Spring 1967:[37] "The very oddity and struggling dumbness of a word for word version is what makes our own imagination jump. A man who has something really serious to say in a language of which he knows only a few words, manages to say it far more convincingly and effectively than any interpreter, and in translated poetry it is the first hand contact – however fumbled and broken – with that man and his seriousness which we want." Of course, "word for word", "literal" and so forth are loaded terms. It is taking a lot for granted to suppose that an *ad verbum* translation will produce anything more than an inchoate string of words. There is a distinction to be made between scholarly cribs or trots and what Ted Hughes was trying to describe in, say, the Israeli poet Yehuda Amichai's own versions of his poetry. Nevertheless, statements like Hughes's, with which our early editorials abound, indicated at least a readiness to listen to what might seem odd, awkward, *unsmooth*. We wanted to be startled, shocked, even offended, rather than lulled!

This is only partly relevant to the present discussion. Since it was his own poetry that was at stake, Joseph could not simply hope for the best, although it seems to me that there was a roughness, a provisionality, as I've said, about much of the work he offered his readers, perhaps in the expectation that they would understand what he was up to. Furthermore, Joseph's knowledge of English was extraordinary, so that we are not talking here of "struggling dumbness". His own versions, then, his own poems, to a considerable extent rewritten in English, have a particular claim on our attention. This is not to disparage the translations by others, but it surely cannot be denied that Brodsky by Brodsky offers the reader "first hand contact with that man and his seriousness".

"A Part of Speech": Attitude Indeed!

I HAVE ALWAYS thought that Joseph's reason for suggesting I translate the sequence, "A Part of Speech", was that it was as near as he had got (except, perhaps, for one or two of his love poems and such a poem as "May 24, 1980") to writing about himself directly. I surmised that he was especially pleased with the group, written in 1975–6. It could no longer be claimed that he was incapable of writing poetry that put the *self* on the line; he had broken that particular mould, if it was one. Of course, all this is debatable, but Joseph, I thought, could not quite hide his pleasure, his excitement at having brought off something that might surprise his readers. Evidently, he at first thought that this maverick piece might be assigned to me, a sort of maverick among his occasional translators. Later he changed his mind. Perhaps when he realized that the sequence was far more central to his work? OK!

So. I don't remember how much consultation took place. Possibly very little, since there appears to be no correspondence between us on the subject. This is not unusual. Alan Myers tells me that there was little consultation between him and Joseph, but that Joseph would simply use the Myers versions as drafts. Alan Myers was content for this to happen, but I was more proprietorial about my work.

Whether he expressed an opinion on the translation at this stage, I don't know. A card from New York, June 1977, baldly states that the "poems are OK" and that he has asked the editor at Farrar, Straus & Giroux to arrange for payment. He even suggested some other poems of his I might try. The card ends disarmingly: "Some of them are fun, but be in touch" – meaning that we should consult more closely with these poems so that there would be no further misunderstandings.

He referred also to the "bitterness" on my part, due no doubt to his radical revision of some of my versions. Worse was to follow: the Cambridge Poetry Festival, where Joseph presented me with the revised text of "A Part of Speech", took place in 1979. It was then I learnt of his having substituted the revised or rewritten translation for my prize-winning text. (The translation had been published in the March 1978 issue of the august magazine *Poetry* and had even been awarded a prize.) I accused him later of plagiarizing my translation. My outrage had to do with what I considered unethical behaviour, his disrespectful treatment of me, even more than with the revisions as such. I had no doubt that I was morally justified. I was also convinced that my version was demonstrably better than his revised one, even though he had reworked it with the help of Derek Walcott.

I felt humiliated! Everything I had done, it seemed, was subject to scrutiny; not an iota was to be taken on trust, nor was my judgement, as a native speaker of English, to be respected. How could I get it across to Joseph that no two people would translate a text in the same way and that though hardly a line could be expected to coincide, it did not follow that one version would be superior to another. Each honest and painstaking version represented a reading of or set of perceptions about a poem. Of course, Joseph wanted the reading and the perceptions to be his own, and in the end the only way of ensuring this was to translate the poems entirely himself or with the aid of drafts that were no more than bags of ideas to be developed or ignored. Joseph's reference to my well known "attitude" did not make his actions more palatable. Attitude, indeed! Evidently, he would not or could not accept that it was not a question of the translation being improved or damaged, but of ethical standards! In short, he refused to distinguish between the ethical and the aesthetic. For him, as we know, aesthetics was the mother of ethics.

"On Love"

ANYWAY, I WAS too upset to appreciate Joseph's overriding commitment to poetry, to language, his despair at the loss sustained by his work in translation, loss to which his closeness with English made him preternaturally sensitive. He tried, with some embarrassment but no less stubbornly, to specify just why, with Walcott's help, he had revised my versions: "What I mean, for example, is that all the poems that deal with love . . . are in iambic pentameter and rhymed. I just thought that the pattern should be sustained."

So, what am I saying? At least I now find his wish that "the pattern [of rhymed iambic pentameters] should be sustained" in the love poems more reasonable, more understandable, even if I did not really appreciate the *extent* of his almost mystic reverence for form. In his scathing (and unpolitic) review of the Clarence Brown and W. S. Merwin free-verse translation of Mandelstam's poetry,[38] Joseph had written: "Meters in verse are kinds of spiritual magnitudes for which nothing can be substituted . . . They cannot be replaced by each other and *especially not by free verse.*" Of poetic form (described as "noble") he added: "It is the vessel in which meaning is cast. They need each other and sanctify each other reciprocally – it is an association of soul and body. Break the vessel and liquid will leak out."

Nevertheless, I seem to remember that there was a tremor in his voice when he announced that he and Walcott had reworked my versions of those two poems. Doubtless he felt he was making amends rather than compounding the injury when he added: "Still I want both of them to appear under your name . . . 'Translated by Daniel Weissbort with the author' will do, although I'd prefer it without 'the author'." It had the opposite effect, fuelling still further my indignation. Did he imagine that all I wanted was to see my name in print! I rejected his proposal angrily, at first insisting that all who had had a hand in

the translation be named, and in a still angrier letter that immediately followed, demanding that my translations either be
dropped from the collection or that they be used in their original
form. If in the end they went in, in the revised form and with my
name still there, it was either because Joseph decided to ignore
me, on the not unreasonable assumption that I was cutting off
my nose to spite my face, or because I was not quite prepared to
dissociate myself entirely from the making of the book. He
ended his letter, "Kisseskisseskisses", followed by a Joycean
"Sinceearly years . . ."

Joseph (in this same letter) said that he could not take his old
poems seriously, resented having to spend time on them. He
was, or seemed always to be, in a hurry, with poems crowding in
and himself directing the traffic as expeditiously as he could,
while also paying the closest attention to the way the poems were
turned out. There was, in fact, no time to go back over old
ground, even if he had wanted to, and Joseph was not nostalgic
or sentimental.

As he had done several times before, he stressed the importance for him of a "sense of the *inevitability* of the statement"
(earlier he had spoken of "a certain air of ominousness, of
inevitability"). Rhyme had to be positive; it was an indispensable
means of conveying that sense of inevitability.

An example is to be found in the last stanza of "On Love".
First, my initial translation (this was the last poem in *Post-War
Russian Poetry*), followed by the revised version.

> . . . this time I'll
> not hurry to the light-switch, nor
>
> will I remove my hand; because I've not the right
> to leave you in that realm of silent
> shadows, before the fence of days,
> falling into dependence from a reality
> containing me – unattainable.

Revised version:

> ... This time I will restrain
> my hand from groping for the switch, afraid
>
> and feeling that I have no right
> to leave you both like shadows by that sever-
> ing fence of days that bar your sight,
> voiceless, negated by the real light
> that keeps me unattainable forever.

Though at the time I rather liked the paradox: "containing me –
unattainable", which is literally closer to the original's "with my
unattainability in it", he has a point. Actually, as is painfully
obvious ("falling into dependence from a reality"), the last
stanza simply defeated me, even though I somehow persuaded
myself that I had deciphered it, and Joseph's far more interpretive and comprehensible English version corrects at least one
crucial misunderstanding. That he failed, at the time, to point
out mistakes shows either that he didn't want to cast aspersions
on my linguistic competence or, more likely, that his attention
was so focused on the prosodic defects of my version that he
could not be bothered to point out errors, or perhaps did not
even notice them.

It seems that for him "inevitability" meant, above all,
unequivocal rhyming. That is, there were certain rules: if you
couldn't manage a whole quatrain, then rhyme the second and
fourth lines, not the first and second: substitution of an *a b b a*
pattern for an *a b a b* one was not acceptable; slant rhymes were
nearly always unacceptable. I was not the only one to complain
about this, insisting that in English, with its paucity of rhymes,
it was necessary to take advantage of assonance and consonance,
as this gave the translator more room for manoeuvre and allowed
him to stay semantically closer to the source text. Joseph would
have none of this, regarding it as spurious, or opportunistic.
Gradually, though, his ear for English became more acute,
and he not only recognized a wider range of assonances and

consonances, but was confident enough even to experiment with feminine rhymes. Still, he detested what he regarded as the "take-it-or-leave-it" attitude (by which he meant casual, indifferent, unfocused, uncommitted, rather than forceful or regressive) of so much contemporary English poetry, characterizing it as "cowardly", these being epithets he applied to me, after first trying to appease me by complimenting me on my "notions of poetic technique". He felt that poetry in English had degenerated, lacked structure, formal definition, intellectual discipline, etc. All these qualities were latent in the language, of course, but the latter was not being heeded. Misguidedly, foolishly, poets were listening to themselves instead.

Choices

THAT HE WILL not answer if I ring his number is somehow inexplicable. Perhaps if I had seen his body, at the lying-in-state in Greenwich Village? Irina phoned to tell me about it. I made a note of the time: Friday, 2 February, 7.30 pm. "He was peaceful. A light surrounded him . . ." She left a rose for me. How did I feel about that. I was touched by her gesture, by her thinking of me at that moment of private grief . . .

Had I been there? Had I seen the Russian Prime Minister Viktor Chernomyrdin arriving, at the last moment, in a stretch-limousine and immediately voicing objections to Joseph being buried outside Russia, because after all he was a great *Russian* poet (*Velíkii Rússkii Poét*), perhaps I would have found it easier to believe that he truly was gone. Since *they* had come to claim him, he had to be gone! He belonged to the Russian language, not to Russia, either Soviet or post-Soviet.

Of course, I know that the lying-in-state is customary. I recall the photographs of a tranquil-looking Pasternak in his coffin. And there are the famous pictures of Joseph in the forefront of the crush about Akhmatova's open coffin. Joseph, his hand over his mouth, as though to stifle a groan. Evidently he is unable to contain his grief. He is staring at her in amazement, in horror, wildly and privately at the same time.

Had I seen his, Joseph's corpse, would I then have believed in his death? If his former homeland wanted to appropriate his body, he had to be dead.

We had saved our pennies and taken the 1980–81 academic year off to concentrate on writing. Part of the time, the winter months, we spent in my flat in Ostend, with its view of the sea. Now we were back in England, having rented a few rooms in

Olwyn Hughes's house in Cambridge. Spring in Cambridge, walks to the American cemetery, ambles in the botanical gardens, which were not far from the house in Lensfield Road.

That summer, 3–9 June 1981, there was another international poetry festival in Cambridge. I had been invited, on my own account this time, to take part in a panel with Paul Engle, Hualing Nieh Engle,[39] and Peter Jay on the teaching of creative writing, entitled "Poetry in the Making: the Example of Iowa". But although I was listed in the programme, it felt anomalous to be part of a presentation about the Iowa Workshop. True, I had spent nearly a decade in Iowa, as director of the translation workshop, but I still could not bring myself to endorse workshops. Furthermore, it felt wrong to be appearing on the same platform as that quintessential man of the American heartlands, that Midwestern internationalist Paul Engle. I who did not even feel myself to be an *echt* Englishman; at best, the Jewish parvenu!

In his introduction to a double issue of *Modern Poetry in Translation* (Nos. 19–20, Spring 1974), dedicated to the International Writing Program, Paul Engle, in somewhat Ciceronian terms, declared that:

Translation is not putting down in one language equivalent words from another language. That is not how the poem was written: not a literal version of the mind, but an imaginative one. So must the translation be imaginative, with something of the same talent for language which formed the poet's own primary text. [. . .] The translator must try the same process. This is why poetry should be translated by poets, so that the end result is close to a poem as well as to the poem.

Forceful and optimistic, this seems or seemed uncontroversial enough. Still, there is a particular ring of confidence to it. While offering no practical advice, it *sounds* quite businesslike, unpretentious, even democratic, although paradoxically the sentiment might be regarded today as élitist or at least romantic, with the special privileges that are claimed for poetry and for poets.

97

Ted Hughes and I, with the magazine *Modern Poetry in Translation*, also believed poetry could be translated, but were suspicious of "poetic" translation. The latter evidently was precisely what Engle tried to promote, although it should be said that the versions he favoured had a grittiness which may not have "reeked of the translator's sweat" but which marked them as something other than just poems written in English. Ted Hughes, in his introduction to the first Poetry International readings in London, in 1967, had written: "However rootedly national in detail it may be, poetry is less and less the prisoner of its own language. It is beginning to represent, as an ambassador, something far greater than itself. Or perhaps it is only now being heard for what, among other things, it is – a universal language of understanding, coherent behind the many languages, in which we can all hope to meet." Engle might have concurred with this sentiment, but Ted and I, with the example of post-War East European poetry before us, believed that the route to a "universal language" lay through a kind of literalism, best served by non-professionals, and consequently that one should beware of poets, with their libertine ways, translating other poets. To some extent, while more optimistic (and less scholarly) than Nabokov, we agreed with him that attention to the text, that is, to the words, even to the order of the words, was desirable. That this smacked of cabbalism or numerology, if anything reassured us.

Where did Joseph stand? His attachment to language, specifically to the genius of Russian, should have made him doubtful about translation. He might have been inclined to settle for Nabokov's scrupulous literalism. And one would expect him to have been scornful of the vague idealism of an Engle. Finally, though, he developed a "theory" of his own, based on his personal situation really, on personal experience as poet and self-translator. If poetry translation was impossible, in an absolute sense – and would Joseph accept anything less? – then it had to be circumvented, an alternative found.

So, even though he had wanted others to translate his poetry, he was not content, even after quite detailed consultation, to relinquish control. It seems that he made use of his translators' talents or inner knowledge of their own language to empower himself. And this was a temporary expedient, pending his assuming the entire task, though he also complained that he would far rather have left it to others, so that he could get on with the primary business of writing his poetry in Russian. Increasingly, he seemed to conceive of the translation process as a single unified one, even though it might involve more than two individuals. In his efforts to achieve prosodic consistency, he began to fiddle with the target language itself. Writing poetry directly in English gave him a greater stake and helped him to strengthen his grip on it. Evidently he believed in the possibility of a rapprochement between English and Russian. Should one, therefore, conclude that he was essentially optimistic about translation, even if he was often brusque with translators, who were simply a means to an end, the end being what mattered? It could be argued on the contrary that he was deeply pessimistic about translation, conventionally or even unconventionally defined, and for that reason had to re-invent it. Brodsky's approach constitutes a new kind of literalism, a rhetorical, prosodic literalism, the emphasis of which is distinct from that of the semantic literalism espoused in the early issues of *MPT,* or as proclaimed by Nabokov. On the other hand, his position is still further from the inspirationalist one of a Paul Engle, or even a Robert Lowell.

But what of another kind of literalism, which rather than suppress or domesticate the foreign text in translation, on the contrary emphasizes its foreignness, allowing the language of the translation to be changed through contact with the foreign?

June 1981, the Cambridge Poetry Festival. Joseph is sitting in an armchair in the lobby of the Royal George Hotel. Facing him is the 76-year old American poet Stanley Kunitz, who is lecturing Joseph on English prosody. Standing, is the burly, charcoal-browed Yugoslav (Serbian) poet Vasko Popa. I am standing beside Vasko.

Kunitz's arguments are impeccable, incontrovertible, it might seem. In any case, Joseph offers no resistance, although Stanley is insisting that rhetorically mimetic translation is simply misguided. In his "Note on the Translation", in *Poems of Akhmatova*, co-translated with Max Hayward (1972), Kunitz defines the problem as he sees it:

The poet as translator lives with a paradox. His work must not read like a translation; conversely, it is not an exercise of the free imagination. One voice enjoins him: "Respect the text!" The other simultaneously pleads with him: "Make it new!"

Of course, one might query what is meant by *read like a translation*. The commonsense approach is: We all know what it means. And the changes made by the translator, intent on eliminating "foreignness", are often, as has been said, defended on the unprovable grounds that this is how the author would have written had he been writing in English. "The only way to translate Akhmatova", Stanley insists, "is by writing well." Although Joseph also believed that the writer's primary (or only) obligation was to write well, he might have defined it somewhat differently, at least in respect to translators, having in mind an enlargement of English, enabling it to match effects commonly regarded as achievable only in Russian. He will, for example, have objected in principle to Kunitz's assertion that

To insist on a universally rigid duplication of metrical or rhyming patterns is arbitrary and pointless, since the effects in any case are not mechanically transferable to another language. Instead of rhyme, our ear is often better pleased by an instrumentation of off-rhyme, assonance, consonance, and other linkages.

I once asked Kunitz point-blank what he thought about formal translations, particularly having in mind Brodsky's strictures. His response is worth quoting in full, I think, since it elegantly encapsulates a particular point of view, with which few would argue or would have argued at the time:

The genius of each language is unique. Each poem is also unique, with its individual inflexion, rhythm, pitch, pacing, auditory pattern, etc. So much of it can only be implied in translation. What is most readily translatable is the matter of a poem, its substantive ground, which there is no excuse for betraying, even in the absence of equivalents. All the rest — its music, its spirit, its complex verbal and psychic tissue — one tries to suggest as best one can. It's foolish to argue for the exact reconstruction of a poem in another language when the building blocks at one's disposal bear no resemblance to those of the original.[40]

To make matters worse, Vasko Popa, who inevitably had been left out of the conversation but had been staring thoughtfully at Joseph, now hissed: "*Dis à Joseph qu'il devrait s'occuper plus de Saint Vladimir, et moins de Pierre le Grand! Traduis-le!*" I obeyed, briefly interrupting Stanley's diatribe: "Vasko says that you should attend more to St. Vladimir and less to Peter the Great." Joseph stared up at me mutely. Was Vasko saying that Joseph should return to the true, the real Russia of the steppes, the tundras, the wooden villages; that he should look rather to the pre-Petrine Russia of the Igor Tale, and turn away from that anachronistic Venice of the North, built on a swamp, at a catastrophic human cost, by architects imported from afar?

While Joseph, like Mandelstam, was "hungry for world culture" and while Leningrad-Petersburg, in its splendour, was his city, he was no étatist. I never discussed Peter the Great with him, but he made fun of tyrants and dictators, even if his jokes were at times in rather questionable taste, as when on my birthday, on a walk through New Yorks's Little Italy, he bought me a tee-shirt with the image of Mussolini giving the fascist salute. Actually, Joseph's "dissidence" was the most dangerous, most corrosive kind, being that of indifference to politicians and rulers. And he was, after all, a Jew, which, while it might not have prevented his identifying to some extent with Russian Orthodoxy and its founding Saint, perhaps stood in the way of the sort of identification that Vasko seemed to be urging. Was Vasko unaware of Joseph's Jewishness? Surely not. Did he, perhaps, regard it as irrelevant? The Jew, in his apartness, is paradoxically so much a *part* of the jumble of peoples, religions, traditions that is Central and Eastern Europe.

In her evocative essay on Brodsky the teacher, Rosette C. Lamont reports a conversation with him.[41] After commenting on the wonderful primitive quality of the Georgian and Armenian poets, Joseph remarked: "They are peasants, and that's fine. That's also what I like about Yugoslavian poetry. It is deeply rooted in folklore. Of course folklore is full of what we might define as early examples of Surrealism: houses on chicken legs, winged humans. It is easy to combine modern techniques with folklore, and this is what the Yugoslav poets have done . . . Do you know Vasko Popa? He creates his own mythology." This took place in the fall of 1973, when Joseph was teaching in New York. He also quoted from the "Homage to the Lame Wolf" cycle, in Anne Pennington's *Selected Poems of Vasko Popa* (1969). Ted Hughes, in his introduction to this book, speculates along similar lines, though in somewhat more uncompromising terms, distinguishing between what he calls folk surrealism and Surrealism, the literary movement. It seems likely that Joseph was familiar with Popa's poetry before he left the Soviet Union in 1972. If he appears to be echoing Ted Hughes here, it is with a difference, his remarks being altogether more urbane (more urban?) than Hughes's. It is clear that, while he admires Vasko and the "folk surrealists", he is also far from them in spirit, whereas Hughes is not.

To sum up, I like to think that Vasko was simply suggesting Joseph rely more on his instincts, feelings. At the same time, I do not think that Joseph was prepared to argue with Vasko. It is as if he knew that there was too much distance between them, just as there perhaps was between himself and Stanley Kunitz. Whatever the case, Vasko's remark seemed to make him uncomfortable, almost disconsolate. But there was a mutual regard, even love, between these two men.

Words Aloud

WHEN I THINK of him, I think of words: words as worship, as celebration, as the sound of ideas. "A poet in his development, if he is a true poet", he said in an interview with Natalya Gorbanevskaya in 1983, "repeats the development of language; he begins with some sort of childish babble, then moves to maturity, and to greater maturity and, finally, to language itself".[42] He gave reading after reading, as if he wanted as many people as possible to *hear* Russian. He showed his native language off, with increasing virtuosity but always in the capacity of a servant. If he displayed pride, it was pride in the language, not in himself. In answer to a question put by Valentina Polukhina at a seminar at Keele University, in 1978, he said: "I merely pass on what exists in the Russian language, there is no special merit of my own." Or again, in a 1981 interview with Bella Yezerskaya, responding to the question: "Do you consider yourself an innovator?", he said: "No, I don't think so. Innovation is, in any case, a silly concept [*Joseph was rarely diplomatic!*]. My rhymes sometimes turn out to be quite good [*no false modesty either!*], but to consider them 'new' is senseless; they're taken from the language in which they have always existed."[43] Genius artlessly describing itself? In any case, though skeptics will remain unconvinced, he was not being disingenuous. However partially, he was reporting the facts as he saw them. His was a reverential attitude, but free of that piety which is a kind of self-indulgence, self-aggrandisement.

So, when I think of his readings, I think, well, of words. First, as has been noted, he was in a hurry. The words, Russian or English, seemed already to be champing at the bit, before he released them: "Yet until brown clay has been crammed down my larynx, / only gratitude will be gushing from it." A fountain or eruption of some kind, though he might have objected to this notion as too grandiose for his workaday dealings with words;

the Russian *razdavatsia* (ring out) is less violent. (Once, when asked how he "composed", he responded: ". . . *if* I compose . . . *Compose* is too big a word for it.") The impression, nevertheless, *was* of a natural force that he somehow directed from within, at the same time submitting to the surge of it. As he concentrated, he seemed to repeat words that only he had heard, barely keeping up with them. He stood, his hands out of the way, in his jacket pockets, leading with his jaw, reciting by heart. And yet not exactly by heart either. It was more as if he saw and heard, as if he were reading or being prompted. Bracing himself and then staring over the heads of his audience, or within, at that prompter. His verse seemed to crave the dimension lent it by his own voice. Of course, the vocalization was not essential for the life of the Russian; but I suspect that live performance, particularly in connection with Joseph's own idiolect, was needed for the life of the English. Now, as the memory of him, the memory of the sound of him, fades (recordings are not enough), some other English manifestation will be called for if he is not simply to rejoin the ranks of "untranslated" Russian poets.

The day after one of Joseph's readings in Iowa, a poet colleague stopped me in the hall and let me know how much he had disliked Brodsky's stentorian rendition. I hazarded an explanation along these lines: "Of course, poetry is more important there, insofar as other avenues of expression are closed off or restricted and so people turn to poetry far more than they do here. There's a tradition of that sort of thing. Poetry draws larger audiences, and therefore the readings are more theatrical, more declamatory . . ." The trouble is that I more or less agreed with my colleague. I was embarrassed by the vatic manner, had grown accustomed to the casual style of so many American poetry readings. It is true that, in spite of this, I still got a thrill from Joseph's performance, but I also disapproved and was suspicious of it. Wasn't it just so much hocus-pocus? To put it unkindly, his readings were alike, the same crescendos and decrescendos, a truncated chromatic scale, an unvarying pitch, etc. And the big voice, and that jaw, like . . . Well, *didn't* it, after all, make you think of *il Duce!* At the same time, can't you see he's in pain, barely getting by! Hugging those words to himself and simultaneously letting them go, words whose life is his own.

Joseph was fond of quoting Herodotus's *History*, in which it is said of the Scythians, those nomadic precursors of the Russians, that "they exist in a state of constant surprise at their own language". One remembers Walcott's: "the man is excited, he's physically excited, the same as a footballer . . ." – he was one! He was keen on the game and played it in his youth, apparently. This excitement or innocence never deserted him. One imagines that it made him especially vulnerable as well. But it also protected him; however grim his vision of the human lot, that joy in language, that excitement, that capacity for being constantly surprised sustained him.

"Bully for you!" I should have told my colleague.

So, Joseph's reading exalted *language* as such, or *the* language in particular. There was an obligation to speak out forcefully, without dissimulation, because linguistic dignity, not his own, demanded it. And it couldn't be helped if, in the eyes of some, all this was misjudged. You can't please everyone, nor would you wish to, if you value your independence!

And as for his performance, he was not striving for histrionic effect. His poetry, his reading of poetry, his own or anyone else's, began from the rhythm, metre, acoustical shape made by the words. He recited from within or among words. And he always seemed to be hurrying as well.

As far as I know, Joseph never submitted to the indignity of having most of the reading in English translation, with but a few samples from among the source texts, to satisfy audience curiosity, to authenticate the event or give him, as the foreign poet, the maker of the source text, some reason for being there. Such was his faith in language that he did not doubt that the Russian sounds would be memorable. To deprive his public of the Russian would have been to cheat it.

The original London Poetry Internationals of the late sixties and early seventies featured foreign poets reading their work in the source language, with accompanying translations read by native readers (occasionally the translator themselves). But objections were raised. Some of the foreign poets were dreadfully boring to more than a few in the audience, and in any case wasn't the strain of listening for two or three hours to poetry, half of which was in languages unknown to most of those present, intolerable?

But what has this to do with Joseph? A poet of the page, he was also a poet of the voice. Revering both Russian and English, he was also instrumental in bringing them closer than they had been before, as he struggled to create an English that embraced the two traditions. He was an exceptionally versatile improviser, or at least gave the impression of so being. Meaning, that he also gave the impression of knowing where he was going, even if he was determined not to let on about it. He was a pied-piper who needed all the guile he could muster.

There was no contradiction here between writing to be read and writing to be heard. Poetry antedates literacy and for many it is the sound that both precedes and underlies sense. Joseph, I surmise, believed in a flow or current between languages, as a prerequisite for that crossing over of sense, which in our *sensum-sensu*, Ciceronian tradition has dominated translation practice, even if it has meant different things to different men.

Proselytizing Students

Friday, 12 April, 1996

LAST WEDNESDAY I presented to the translation workshop a few early poems by Brodsky that I had just translated. I included "May 24, 1980": the Russian original for the three students this semester working with Russian, Joseph's translation, and a literal or "literate" version. I brought along as well the tape of Joseph's Iowa City reading, since he started, as he frequently did, with this particular poem. I talked for much of the time, trying to persuade the students – anticipating their resistance to the notion – that Joseph was submitting English to the test of Russian. The idea, as an idea, might appeal to them, I thought; but what would they make of it in practice? *My* literal version showed how far Joseph was prepared to depart from literal sense, changing, dropping, even adding – new metaphors, for instance. If another translator were to make so free, it would surely be regarded as presumptuous, irresponsible, or reckless. And there were losses. However cleverly disguised or integrated, what amounted to padding could only weaken the poem semantically and prosodically. My discourse was overlong, partly because it was easier for me to continue in this manner than to stop and let things take their course; partly for tactical reasons. I hoped that if my own commentary embraced nearly all conceivable negative reactions, the revelation that it had all nevertheless been worth while would come as an even more salutary shock.

Actually, I was trying to show the students in advance that the objections inevitably forming in their minds were jejune, that it was reasons such as those they were about to advance (or would have advanced, had I not saved them from making fools of themselves!) that accounted for the failure to give Joseph's innovations a fair hearing; that the method itself was at least as significant as the practical results, which should be evaluated

in this wider context. The students interrupted this monologue
only to ask one or two factual questions. Finally it became clear
even to me that I was hardly inviting open discussion.

As I listen to the tape, with Joseph reciting "May 24, 1980",
preceded by his introduction to the reading, full of "well's" and
"actually's", I can see him leaning forward, wrinkling his brow,
stretching his neck to peer at the audience, with that inward,
anxious look on his face, his hands shoved into his pockets:
"Well, Mr Weissbort will read the English, and then I'll follow
with the . . . well . . . with the Russian. Actually, I could read the
English too, but . . . well . . . you see . . . the poems are . . . well
. . . translated, that is . . . actually . . . they have already been
badly damaged, and I . . . well . . . I wouldn't want to add accent
to injury . . ." Joseph tries to continue, but has to pause for the
laughter. As a translator, I grit my teeth and then I read, doing
the best I can. And then Joseph's voice . . .
   I stop the tape, glance at the inscrutable faces before me and
start talking again. My concern, now, is to show that I am still in
charge. Is anyone deceived? Does anyone even know what's
going on? I can at least show that speechlessness has not overwhelmed me, that I am not overcome by emotion! I fill the
silence, improvising desperately: "Could it be that Joseph's
English version of the poem somehow makes the English reader
sound like the poet himself, not as the poet might be supposed to
sound if he were writing in English, but somehow as he *actually*
sounds, *in Russian?*"
   This fanciful, but actually quite simple idea seems to break
the ice. At last the comments begin to come. It is hard for me to
follow. Contrary to the impression I was trying to give, I am far
from cool-headed. "His English loses the ironical element; it
mixes registers, levels." Well, it does. I try harder to understand.
Loses the ironical? Joseph was certainly not lacking in a sense of
irony, although wasn't it a rather gentle kind of irony? (Or is that
a contradiction in terms?) So, what does she mean? And anyway,
this is not really an ironical poem, although one can see why
she might think so – it is, after all, mock-heroic: but surely it is

obvious that Joseph is not *really* mythologizing himself? Still, what *does* she mean? Mixes registers, yes. But irony . . . "Let knives rake my nitty-gritty . . ." I'd already allowed that this was unacceptable and that I wouldn't attempt to defend such a euphemism. That is, I might defend it, but not straight off; a lot of ground had to be laid, before one risked taking "nitty-gritty" seriously! Anyway, here it comes: "'Nitty-gritty'! It's like at school, when you're given some theme or other and told to write a poem on it and this is the sort of thing you come up with . . ." I am shocked, but do not respond. That is, I don't know how to respond. Is this the way it strikes people? Did his reading leave them cold? Or could this be how *they* deal with difficult feelings? Perhaps they are embarrassed by them? Or am I deceiving myself about his translations, not to mention his own poems in English? Is what he has set out to do simply impossible, or perverse, or worse, presumptuous?

But, finally, I give up; I've not allowed enough time for proper discussion. Aren't they, in spite of all my precautions, my attempt at a pre-emptive strike, responding exactly as feared? Nevertheless my discourse has given them something else to get their teeth into: for instance, that Joseph was using language, English, in a boldly experimental manner; also that the fact that English was not his mother tongue was in a way advantageous, since one is somehow freer in another language (or in another country).

Hard to let go of this! Of course, I wanted to prove – to my students – that Joseph's English was a legitimate creation, capable of effects of which our (or my) English, for instance, was not. But how can this be shown, short of reading the poems and translations aloud, over and over, perhaps reading the latter *immediately* after, or immediately before the Russian – miming the Russian? Maybe the original and its translation texts could even be read simultaneously? Could it be shown that the shape of the poem – the shape of the sounds – was answered, echoed in the translation, Joseph's translation.

I remember "teaching" Gerard Manley Hopkins to American students. Rather than interpret, rather than talk about the poems – influences, structure, even phonology – I recited or spoke the poems. At least that gave *me* pleasure and was rewarding, because in class I was simultaneously reader and listener, which cannot quite be done on one's own. So, I was also free to enjoy myself, if exhibitionistically! I hoped, and rather presumptuously believed, that the pleasure I was experiencing was also being conveyed. Regrettably, I lacked the nerve to make the class one of poetry-recitation. Some might think that this is the easy way, that to stress performance shirks the responsibility of explication, of discussing the poem as a cultural artefact, etc. But perhaps the "easy" way is also the right one.

Then again, with Joseph perhaps this would be cheating. And am I trying to usurp his place? As though he couldn't look out for himself. So afraid, indeed convinced that he'll be misunderstood – because, after all, I too misunderstood him – that I try to anticipate the doubts, the sarcasms, etc. As if my heading them off might win the skeptics over. Or, even if they still believe that they are right but have to allow that their arguments have somehow been pre-empted, they will in all fairness have to give what is being said on Brodsky's behalf a fair hearing. It will then become possible to acclimatize *their* ear to *his* English.

Here is the gist of what I told the workshop: "It's like a new kind of music. You may not like it, may find it absurd, outrageous even, but admit, if only for the sake of argument, that this may be due to its unfamiliarity. Give it a chance, listen!"

The Self Projected

ON THE OTHER hand, when Joseph left Russia, when he read for the first time in the West, at that poetry festival in London, he may well have been quite surprised at the enthusiasm of the audience. It is conceivable, even likely, that he had no inkling of what to expect. Of course, though still young, he was not new to the game. He had been translated, had become the object of what were in effect cultural pilgrimages, had been pilloried by the state, was close to the last of the great ones, Akhmatova. And then there were his readings in Russia (remember Etkind's description, cited above). I suppose he was already a cult figure, whatever that may mean, or well on his way to becoming one. So he was surely aware of the hallucinatory effect of his performances. Even so, there was no telling whether this would turn out to be exportable. Traumatized as Joseph evidently was, that first reading at the Queen Elizabeth Hall at once set him on the path. He gave reading after reading. He did not let the sound fade, or himself go out of fashion, be lost sight of. He kept himself, the sound of himself, current. In one respect, this can be seen as a triumph of the will to survive, though he may also have needed constant exposure of this sort to compensate for the loss of a native audience. And in any case, as we have seen, he regarded it as his particular mission – though he might have balked at putting it so grandly – to bring Russian to English. And beyond that, of course, was the larger mission, on behalf of Poetry itself. And there must have been a price to pay, that of privacy, of the seclusion most artists need. Still, he also had the invaluable knack of being just himself. And periodically, as at Christmas when he went to Venice, he became a "nobody in a raincoat".

Or do I exaggerate? Was he, in fact, misled? Did he misunderstand the interest his person or presence aroused? Perhaps it was more a matter of curiosity. He had become a sort of institution, America's Poet-in-Exile. And as for his odd English, well, who cared really. It had seemed to me, from the start, that Joseph was a great improviser. He had not quite anticipated the reception he received, but he adjusted readily enough to it. And as for his style of reading, well, as noted, he claimed it was simply the way poetry was read in Russia. But even his disingenuousness worked to his advantage. So, perhaps it was *all* a kind of improvisation. He relied on the challenge of live situations, on his wit and his wits, on language itself. Joseph had faith. He adopted a casual manner, even though the delivery of the poetry was quite the opposite to casual. He resisted being turned into a monument, an institution, although he himself raised monuments to those he regarded as his mentors: Tsvetayeva, Mandelstam, Akhmatova, Frost, Auden.

Joseph had no training as a teacher. And not only did he not possess a so-called further degree, he had no degree at all. Nevertheless, in '74 or '75, having been invited to teach a poetry course at Iowa, I visited him in Amherst, seeking his advice. The very idea of teaching, for which I too had no training, petrified me. I simply could not visualize myself in front of a class, for three or four months. How did I get myself into this!

We met for dinner, in the home of a mutual friend, Stavros Deligiorgis, who had been directing the Translation Workshop in Iowa, but was at this time a visiting professor at the University of Massachusetts. I remember next to nothing of the evening and nothing of Emily Dickinson's home town; when I went there, a few years later, to give a talk at Amherst College, it might as well have been for the first time. But what *does* remain is Joseph's attempt to fill me with confidence. It went something like this: "There's nothing to worry about! As a European, you already have a huge advantage: you know things, this comes with the territory after all. So, all you have to do is talk. Anything you say will be news to them!" This advice turned out to be well founded. Plus my own realization that validating students is the key to "teaching". Though he validated *me*, Joseph apparently was not always so gentle with his students. Indeed, I am told that he was often quite scornful or sarcastic. However, he usually got away with it, maybe because he wasn't mean, though probably not everybody would agree with this.

It distresses me that I cannot remember his *actual* words. Joseph remembered his poems. Did he, like an actor, deliberately memorize them for readings, or were they already in his memory, retrievable at any time? I think the latter. They were there, together with many other poems, by other poets, Russian and English; Mark Strand recalls how at their first meeting Joseph recited a poem of his (Strand's) which Strand himself had forgotten. He remembered poems as sound, metrically, accenting the English ones in a Russian manner. Obviously, there is a difference between remembering verse and remembering spoken words, but I am still upset by my own very poor memory. Generally what I have at my disposal is an imperfect or approximate *translation*. And not just imperfect, incomplete, but often incorrect as well: in faulty English, or in a kind of translatorese; or even worse, a kind of pre-English, so that translating myself, as it were, is as frustrating as translating the poetry of others!

To be fair (or fairer) to myself, at least in Amherst, I may also have been embarrassed or uncomfortable with what he was saying. He seemed to be advocating what amounted to a kind of con. Instead of really applying myself, all I had to do was *be* European. And wasn't it invidious to suggest that young Americans were so ignorant, so impressionable and simple-minded really that we crafty Europeans could easily hold their attention simply by bullshitting? I felt it was dishonourable to concur with this – I was a Brit in the US, not a Russian political exile; perhaps he could be excused – but I raised no objections at the time. His assumption that, like him, I must have the wherewithal to instruct and entertain was flattering. And anyway, hadn't I rather invited this complicity by sharing my anxieties with him?

To sum up. From exile to commanding presence, despite his relative youth. Nothing could stop Brodsky. What if he *had* removed himself, become a recluse, like J. D. Salinger or Henry

Roth? This was not an option. He made use of his *renommée* to do what had not been done before, to translate himself, to make the American "scene" move over for him. And he found friends, supporters, as well as admirers. I do not believe that his poetry alone, however brilliant, created the opening. Something to do with his actual presence, what he projected as a man, his fate or destiny, was responsible, even if he continued to insist that this destiny, Nobel prize and all, was an accident. And his poetry was more than the poems or even the sum of the poems. It represented and still does a kind of conjunction or collision of prosodies.

It occurs to me that, although I might not initially have taken to Joseph's poetry, I had from the start responded to his reading. I may have tried to find reasons not to do so, to resolve this apparent contradiction, to align myself, my responses, with what I thought, or thought I thought. But I failed. Joseph was extremely inventive, but his imagery often seemed contrived, fanciful. The conceits might entertain or impress, but I could not visualize them; they had no sensorial presence for me. At the same time, Joseph seemed to equate rhyme and metre with virtue, with ultimate worth. Incidentally, he also wrote about Mandelstam: "For him, a poem began with a *sound*, with a sonorous molded shape or form." Of course, many poets (Housman, Eliot, for instance) have similarly tried to explain what happens when a poem is coming into existence; but somehow I had not thought of Brodsky as being in that company.

How Does Brodsky or Anyone Else Translate Brodsky?

BUT HOW TO translate his poetry? Later, as we saw, Joseph himself began to take on the rôle, applying as much of his skill and ingenuity as he could spare from his main task of writing poems in Russian. He may have been reluctant at first (judging from his letters to me) but I imagine that eventually – or maybe from the start? – he also saw this enterprise as part of a larger literary one that had to do with English-Russian reciprocity. After all, he imported into Russian elements drawn from Donne, from Auden; and he then re-imported these into English, transformed by his earlier Russianizing of them. That is, he did not simply attempt to impose Russian syntax, Russian phonology or metres on English; he also permitted his Russian to be changed or charged by the English language, by English patterns of thought and behaviour. Yet so complete was his mastery of traditional techniques, that the hybrid he created was alive (not just because its author was) even if it was not easily come to terms with.

So, how *does* one translate Brodsky? Ezra Pound's well known, no-nonsense definition of poetry comes to mind. According to Pound, there are three "kinds of poetry": *Melopoeia*, "where the words are charged, over and above their plain meaning, with some musical property"; *Phanopoeia*, "which is a casting of images upon the visual imagination."; *Logopoeia*, where words are employed "not only for their direct meaning, but [taking account of] habits of usage . . ." Of these melopoeia is practically impossible to translate; phanopoeia *can* be successfully translated; and logopoeia is not translatable, though "the attitude of mind it expresses may pass through a paraphrase. That is, you cannot translate it 'locally', but having determined the original author's state of mind, you may or may not be able to find a derivative or an equivalent." This last observation is, of course, problematical. How do you determine "the original author's state of mind"? Or maybe it doesn't matter, so long as you, the translator, confronted by the text, have determined your *own* state of mind.

Pound has a point. Although Brodsky may be regarded as strong in all three departments, his poetry has most to do with logopoeia, which Pound saw as virtually untranslatable "locally". Also, I imagine that Brodsky's poetry, whether in English or in Russian, is to some extent, the product of an interaction between Russian and English. One can understand why he should have attempted to control and eventually take over the translation process. Uneven as the results may have been, in an ideal world he was the proper translator of his own work, at least the proper primary translator. Since he is no longer among us, the question arises as to whether his future translators should or will follow in the path of prosodic literalism that he trod. Perhaps only Joseph Brodsky was in a position to undertake such a project. Perhaps, that is, author and translator have to be the same person; and even then, it is quite likely that Brodsky was uniquely endowed or qualified.

And then, as I suggested earlier, there is the question of his voice, his living voice, his actual readings, his polemical, vocal presence.

Two Jews

AN INVOLUNTARY exile, Joseph was a *kosmopolit*, more avid for world culture than he was curious about Christianity. The Jew-as-writer, it seems to me, is committed to language as such, to the living language. He does not write for the future, even if his writing is "ahead of its time". Nor does he write out of reverence for the past: past and future can take care of themselves. Joseph, of course, was engaged in something else as well, making the two languages more equal, adding, subtracting, but above all mixing. Even before he became a wanderer, Joseph was a transgressor. As a translator, in the wider sense, he crossed and recrossed frontiers. "All poets are Yids", said Tsvetayeva.

Joseph dispensed with the supposed privileges of victimhood. Jewishness, inescapably identified with persecution, was not likely to appeal to him. He made light of exile, stressing the gains both material and spiritual or intellectual, minimizing the losses. He was clearly scornful of those intellectuals who gathered periodically to discuss such issues, insisting that while the delegates talked, under the auspices of this or that foundation, others were suffering on a scale and to a degree that rendered their complaints laughable, even contemptible. He was not a whiner, and he was quite intolerant of the pervasive "culture of complaint". Naturally, this did nothing for his popularity among fellow exiles. In short, if he made a career, he did not actively make it out of the sufferings he had endured as a Jew or as the victim of a régime that still had totalitarian aspirations.

There are some similarities between us. He left a son and two daughters (one of them born the year of his departure, whom he never saw); I left a son and two daughters. The pain of those separations virtually defined my existence.

Was he *family*, as Jill maintained? In that mysterious and at the same time artless way that family *is* family, perhaps. Which somehow distanced me also from his circle of literary friends and acquaintances, the poets, the publishers, the colleagues, even if, as an occasional translator of his work, I too had professional dealings with him.

But did Joseph feel that way about me? At the very least, he was ambivalent about my work as a translator, and yet he stuck by me, as in a way I stuck by him as a poet, although I was ambivalent about his poetry. Joseph's views, in particular his insistence on the primacy of form, made him less than tolerant of what he regarded as slapdash practice, associating this with cultural ignorance, irresponsibility, or worse; it is hardly an exaggeration to say that for him, "crimes" against language were almost tantamount to crimes against humanity. And yet, it seems, he forgave *me* my crimes or sins; surprisingly tolerant, even tender, he held out the prospect of redemption and tried to lead me onto the paths of righteousness! He did not remain neutral, as he might have done, but urged me to continue translating his work, although of course under guidance.

I resisted. That is, in order to preserve rhymes, I was not prepared deliberately to sacrifice literal accuracy. I railed at Joseph, trying to convince him that, in any case, as a non-native speaker, he could not possibly *hear* my off-rhymes, my assonances, and that it was perverse of him to insist on strict formal imitation, when this must lead to distortions, preposterous rhyming and, finally, despite all his efforts, major alterations in sense, tone, etc. It infuriated and frustrated me that he refused to be moved by these arguments, which seemed incontrovertible. He would not acknowledge his indebtedness to his anglophone translators, nor honour their sensibility as native speakers. Surely he must realize that you could translate only *into* your native tongue, especially when it came to poetry. He should chose his translators with care, and be ready to provide them with contextual and linguistic information, but he should not second-guess them or try to manipulate them. On the contrary, he should be guided by *them*. They, after all, were responsible for the final version. The translation was not – could not be – identical with the original, just as English did not mesh perfectly with the Russian, however much translators of Russian might wish it did. The translation was a derivative text, but it also represented the poem's further life, or one of its several possible further lives. But for it to *live* in another language, it had also to *be* another poem; in the final analysis, whether he liked it or not, it had also to be the *translator's* poem.

Joseph would not be budged. He heard me out, evidently unimpressed by what I had to say, merely repeating from time to time that English was richer in rhyme than was supposed. That is, he seemed stubborn or, one might say, pig-headed, except I could not help feeling a certain compassion for him in this predicament. On the other hand, it was also as if he were just waiting for me to come around, convinced that eventually I must. Under the circumstances, it surprised me that he continued to encourage my forays into Russian poetry, as translator and editor. We could hardly have been more at odds, and yet he behaved (and I behaved) as though this were not so. In a way, it wasn't.

Complain as I may (and as I did) I would not have wanted to be other than a stranger in America where a different English was spoken, and before that to have been an Englishman who, with his immigrant family, was not *echt* English. I was, or thought of myself as being, between languages. This made me acutely aware of the provisionality of language, which was a kind of advantage. Language was distinct, apart. For that reason (paradoxically?) its dimensions too were more acutely sensed. This sometimes had the effect of reducing or more sharply focusing existence itself.

Joseph spoke of language as *directing* consciousness. For instance: "Reading him [Dostoevsky] simply makes one realize that stream of consciousness springs not from consciousness but from a word which alters or redirects one's consciousness" ("The Power of the Elements", *Less Than One*), or: "A poet's biography is in his vowels and sibilants, in his meters, rhymes and metaphors [. . .] With poets, the choice of words is invariably more telling than the story line; that's why the best of them dread the thought of their biographies being written" ("The Sound of the Tide", *Less Than One*). (That "the best of them" is rather desperate.) So, presumably, he would have taken a dim view of what I have been saying here. Still, I am not inclined to ignore what he would certainly have regarded as irrelevantly biographical. Languages as something *out there*, in that one finds oneself between them, is quite a seductive notion. Joseph, though, combined this alienating or hyper-linguistic awareness, a form of self-consciousness really, with a genial determination to know his language(s) literally inside out. A Jew, he was also quite adamant about being a Russian, at least insofar as the Russian language belonged to him and he to it ("From Russian with Love"). I envied him and was a little suspicious of this devotion to the Russian language, if not to Mother Russia, since I did not really feel that way about English. As a Jew, Joseph was able to objectify his apartness from the language. It was this, I dare say, that allowed him to be so entirely devoted to it. One might almost call it romantic love, in that the beloved was unattainable.

Improvising the Whole: D. H. Lawrence

I HAD SET myself the certainly presumptuous task of validating Joseph's translation methods, of pointing out their originality, their potential. But while I can discuss this in the abstract, words fail me – or I fail words – when it comes to actual examples. Publisher friends are not encouraging. One writes: "I hope you are saying how bad his poems in English are. I re-read them and found it hard to be generous." "The Brodsky proposal does not, I regret, look like something I could take up, even if you were able to persuade me that there were good reasons for the sort of English he uses to translate his Russian poems", writes another. But then, didn't I already know that the likelihood of convincing my compatriots was slight?

Since so far I have not even been able fully to convince myself, this is hardly surprising!

Joseph's English, after all, is often beyond the pale, and the English poems are at least questionable. On the other hand, they *were* improving. Or it may have been that by sheer force of will, personality, argument, survival he was getting some of us (the more impressionable or perhaps less "native" among us) to reappraise them. In our clash over *The Poetry of Survival*, Donald Davie called me "insubordinate on principle, a Leveller". (I was rather flattered by this, which perhaps shows that he was right?) He argued that I and my cronies (Ted Hughes, A. Alvarez! . . .) believed "emotional 'closeness' makes up for technical incompetence" and he alluded to my alleged "squeamishness" about the words "master" and "mastery", when discussing poetry. My contention – romantic, irresponsible, in short insubordinate – is that Brodsky's English poems are problematical or un-English, for obvious reasons but also because they have to be.

To return to the not unrelated question of translation. In his long letter to me of December 1979, Joseph tried to define what he was looking for. My translations lacked "that element (or device) which creates the sense of the inevitability of the statement". Sometimes, there was too much of the "take-it-or-leave-it" attitude, which he thought "cowardly". He did not mince words, but anyway I'm not looking for excuses. Perhaps I just hoped for the best. Was this a weakness? Joseph saw it differently; he tried to explain: "I think that the main problem between us is not so much the aesthetics but that you never dealt with an author who had this kind of attitude to the language, who was as opinionated. I am not a Swede or a Hungarian who, for all their knowledge of the language into which they are trans-lated, would wave the whole thing, believing that the lads know better and that modernism means looseness of form, etc."

On reflection, I don't think he was being quite fair! After all, I was no proponent of "modernism" or, as far as I know, any other "ism". I had my own notion of form and formally mimetic translation. The trouble is I was not able to project it in a way that got through to JB. And so, there was no dialogue.

The minimalism of East European poetry of the late fifties and sixties, the break with traditional prosody, the content-driven form that so appealed to me were less appealing, it seemed, to Joseph. In fact, Joseph's admiration for Beckett, of which I became aware only later, has rather puzzled me, except insofar as Beckett writes out of a universal rather than local *angst*. Besides, he belongs to the grandfather generation. Poets like Popa or Herbert were almost father generation for Joseph, whereas for me they were like older brothers. Be that as it may, an anthology that concentrated, as mine did, on this generation was for Joseph problematical. What might be construed as a reproof to a tradition that had set no barrier to tyranny and barbarism, whether fascist or communist, had to be resisted. Was it not, after all, a version of the pathetic fallacy to lay the blame at culture's door? On the contrary, instead of condemning culture, our task and rôle was to re-affirm it. Czeslaw Milosz, revered by Joseph, wrote of Tadeusz Różewicz: "His scorn for 'art' is quite programmatic, with all the contradictions such an attitude involves [. . .] It seems that his tragedy is to deny the values which are affirmed by his revolt."[44] This, I imagine, would fairly represent Joseph's view as well, whereas for me what distinguished Różewicz was his having taken responsibility, however reductively, for voicing the "unspeakable", without aestheticizing it. Culture could not be absolved. I was more affected by Różewicz's radical approach to poetry than by that of his (as it seemed to me) more temporizing Polish contemporary Zbigniew Herbert, with whom Milosz was closely associated and whom Joseph admired too – although to what extent I was never quite sure.

But lacking "subordination", or perhaps for other environmental or historical reasons, I did not follow the example of my East European friends. Here's my attempt to come to terms with my own allegiances: "Of course, he [Eliot] was right: an objective correlative is necessary. Words uttered under the influence of feelings manifest rather than articulate. Still, most poetry leaves me cold. My own won't give up trying to hitch a lift. I fall, hang on, am dragged along by my feelings. One foot trails, the other scrabbles."

I realize that the aesthetics, clumsily represented there, are at odds with those of my admired East European poets. The political system itself made a kind of objective correlative obligatory, since unmediated criticism, accessible and unambiguous, was not tolerated by the state. Furthermore, while I spoke for myself, those poets spoke for humanity, or at least for the individual as such. Nevertheless, it was almost with a sense of relief that I read Różewicz, Popa, Holub, this having something to do with what I took to be their particularity, their ability to anchor the stultifying generalities, especially those concerning nationalism or étatism. Perhaps Joseph and I were not as far apart as one might have supposed. In the end, though, it was not that he didn't support my enterprise, but that there really was no room for two at the helm of this particular vessel. My sense of having discovered, or more modestly of having been among the first in

England to recognize, these poets made me reluctant to collaborate with anyone, even Joseph.

D. H. Lawrence – a dodgy poet! Certainly he published a lot of mediocre stuff. Lawrence stressed the moment, the alive moment. But is it *still* alive seventy years after his death? In a letter to Edward Marsh, he wrote: "It is the hidden *emotional* pattern that makes poetry, not the obvious form." And in his Introduction to *New Poems* (1918):

The poetry of the beginning and the poetry of the end must have that exquisite finality, perfection which belongs to all that is far off. It is in the realm of all that is perfect. It is of the nature of all that is complete and consummate. [. . .] But there is another kind of poetry: the poetry of that which is at hand: the immediate present. In the immediate present there is no perfection, no consummation, nothing finished [. . .]

And then to specifics:

Much has been written about free verse. But all that can be said, first and last, is that free verse is, or should be, direct utterance from the instant, whole man. It is the soul and the mind and body surging at once, nothing left out. [. . .] In free verse we look for the insurgent naked throb of the instant moment [. . .]. Free verse has its own nature. That it is neither star nor pearl, but instantaneous like plasm.

And in his Foreword to *Pansies*, 1929:

I offer a bunch of pansies, not a wreath of immortelles. I don't want everlasting flowers, and I don't want to offer them to anybody else. A flower passes, and that perhaps is the best of it [. . .] As for the pansy poems, they are merely the breath of the moment, and one eternal moment easily contradicting the next eternal moment.

Why do I drag Lawrence into this? His position, after all, seems diametrically opposed to that of a Joseph. Perhaps it is because he speaks with comparable vehemence and conviction. But then, vehemence and conviction do not in themselves constitute a proof. So, what's the point of this comparison? That Lawrence and Brodsky were equally driven, fundamentalist, absolutist? That in their poetic universes, the distinction between "good" and "bad" ceases to mean anything? Except that "badness", as conventionally defined, actually has positive connotations!

I imagine that Lawrence's defence of *vers libre* might have been anathema to Joseph. He talks of the sanctity of form and of rhyme as a mnemonic device to ensure memorableness. If I have doubts about Lawrence's *Pansies*, it is because they are *no longer* necessary, memorable. But that their memorableness is by now all used up is to their credit; paradoxically it's what makes them still readable. The pansies have done their *job*, to use one of Joseph's favourite words.

And Joseph's English verse, too, has a job to do. It is of-the-moment alive; in its work with language, it is as much impro-vised as planned or foreordained. It seems to me that in his English verse, possibly more than in his Russian, he is thinking on his feet (pun unintended but appropriate). And he takes chances; he stumbles, even falls, but gets up again, keeps going. In typical free-verse fashion, Joseph treats the language as though it were something plastic. If, as Auden said, "in their attitude towards art, the formal verse writer is a catholic, the free verse writer a protestant",[45] Joseph was probably both. To be theologically fanciful, the free verse writer – Joseph was moving from syllabo-tonic towards a more flexible (looser?) accentual verse – represented the Jew in him. He treats English rough, with scant regard for its sensibilities, deaf to its protests. Did he really believe that keeping to a regular metre and rhyme pattern (at least visually, since the eye does not immediately register the enjambments or the segmented words) made the whole package acceptable to us natives? He tried out this and that, and after-wards stood his ground – he was his own flack-catcher. He knew where he wanted to go, even if he couldn't yet get there. Perhaps it would have been better for him or his enterprise, if some of these experiments, these improvisations had been kept private, not acted out in public? But there is a pedagogical side to it. One can learn from other peoples' failures. If you ignore the malapropisms, the mangled idioms, the excruciating puns, Joseph's failures look more interesting than many so-called successes (to paraphrase what he himself said of Auden).

The analogy with Lawrence is certainly extraneous and I feel duly contrite. Nevertheless, these poets – both also had their say in prose of various kinds – share a quality of "badness" or perhaps of excessiveness, which may be unavoidable when you are working so close to the edge or end of a tradition. While Joseph was, for polemical purposes, a traditionalist, devoted for instance to classical prosody, he was also an experimenter; at least, one recognizes in his work the experimentation of the earlier part of the century. In his translations or his collaboration with translators, he tried to formulate a kind of inter-language. This encouraged him to take risks, which he was arguably more able, freer to do, because of his outsider status in the target language. He battled on, regardless of the inevitable and understandable, even legitimate, rebukes. So, if he followed the lead of language, proclaiming himself its servant, a point was soon reached where leader and led merged in the person of a lone prospector, pressing on with no guarantees – as he himself said, nothing *can* be guaranteed.

"WHEN YOU SPEAK, cherish the thought of the secret of the voice and the word, and speak in fear and love, and remember that the world of the word finds utterance through your mouth. Then you will lift the word." This is from Martin Buber's *Ten Rungs, Collected Hasidic Sayings* (1947), a section entitled, "Of The Power Of The Word". Later, in "How To Say Torah", the compiler warns: "You must cease to be aware of yourselves. You must be nothing but an ear that hears what the universe of the word is constantly saying within you. The moment you start hearing what you yourself are saying, you must stop." And further: "[The proud] are reborn as bees . . . that hum and buzz: 'I am, I am, I am.'"

If Joseph did not allude directly to "the word of God", did not set his devotion to language in a specifically Judaeo-Christian context, it was perhaps because he felt that "the twentieth century has exhausted the possibilities for salvation and come into conflict with the New Testament." "Christ is not enough, Freud is not enough, Marx is not enough, nor is existentialism or Buddha." He concludes, in a kind of last ditch appeal to the power of the Word: "All of these are only means of justifying the holocaust, not of averting it. To avert it, mankind has nothing except the Ten Commandments, like it or not."[46] Such statements seem to contain little or nothing of Christian charity or belief in redemption, but a great deal of misanthropy and Old Testament fatalism. Only the Word, specifically the *words* of the Ten Commandment, stand between us and the triumph of Evil. At the time, I thought this rather simplistic. But there was also something quite empowering about it. It is not so much that the Word saves, as that language is identified as the arena of contention or engagement. Joseph acknowledged this when he gave up the various consolations on offer. However different the timbre of his voice, he was after all – I came to this only lately –

of that company I had so admired in my early days with *MPT*. It reminded me of what Ted Hughes, in his Introduction to Vasko Popa's *Collected Poems* (1978), had written of this generation: "They have got back to the simple animal courage of accepting the odds." If you accept the odds, you do not obliterate them, but paradoxically you do take control. Joseph was never one to surrender control.

Let me try something! He was not meek in his fatalism, his resignation. Rather, he was fierce, even angry. Like a moralist. But this anger, which sometimes showed itself in his encounters with the press or others, was not manifest in his writing, in that which was destined to remain. Language, as written down, demanded more of him. A certain ceremony or decorousness was required. But he did not, as I sometimes supposed, hide behind it. He just paid his dues to language and earned the right to import more and more of the whole man. This apprenticeship was an intensely moral affair, a training in morality, in ethics as well, morality being engagement but with the ego under control, providing the charge of energy but not dominating the proceedings. Come to think of it, wasn't Joseph a Protestant rather than a Catholic? A Calvinist actually.

I am not being captious, merely speculating about Joseph's approach to the business of writing. His vision of the self was a useful one. Perhaps, after all, I was misled when, in the early seventies, I conjectured that "His refusal to play any part other than himself should protect him against blandishments in the West, as he was, in a sense, protected against pressures of conformism in the Soviet Union by the refusal of the orthodox literary establishment to acknowledge his artistic existence." The second part of that statement is, in any case, tautologous. And the trouble with the rest of it is that I was probably fearing the worst, that he would end up wholly owned by the media, typecast as America's tragic resident exile. But at the same time, knowing him, having sensed, even experienced the strength of his resolve, I also hoped that he would be able to preserve his integrity, even if I presumptuously couched this hope in para-doxical, skeptical, or political terms, when I talked of his not *playing a part*. It would have been wiser to have stated the obvious: that it was *being himself*, answerable to none except his great predecessors and finally God or Language, that got him into trouble in the first place. But at least that, if he were successful from a worldly point of view, as seemed likely, it would be largely on his own terms.

Obviously his insistence on the primacy of language and his own subordinate rôle, helped him to combat pride. He kept reiterating, almost like a mantra, that the biography of a poet has to do not with the life he has lived but with his words.

On the one hand, this smacks of a certain counter-élitist élitism, a romantic "not myself but the force within me"; on the other, it is simply foolish to claim for oneself what properly belongs to language, since one is the latter's servant or, more precisely, its artisan. If Joseph was a pedagogue as well – and he certainly was – it was not out of some exaggerated notion of his own importance. But, as I have said, there was no false modesty either. He could be the most natural of men. For instance, in response to the question posed by Bella Yezerskaya, mentioned earlier: "Do you consider yourself an innovator?" he replied: "No, I don't think so. Innovation is, in any case a silly concept. My rhymes sometimes turn out to be quite good, but to consider them 'new' is senseless; they're taken from the language in which they have always existed". Which is, of course, *literally* true. Nevertheless, more than a little satisfaction is expressed also by the modest "quite good"!

Rhymes Galore

Friday, 10 May, 1996

FOR SOME TIME I have been promising myself to look more closely at Joseph's English rhymes. Baranczak holds that the rôle of rhyme in Brodsky's poetry is particularly significant. At any rate, Joseph himself left one in no doubt as to the importance he attached to it. Baranczak, as a translator, was referring, of course, to the Russian rhymes and the obligation to find a match for them in Polish. My interest at this time is in how Joseph *himself* deals with this in English, either in the self-translations or in his original English poems. When the former are compared with the Russian originals, the significance he attaches to rhyme becomes even clearer. He is prepared to take such liberties with the text that it is no longer so much a question of a different language as of a different poem. Translation shades into "meta-poem".

A stroll through the opening pages of *To Urania*, omitting "May 24, 1980", produces the following: *Partly / paltry*; *livers / beavers*; *all over / Goncharova*. Obviously he is on the lookout for polysyllabic or feminine rhymes, attentive to consonants as well as to vowels: *p . . . t . y / p . . t . y*; also quite prepared to use proper names, he'll rhyme anything with anything. *Sentence / entrance*; *curtains / importance*. The latter consonantal rhyme *t-n-s* is unusually muted. On the other hand, since the reference is to someone who is no longer there, for whom the living friend's farewell is of "no importance", a rather indeterminate rhyme seems apposite. Note that the masculine rhyme words, mostly monosyllabic, tend to be more conventional, less witty, entertaining, or outré. They can even be quite banal, of the *love / dove* type: e.g. *cask / task*; *tears / gear*; *mud / bud*, etc. Maybe they function as sober counterparts to the rather exotic, even flighty foreign imports: *healing / helix*; *horizon / light on*; *tamper / downpour*; *naked / make it*; *patterned / passion*; *Lady*

Godiva / saliva; *mollusc / Pollux*; *minute / in it*? Provided the accented syllables are assonantal, Brodsky will allow endings to vary considerably: e.g. *patterned / passion*. Granted, this kind of rhyme is less irregular in American than in British English. If both accented and secondary vowels are assonantal: *healing / helix*, the fact that the endings "ng" and "x [*ks*]" are not easily elided may be ignored. A consonantal variation can also occur in the middle of a polysyllabic rhyme: *horizon / light on*. Another favourite device, rather witty in its dyslexic way, is to reverse double consonant endings: *sk / ks* in *mollusc / Pollux*. The *Godiva / saliva* rhyme, of course, is delightfully incongruous.

The shapeliness or symmetry of Joseph's verse is edifying. *Felt / Geld; wish / quiche; flash / flesh . . . Arrivals / rivers*, another consonantal (partly visual) rhyme, is more muted. Similar is *corners / coroners*, which works particularly well visually, since the only difference is the "o" between "r" and "n" in *coroners*. Also pronounce "corner" in the American way. The final rhyme is *lordly / laundry . . .*

These last come from an original poem "Dutch Mistress", and it is noteworthy that the outlandish feminine rhymes are, for the most part, balanced by strong, simple masculine ones: *rain / brain; ear / where; curls / coils*, the last being less emphatic, relying more on consonantal symmetry. Joseph deploys semantically shock rhymes such as *spliced / Christ* with great aplomb.

He delights, too, in *tours de force* like *bogus / hocus-pocus / locus / focus; waters / foetus / photos*. *Foetus / photos* is intriguing, with its differently represented "f" sound, and the nudge to slightly mispronounce (at least from a British point of view) the "-tos" of *photos*, bring it more into line also with *focus*. Joseph is attentive to visual as well as to sound effects, and these complement one another. His boldness or adroitness in what, after all, was still his second language is remarkable (*actor / factor / back two*!) If there are some non-idiomatic moves, they are so well integrated soundwise, so semantically ingenious, that, as far as I'm concerned, he gets away with it.

Leafing through collections of some of Joseph's favourite poets (Donne, Hardy, Auden, Frost, Wilbur) I find nothing much resembling the above. Relatively few feminine rhymes, mostly masculine rhymes, only a minority of which are just assonantal or consonantal. Hardy's inventiveness has more to do with the form, although it is true that he also uses an expanded vocabulary, including a number of rare or archaic words and eccentric, archaic or regional usages. In late Auden (actually, to my surprise) there is comparatively little rhyme . . .

So, perhaps I should rather search the works of Ogden Nash, Lear, Gilbert? Or Swinburne, Kipling? Betjeman? Many of Joseph's English poems, after all, are playful or semi-humorous (semi-serious?), as if he had chosen to begin at that end of the spectrum. Betjeman, as befits so topographical and socially conscious a poet, frequently rhymes on proper nouns: *Penmaenmawr / shower* (which, incidentally, also tells the reader – not quite politically correctly, by today's standards? – how to pronounce a difficult Welsh place name!); *Miguel / sell*; *cleaner / Cortina*; *Chatsworth / that's worth*, etc. Occasionally, he also resorts to mere assonance (or to no-rhyme at all), especially in the first and third pair of an abab quatrain. It is not surprising that Betjeman should make considerable use of polysyllabic rhyming: *digits / midgets*; *neuter / computer*, etc. But even he, for the most part, employs plain English monosyllabic rhymes of the *wood / stood, noise / toys* type.

How about Gerard Manley Hopkins? Consider sprung rhythm, "measured by feet of from one to four syllables, regularly, and for particular effects any number of weak or slack syllables may be used". The breath units in Joseph's poetry rather resemble those of Hopkins. The number of syllables between accents varies, but in any case it is the strong, if irregular, stress that structures the poem. As we know, Hopkins was influenced by the complex Welsh system of alliteration and internal rhyme, *cynghanedd*. He scored his poems (though these marks are generally omitted from the printed texts) and, as his notes indicate, intended them to be read aloud (I am increasingly convinced that Brodsky did too): "remember what applies to all my verse [. . .] that its performance is not reading with the eye but loud, leisurely, poetical (not rhetorical) recitation, with long rests, long dwells on the rhyme and other marked syllables, and so on. This sonnet ["Spelt from Sibyl's Leaves"] shd. [*sic*] be almost sung ..." Hopkins condenses, agglutinates, working against the grain. In his efforts to achieve "individuation", he tries to energize the language, to make it more directly, onomatopoeically mimetic. In its own time, his poetry was held to be inaccessible, even though the content was far less radical than the form, and the first edition of Hopkins's poetry having been published only in 1918, nearly thirty years after the poet's death. It is almost as if for Joseph the rhyme was intended for the eye rather than the ear. Of course, as far as "long dwells on the rhyme" goes, Brodsky tended to go the other way in his public readings gathering the rhyme up in his enjambments, almost losing it, as if challenging the reader to notice what he had given so much attention to, like a mediaeval, cathedral craftsman's work, which may not be visible to Man though hopefully it is to God.

Joseph's position is rather ambiguous, and in a rather similar way to Hopkins's. It is arguable that his translations of his own poetry, which should perhaps be read alongside his English poems, represented an attempt, as Goethe put it (in his introduction to the *West-östlicher Divan*), to close the circle "in which the alien and the familiar, the known and the unknown move towards each other". For Goethe this was the third kind of translation, the first being a simple prose one, which "familiarizes us with the foreign country on our own terms", and the second being where "one seeks to project oneself into the circumstances of the foreign country, but in fact only appropriates the foreign meaning and then replaces it with one's own." It is as if Brodsky, time being so limited, tried, as it were, to move straight to the "third type" of translation.

Hopkins, Yes; Brodsky, No!

IN HIS REVIEW of *To Urania*[47] Christopher Reid warns against just such an analogy: "it is [. . .] necessary [. . .] to counter the notion that something fresh, healthy, rich in artistic potential and urgently needed is being introduced into the poetic repertoire [. . .]. Milton, Keats and Hopkins may, in their turn, have perplexed readers with their foreignisms, but the most Latinate of Milton's periods, the most convulsive and startling of Hopkins's syntactical experiments, get their strength from a secure and organic understanding of English idiom." And in case the reader might think he is being chauvinistic, he adds: "This is not [. . .] something to which native English-speakers alone have access. It can be learned, as Vladimir Nabokov, for one, gloriously demonstrated. Brodsky, however, has yet to achieve that mastery and, from the evidence here, would appear to have a long way to go before he does so."

It is true that Brodsky's control of idiom is insecure or at any rate eccentric. He has, in a sense, mis-learnt English, or learnt it while never taking his eye off Russian. He has absorbed or filtered English through Russian. His English is idiosyncratic, an amalgam which nevertheless is gradually normalizing or naturalizing itself, or at least becoming more self-consistent and so acquiring greater authority, survival or perseverance being more than half the game. In the meantime, though, readers get a distinctly negative impression of the proceedings. The mixed idioms, archly polysyllabic usages, dubious grammar, etc. make much of Brodsky's English poetry hard to take seriously. It is not a "finished poetry" and Brodsky's own remarks about the sanctity of poetic form have not helped matters. It seems to me to be a poetry in the making. Dense, intricate, it is at the same time diagrammatic or sketch-like, rather than comprehensive, though Brodsky may have hoped for more and in some instances achieved more. Still, I doubt whether *So Forth* will have made Christopher Reid change his mind.

I am interested in Reid's assumption that "it is necessary" we be warned, and that Milton et al. "get their strength from a secure and organic understanding of English idiom". If, indeed, it "is necessary [. . .] to counter the notion", etc., this must be because our language is under threat. I would agree that it is, but not, I think, from the likes of Brodsky. I'm not sure that Hopkins's strength comes from a "secure organic understanding of English idiom", although no doubt he had such an understanding, whereas Brodsky's grasp was not secure. It might have been better had Brodsky not been in such a hurry. But he had to be, and his grasp of English idiom was far from negligible. What he did, in these less than ideal circumstances, is not so easily dismissed.

Of course, Hopkins *was* a native speaker of English, albeit with an interest in Welsh forms, whereas Brodsky's devotion to the language, English, was necessarily of a different order. It is, in fact, quite distinctive. In his essay on Auden "To Please a Shadow" (*Less Than One*), he claims that he wrote in English so as to "find myself in close proximity to the man, whom I considered the greatest mind of the twentieth century: Wystan Hugh Auden . . .".[48] Joseph was seeking a closeness with the language, as with one of its foremost literary practitioners, the language, in a sense, being identified with the poet ("Tsvetaeva the poet was identical to Tsvetaeva the person . . ."). There is no doubt as to his commitment. Again, as Roy Fisher wonders: "It's salutary and quite a noble sight, if a quixotic one, to see Brodsky coming into English and fighting, practically, to reverse its retreat as a matter of principle, and in gratitude for what it's given him." In fact, though, he was shuffling back and forth between two camps, trying to populate a No man's land with representatives of both of them, the problem being that by birth and heritage he belonged actually to one, not to both. Hopkins, for his part, was inviting the proximate foreigner into the fortress, for purposes of experimental miscegenation.

Still, with his ingenious rhyming, his daring (or unwitting) manipulation of syntax, incongruous or macaronic juxtapositions, and in general, through his grouping of words that purports to give this predominantly monosyllabic language a polysyllabic feel, Brodsky does remind me of Hopkins.

When Joseph read his English texts, almost as if they were Russian – even *his* English was far more monosyllabic than his Russian – it was at first hard not to be skeptical, hard sometimes even to understand him. After all, English can readily be made to sound like Russian or any other language. My point is that, at first, Joseph's performance of his English poems seemed a kind of illusionism. At any rate, these poems contrasted, often quite shockingly, with his magisterial Russian ones. Was he aware of this? If not, was he deceiving himself? In his Iowa City reading, as noted above, he had ironically remarked that he did not wish to compound the violence already done to his poems through translation by reading them himself with his foreign accent. That was why he had an English reader. However, it would not have been surprising had he preferred to read the English as well, since he alone knew how the poems should be phrased. Or was it really that he made the English sound more like the Russian through mispronunciation and by yoking words together in a most un-English manner. At any rate, on that occasion, in Iowa City, he could not resist taking the stand himself at the end of the evening. Evidently he was experimenting and wanted to try his English out in public. Gauche though his efforts may have been, they were also impressive. Since he had just been reciting his poems in Russian, what he had in mind was obvious enough. That he could not expect a native speaker like myself to read in the same way was neither here nor there. Or perhaps he didn't like to ask. Maybe he was hoping eventually to take over the reading of the translations just as he had taken over the making of them.

An Irish Tribute

YESTERDAY, Seamus Heaney was in Iowa City, to speak at a reception for this year's winner of the Truman Capote Prize for Literary Criticism, Helen Vendler. He was also to give a reading of his own. I mentioned that I had been in New York at the memorial service for Joseph, and he remarked that Joseph would have appreciated the event: just poems, no speeches. I told him that I was writing about Joseph's prosody in English, and we talked a little about Joseph's English, Seamus alluding to the enjambments, referring me also to his own poem "Audenesque", in memory of Joseph Brodsky.[49]

Seamus ended his reading with "Audenesque". His wife Marie had told me that he wrote it more or less straight off, on learning of Joseph's death. I'm not so sure about the memorial service, but I do think "Audenesque" would have pleased Joseph. It is yet another reprise of Part 3 of Auden's "In Memory of W. B. Yeats", and Joseph's imitation of that in *Na Smert' T. S. Eliota* ("Verses on the Death of T. S. Eliot"). Yeats died on 28 January, Eliot on 4 January, and Joseph Brodsky on the same day of the same month as Yeats. An Englishman on an Irishman; a Russian on an Englishman; an Irishman on a Russian, better perhaps now described as a Russo-Anglo-American.

Heaney's poem sounds quite spontaneous but is, at the same time, a finely wrought tribute, stopping for a while in Brodsky territory, or in Brodsky-adopted Auden territory. It is both *tender* (a word Joseph often used) and also humorous, as it imitates Joseph imitating Auden, celebrating Yeats and employing the latter's own measure in his self-epitaph "Under Ben Bulben". In "To Please a Shadow", Brodsky, as noted, explained that he wrote in English so as to be close to Auden. I like to think that Heaney, Russian itself being inaccessible to him, wrote "Audenesque" also "to please a shadow" – maybe two shadows for the price of one.

Joseph would have appreciated Heaney's rhyme in stanza 8, *produced / Massachusetts*; and there is his reference to enjambments, "Jammed enjambments, piling up . . ." A wonderful picture, too, of Joseph, *driving* English: "Nose in air, foot to the floor, / Revving English like a car . . ." And what of those enjambments? Presumably Seamus was referring not only to the actual enjambments but also to Joseph's habit of "roving over" as he went, even when the syntax or sense did not call for it. It was as if he got an extra boost each time he did this. He also seemed to be contending with the form that he himself had established, as though challenging it to make itself felt, or perhaps intimating that, so long as *it* was in place, *he* was free to do whatever *he* liked. I was puzzled by this. His performances seemed at first dramatic rather than shapely or attentive to acoustics. But Joseph's mixture of syntactic and non-syntactic, semantic and non-semantic enjambments was different. And as for expressiveness, dramatic effect, his readings, while resonant, were actually even-paced with little *chiaroscuro* or *Sturm und Drang*; in short, they were classical rather than romantic, stately rather than tragic. In any case, there were no histrionics. He might wipe his brow, but that was about the extent of it.

Joseph's enjambments never "jammed", as such. That is, they never *quite* jammed. They seemed to propel him forward, so that he had to improvise in order not to get tangled up. It was all rather exciting, keeping the audience (literally) on the edge of its seats. Half measures did not appeal to him. Standard prosodic devices were perhaps overused (Heaney: "As you went above the top"). Come to think of it, his omnivorousness with rhyme was an example of this. He was a special kind of enthusiast: his excessiveness kept him going. He thrived on it, rather than being overwhelmed by it.

Rhymes, Especially Feminine Ones

SO, I HAVE been mugging up on prosody. Would Joseph have approved? Not particularly. I can hear him: "Counting again, Danny!" Or maybe even paraphrasing Pound's "compose in the sequence of the musical phrase, not in the sequence of a metronome". Although that's hardly likely, given his feelings about Pound (see *Watermark*).

Perhaps the comparison with Hopkins is, after all, apposite. Particularly in his later poems, Brodsky seems to be writing accentually rather than syllabically; certainly his oral performances suggest this (see various works by Prof. Gerry Smith).[50] Like his beloved Auden, he reaches back, in his sophisticated, late twentieth-century way, to pre-Chaucerian metrics, stress and alliteration, though the alliteration is not so marked in Joseph's verse. Of course, he is eclectic, using rhyme as well. But, as we have also seen, he often mutes the effect of it, riding over those rhyme words almost as though they were not there. Hopkins, not counting unstressed syllables, goes further than Old English in accentualism; Brodsky for his part exceeds even Hopkins. This seemed to upset a lot of people, who regarded it as un-English. To round up his straying syllables, he has to put on bursts of speed. If this is English, it is a greatly accelerated version of the language, more like Italian really! And English tends to stumble when it is hustled along in this manner. But apparently Joseph didn't mind, provided the gist was clear enough. The inner workings are on display, but then isn't it the same with his Russian? Of course, he was much nimbler in his native language, but even then it was a writer's, rather than a performer's performance, although perhaps there is always something amateurish about an author's own rendering, which often tends to be instructional rather than product-oriented or merely entertaining.

Perhaps I was more inclined to be tolerant, because I myself, with my non-English parents, felt at a certain remove from English. And yet it might also be claimed that Joseph was (instinctively?) harking back to an earlier English, before the imposition of metronomic norms. If so, the effect was rather of pastiche. Pastiche, though, may be just another weapon in the eclectic modern artist's arsenal – and Joseph was a modern traditionalist (Baranczak's "skeptical classicist"). His "Verses on the Death of T. S. Eliot", like Auden's earlier one on Yeats, and Seamus Heaney's recent one on Brodsky, is a pastiche. Actually, nearly all Joseph's English-language poetry may be regarded as pastiche, attempts to "please a shadow". But when does pastiche cease to be pastiche? Or am I talking simply of apprenticeship? There is no steady advance towards mastery; rather, mastery begins to manifest itself straight away, in the apprentice's imitations.

The truth is that I am baffled! So seductively plausible did I find him that I could hardly not be won over to his way of thinking. When it came to the English poems, his arguments may have been more persuasive than his texts, even if one regards the latter more as notes, scores for oral performance. Or perhaps his arguments and what he actually produced should be seen as a whole, the product being an embodiment or demonstration of the argument. His English poems – at least the best of them – were dynamic, agitational. And they still are. Time-bombs perhaps!

For a while now I have been intending to take a look at W. S. Gilbert's and Ogden Nash's verse. Joseph's predilection for double, triple, even quadruple rhymes, a component of the comic-verse writer's repertoire and hardly fit for more serious use, has led critics to invoke such brilliant rhymesters.

Take Gilbert. Firstly, the rollicking lyrics, for all their variety, are metronomically regular, though occasionally he will insert non-scanning lines of virtual prose. All the examples here are from *H.M.S. Pinafore*:

Fair moon, to thee I sing,
Bright regent of the heavens;
Say, why is everything
Either at sixes or at sevens?
I have lived hitherto
Free from breath of slander,
Beloved by all my crew
A really popular commander.

However, bearing in mind that Gilbert's verse is intended for singing, irregularities can of course be accommodated. It abounds with jokes, often quite caustic. I have tried to read it to myself, as Joseph might have done, that is, striding or bounding from accent to accent, swallowing what comes between. How staid, even stately, they appear now, when performed as originally intended. But here and there it is possible to make a verse sound Brodskyish: *I know the value of a kindly chorus, / But choruses yield little consolation, / When we have pain and trouble too before us! / I love – and love, alas, above my station!* Read in a monotone, punctuated by widely spaced accents, so that many words must be fitted into a short space of time. Even so, it is virtually impossible to hide the beat, which of course is quite slow. Furthermore, the rhymes are all full. Gilbert does not use slant-rhymes, assonantal or consonantal, although he does exploit homophones: *see / minstrelsy.* He is, on the other hand, fond of feminine rhymes: *tutor / suitor*; *thump any / company*, and the "company" will often, as it were, approve, by reiterating or echoing this. Quite often the "ee" sound is used, the rhyme even encouraging a comic relocation of the accent: *me / Queen's Navee.* Class accents are also exploited: *fe-ar / we are.* Much is made of proper names: *Over the bright blue sea / Comes Sir Joseph Porter, K.C.B.* Gilbert has style and an impeccable sense of timing or pacing. He is, in short, a dramatist, rather than a poet. Though much enjoyment is to be got from his word play, his deftness, characterizations or caricatures, it is an intellectual rather than aesthetic pleasure. There is no particular feel for the organic shape of lines or stanzas, however formally correct they may be. That is, the form is set. Brilliant stuff – witty, satirical, crammed with *jeux de mots*, mimicry, melodrama, mock lyricism, but limited also by its own intellectualism. This is no criticism of it. So clever, secure is the writing, that even without internal music (and after all, there is Sullivan's *external* music) there is a kind of briskness, adroitness that lifts the spirit: *His foot should stamp and his throat should growl, / His hair should twirl and his face should scowl, / His eyes should flash and his breast protrude, / And this should be his customary attitude.* "Customary attitude" is delicious, with each syllable distinctly pronounced, lightly stressed, *cus-to-ma-ry*, then abruptly decelerating to the more staccato, more heavily stressed *at-ti-tude*. And "protrude" literally does, with the accent on "trude".

What of Ogden Nash? Again, the verbal dexterity, the punning, the multiple, often neologistic or macaronic rhymes are not self-contained, not so much linguistically determined, as deployed in the service of urbane social or domestic commentary. The wit and artfulness is pleasurable, but again the pleasure is more of the mind than of the ear. There is nothing particularly compelling about the work acoustically. But this is irrelevant. Ogden Nash wins us over in other ways. It is only in his playing fast and loose with metre, his deliberate flouting of prosodic convention, that he might make one think of Brodsky, at least in the latter's English translations and poems. Nash's absurdist and absurd rhyming is part of the method, which owes a debt, as he ironically reminds us, to "bad" poetry. His use of long (often very long) lines encourages an accelerated, deadpan style of reading, from end-rhyme to ostentatious end-rhyme. Since the distance between the beginning and end of the line is often interminable, there is a tendency to look for stepping stones, the accented words functioning in this capacity. In its prosiness, Nash's verse sometimes reads like a parody of sprung-rhythm poetry. In any case this is talking-verse, based on prose rhythms, or imposing on prose a kind of versified reading. Here is an example of his wait-for-it technique: *Indeed, my vagrant thoughts were many, / And one of them lingered on the distinguished poet who recently wrote that he would "dream of small white stars falling forever in darkness like dandruff,"* and *I asked myself if this phrase could be a subconscious tribute to the late Daily Mirror's immortal bard, Nick Kenny.*

Like Gilbert, Nash employs full rhymes, whether simple or multiple, even if they *are* neologistic, macaronic, or visual rather than aural. A random selection: il est */day*; *heroics / "Yoicks!"*; *bachelor / spatula* (actually, that one is somewhat more Brodskyan); *economy / bonhomie*; *General / Gehennaral* (typically converting a proper noun into an adjective); *Odysseus / delysseus* (a mild distortion, again quite typical); *Euripides / centipedes* (inviting the reader to transfer the accent in "centipedes" from the last to the second syllable and to add a syllable, so as to ape "Euripides"); *wombat / combat* (an incongruous pairing which looks as though it had been picked out of a rhyming dictionary and, indeed, may well have been, since I just chanced on it in Clement Wood's *Unabridged Rhyming Dictionary*, where it is the only rhyme under "om'bat"); *acoustic / Aroostook* (Aroostook, the supposed name of a town, being a bogus proper noun); *thin / minny min* (the latter an affected pronunciation of "men"); *eccentrics / gentry in their gentricks* (an abbreviation, as it were, with the "t" serving both words); *but true/*Chacun à son goo; *fleddest / should-have-stood-in-beddest* (in a verse that plays delightfully with superlative forms). And on and on.

While occasionally Brodsky's syntax or prosody might look as though it had (unintentionally) been borrowed from "bad" verse (in Nashian fashion – sorry!), and while, quite often, his tenuous, more or less gestural rhymes are used for comic effect, his writing is subsumed under a larger poetic scheme; perhaps not always successfully, but subsumed nonetheless. It is simply that he has, without prejudice, drawn on all the resources available to him. With a Nash, a Gilbert (or a Belloc, Lear, Lewis Carroll?) we are in a world of clever, sometimes brilliant prestidigitation. Skilful as is their trickery, there is little else that they can do. In a way, that's the point.

But what, for instance, of the elegiac Stevie Smith? Her rhymes are, for the most part, exceedingly simple, which is what makes them so effective. At the same time, her faux-naif technique permits intriguing metrical irregularities. Her poetry is often quite wildly free. The tragic note is sounded, but has more to do with nostalgia, regret and – however indirectly – her individual pain and suffering.

Joseph's sometimes quite perverse fondness for enjambment finds no echo in the work of Nash, or Gilbert, or even Stevie Smith. Rather the reverse (an anti-echo?). Indeed, the trouble with Nash (if there can be said to be a "trouble") is the monotonous effect of an endless series of mock-aphoristic couplets, of two-liners, gags. Gilbert, too, goes in for end-stopped lines almost exclusively. Stevie Smith, for all her eccentricity, makes comparatively little use of enjambments, and when she does run on, even though she capitalizes the first letter of each line, it often seems quite arbitrary, typographically determined. None of these writers writes simultaneously with and against the grain as does Brodsky. However playfully, they play by rules that for him appear to be only one among several elements.

So Forth: *Who is the Translator?*

T OMORROW I LEAVE for London. I'd thought to be done with this journal well before. I have solved none of the "problems", nor am I any more reconciled to Joseph's death.

And today I received an uncorrected bound proof copy of *So Forth*, Joseph's last poetry collection. It is to be published by FSG in September. Accompanying the collection was a note from Ann Kjellberg, his personal assistant and now the executor of his literary estate. Although Joseph completed work on the collection during the weeks before his death, he did not, in fact, see the proofs. Ann writes: "JB always treated galleys as working things." As long ago as 1979, he wrote to me that it was not so much that he aspired to re-work translations by others, as that he was given the galleys "and found enough time to read them". With his own work, at least he did not have to consider the susceptibilities of translators, or cope with their dismay on discovering that, while they were under the illusion that all was well, their versions unilaterally had been subjected to substantial revision.

I am excited at receiving this collection, which I can bring with me to London. But I am also overwhelmed. Up till now I have been collecting Joseph's English poems, in scrap-book fashion, from various sources, including *The Times Literary Supplement*, which regularly published his work. And suddenly I have 130 pages of poems! To quote the blurb: "[The collection] represents eight years of masterful self-translation from the Russian, as well as a growing body of work written directly in English [. . .] Brodsky firmly demonstrates in *So Forth* that in nearly half a lifetime in this country he had become not only one of the reigning voices of his native language but a commanding presence in his adoptive one."

145

I suspect that the opposition will not be persuaded.

I had not realized that this last book was to be Joseph's first _English_ book, in his own English, not mediated, it seems, through other sensibilities. This is Brodsky by Brodsky, or Brodsky into Brodsky, Brodsky in his own English words.

Glancing through the book, I discover that it is not so clear whether the poem is a translation, "translated by the author", or whether it is an "original" English poem.

Joseph often remarked that he wished he could devote himself solely to writing poetry in Russian and need not concern himself with the translation thereof. But the more he got into English, the more he realized that this would not do. Increasingly he took responsibility for the translation of his work into English, first translating his translators, as it were, and then substituting himself for them. And I believe that it was as a part of this process, that he also wrote poetry directly in English. It is unlikely that he would have considered translating his English poems into Russian, there being no need for this, since his native language remained that in which the bulk of his serious poetry was written. Maybe Joseph's rôle as a translator of his own poetry was becoming a wholly invisible one, the distance between translation and original narrowing.

So, his English translations and his English poems were less distinguishable now. That is to say, his reader was invited to approach them in the same manner, not ask himself whether an earlier "version" in Russian existed. This was brave of Joseph, although some might regard it as foolhardy.

So, his English poetry collections show a clear progression from the unauthorized, rarely mentioned, first collection _Elegy to John Donne and Other Poems_ (translated by Nicholas Bethell, 1967) and _Selected Poems_ (1973), the first authorized collection, translated by George L. Kline. _A Part of Speech_ is translated by the author, the author in collaboration with others, and by others on their own (of its thirty-seven poems, two, including the title sequence, are translated by the author, ten with the author, twenty-four by individual translators, and there is one original poem in English). As for _To Urania_, of its forty-six poems, twenty-two are translated by the author, eight with the author, four only by individual translators, (although this includes the forty-page poem "Gorbunov and Gorchakov") and there are now twelve original poems in English. *So Forth* is wholly translated by or written in English by the author . . .

But is it? In small italics, among the credits, is a note indicating which poems were written in English and which were translated by the author *with others* – Alan Myers, Peter Graves (who also co-translated the poetry of Brodsky's Leningrad friend Aleksandr Kushner), Jamey Gambrell, Harry Thomas (admittedly, the forty-page early poem, "Gorbunov and Gorchakov"). The rest, it states, were translated by the author. The emphasis, of course, still remains on the original Englishness or Americanness of the volume, but he had not yet taken over *entirely*. To summarize, of the sixty-four poems, twenty-three were written in English, nearly twice as many as in *To Urania*; thirty-four were translated by the author; and only eight were translated with others. Not a single poem untouched by Brodsky's hand intrudes.

An Inscription

I READ JOSEPH's inscription in the copy of *On Grief and Reason* that he gave me in December 1995 and which I left in London when I returned to the States in January. He had a stack of books, lately come from the publisher and seemed very happy about it. This was the last time I saw him. The inscription is headed: December 15, 1995, New York.

He sat on the floor of his study, the book resting on his lap, thought for a moment, and then wrote rapidly. Then he handed me the book. He was more than pleased with what he had written. "It's rather good!" he said. I cast an eye over it and agreed, without really reading. (I wonder if I had been lamenting my lonely state, talking about growing old?) Now I read: "May what's behind be at least matched by what's ahead." Perhaps it was the ambivalence that pleased him. That is, in view of what was behind, it may not have seemed to be hoping for too much. On the other hand, I am now – or was then – sixty years old. When we first met, we were both in our thirties. Maybe the gods could be suckered into giving me a better deal than I might otherwise have expected! I mean, you have to think twice when you read "May what's behind", etc., and then that passive construction "be . . . matched by . . .". In fact, with Joseph's self-appreciative chuckle ringing in my ears, I did not perceive the subtlety of what he had written, although I must subliminally have registered the benevolent intention. And one should not forget the "at least". There *was* some wheedling going on! Knowing how much I agonized, he had invented a kind of mantra for me. The inscription now reads like a blessing from the other side, with Joseph wishing me well in a future life, the piece of a future time that did not include himself. And yet it also recalls his living presence.

I had arrived in New York on December 14th and was hoping to meet him on the 15th, to go over some of the Zabolotsky translations, a selection of the "final versions" of which I had sent him shortly before, as he had offered to send the collection to his publishers with a note urging them to publish it. Then, when I was back in America in January, I wrote to him. It was eleven days before he died. Did he read that last letter of mine? I told him how good it had been visiting him in Brooklyn Heights and how helpful I had found his comments. I also told him about a reading of Zabolotsky that I had given at the Pushkin Club, in London. The translations, I assured him, had "read well" in English. I knew he still had reservations about my translations, but my impression was that he now thought them at least redeemable.

However, Joseph was hardly likely to allow the fact that I'd had a successful reading influence his own opinion of the translations. Probably, I was simply trying to boost my own ego, to give myself more strength for the anticipated argument with him. Actually, though, I had lately come round somewhat to his way of thinking, having more or less abandoned my earlier *vers libre* approach. I told him that, on his advice, I was also trying to make the translations more "sprightly", and warned him that I would be sending him my own latest poetry pamphlet; my own verse, too, seemed to be getting sprightlier, I noted. On the other hand, my abandonment of the *vers libre* approach was not quite what it seemed. It was just that you couldn't have it both ways. Once it was engaged with, rhyming became a challenge not easily ignored. And I didn't ignore it, although aware that I was not among the best or even better rhymers . . . But just because I had a long way to go was no argument not to get started.

In that last letter of mine, I also transmitted an invitation from Michael Horovitz for Joseph to participate in an international poetry reading to take place at the Albert Hall, London, in July 1996. I concluded: "Life begins at sixty – I hope."

At Sea in English But Not in American: Rhymes

READING JOSEPH'S English poems, it occurs to me that his technique might owe something to translation, that is to what translators get up to as they mediate between Russian and English. Thus, assonantal or consonantal, rather than full rhymes are plentiful. Earlier, before Joseph was quite so involved in the translation of his own work, he was disinclined to accept or even acknowledge the existence of near-rhymes. However, that he began to change in this respect was not, I think, simply a matter of convenience, now that he himself had to grapple with the problems rather than exhort his translators to try even harder. Greater familiarity with English may have something to do with it. He is quite adroit with syntax. Enjambment has become a structural principle, prepositions, conjunctions finding them-selves, almost routinely, in the rhyming position. Occasionally words are broken in two and divided between lines, disclosing, as it were, the rhymes contained within them: the echo, faint but precise, recalls the formal tradition for which Joseph had expressed such reverence. Unless he is using a set form, he tends to write accentual verse, the unaccented syllables or feet being variable. This enables him to approximate spoken rhythms more readily.

For a poet apparently of such classical aspirations, Joseph is remarkably free with the language. That is, he treats the conven-tions not as inflexible laws, but as malleable. At the same time, oddly enough, he sees himself as the defender of English, resis-ting the loose practices of the moderns ("If anything really upsets me, it is not the distortion of this or that passage but a really cavalier disrespect for the English language.") Of course, this is consistent with his view of language, rather than the poet, as the prime mover. He continues: "I don't care that my line doesn't scan well [Hmm!]. But the point is that it's not *my line*: it's the *line in English*." It took some cheek, really, to appoint himself the defender of English! As for the "cavalier disrespect", it was not so much, I think, that he had anything specific in mind, as that he was aware of a general indifference or lack of discipline. He was, in principle, suspicious of free verse, because he believed it encouraged such tendencies. His discipline as a writer in English, though, is quite *sui generis*. But what does strike the native reader is his quirkiness or awkwardness. Time and again he seems to get idioms slightly wrong. Sometimes he simply errs, though usually there is some acoustical rationale. One wonders why these lapses, if they are lapses, were not pointed out to him. (Perhaps they were and perhaps he ignored this, since more was at stake than idiomatic correctitude?) Quite often, though, his stubbornness was justified. At any rate, it paid off, since what he was after was some novel or unprecedented effect. Still, his English did begin to sound more natural. He learnt very fast. This dual movement – the translation of himself into the language and, despite what he said about the latter's preeminence, the translation of the language into himself – gave rise to a distinct form of English, which was not exactly the Anglo-Russian hybrid it seemed to be. To what extent did this idiolect depend on performance, on Joseph's voice, on his being there? I suppose it's too soon to say.

But how about some examples? What is needed, I suppose, is a stylistic analysis of Joseph's English. In the absence of a comprehensive dictionary of his tropes, however, that would be dauntingly speculative, Still, it is agreeable to wander through the poems, on the lookout for interesting features. What, for instance, do I mean by unidiomatic? Firstly, there is the intonation. Joseph's poems are discursive and his voice can be heard in them with almost eerie clarity. It is a Russian voice, albeit macaronic, with its Oxford-English (note his liking for "one", rather than "you" or "we") rendering of American (Manhattan?) English. Furthermore, since he is apt, rather incongruously or surrealistically to juxtapose quite elaborate, even precious images, apparently more for acoustic or formal than semantic reasons, there is often a made-up quality about the language. Sound, metre, structure seem of more immediate significance than the actual meaning or even imagery (at least as a visually descriptive device). The demands of rhyme, and in particular Joseph's readiness to employ double or triple rhymes, as if in defiance of the monosyllabic norm and the humorous associations of polysyllabic rhyme, encourage also the use of rare or archaic words, of Latinate diction, where more informal language seems indicated.[51] (This perverse formality echoes his personal accent, its Oxford component.) The effect, therefore is of unidiomatic or mannered speech, which at the same time *seems* organic, natural-sounding, necessary.

He ended his Iowa reading with a love poem, written in English ("A Song"). I was worried by such lines as: "the water / that sighs and shifts in its slumber", when "in its sleep" would be more natural (or maybe "as it slumbers"), although "slumber" is more suggestive of water and moreover supplies the tongue-in-cheek feminine rhyme with: "I wish it were still a quarter / to dial your number." Joseph's exploitation of synonyms in English to increase the rhyme stock and compensate for the lack of inflections, has precipitated the substitution of the more expressive "slumber" for the monosyllabic and more idiomatic "sleep". (I wonder if the first choice, the idiomatic choice, generally *is* a monosyllabic word?)

I cringed, waiting for the groans. But presumably nobody else cringed. In any case, there were no groans; and not just because Midwesterners are courteous. The poem touches more than one nerve, and the final lines: "What's the point of forgetting / if it's followed by dying?" uncover the helplessness, the tragic or hellish dimensions of love, of life. The naively consecutive, elementary rhymes (*dear / here / near*; *dear / here / gear*; *dear / here / appear*; *dear / hemisphere / beer*), seem those of a plain man, trying to find words to dignify the grief of separation. He achieves a kind of pathos, and with that last quatrain something more: "It's evening, the sun is setting; / boys shout and gulls are crying. / What's the point of forgetting / if it's followed by dying?"

Sometimes he will manipulate – I'm trying to find less negative words than "distort" or "twist" – the syntax for the sake, apparently, of a quite tenuous rhyme (in "Star of the Nativity": "a child was born in a cave in order to save the world; / it blew as only in deserts in winter it blows, athwart."[52] Of course, Joseph's pronunciation of the "or" in "world" was closer to that of the "aw" in "athwart". But "blows, athwart" is hardly English . . .

Or is it? I'm speaking of *my* English, which I learnt to question here, in America. As often as not, when I draw attention to it, for instance, in the Translation Workshop, a student will say something like: Sounds all right to me! Little does the class know what inner turmoil this produces in *me*! That English, *my* English, is all I have, all I have ever had. And as the only "native" English speaker in my family – and the only British-speaker here, in the Translation Workshop, in Iowa – I am terribly unsure about it.

This problematical rhyme, *world / athwart*, however, *is* integrated into the poem, echoing "cold", twice repeated, in lines one and two: "In the cold season, in a locality accustomed to heat more than / to cold, to horizontality more than to a mountain, / a child was born in a cave in order to save the world . . .", etc. The rhyme, based on Joseph's Russian-American pronunciation, follows the unquestionably faint *than / mountain*. He is playing a subtle almost, subliminal game of formal or prosodic irony. He has enlarged the field, giving himself more room for manoeuvre. Anything goes, or so it at first seems. In fact, rules are no less firm for being, shall we say, more accommodating. And if that is a contradiction in terms, so much the better! I might add that the "aw" sound is also echoed in the following line (a new stanza) by the middle syllable in "enormous". And the awkward apposition of "athwart" ("blows, athwart") is grammatically paralleled in the second stanza: "their presents heaped by the door, ajar." (to rhyme with "star"; there is a further problem, of course, in that grammatically "ajar" might also refer to "presents").

"Natural" English word order evidently was not the highest priority for Joseph. He treated the language rather like Russian. That is to say, he was not prepared – or able, given his needs – to forego the advantages of flexible word order. But even in this respect, there was "improvement", due in part to his making the idiolect more self-consistent (and perhaps to the familiarizing effect on his readers of his consistent employment of it!) and in part to his versatility and alertness in English. Nevertheless, compromise and compensation were still the name of the game.

A typical example, in the third stanza: "through pallid, stray / clouds . . .", where "stray, pallid clouds" would be more natural. He has reversed the order, on account of the "stray / away" rhyme, and I cannot help wondering whether adjectival word order meant anything to him. If it did, clearly it did not matter as much as the overall acoustics, to which he was acutely sensitive, in English as in Russian. It is this acuity that helps him recognize and control the assonances and also accounts for the congruence of his consonants in the rhyming words. While he rings the changes, almost with abandon, rarely does he err. His sense of design was as secure as his command of idiom was not. But idiom is probably the last bastion. Even with native speakers idiom can crumble after prolonged exposure to a foreign linguistic system. Joseph did what he could, and presumably he reckoned that what was gained when he himself was in charge outweighed what was lost when he let others have their perhaps more idiomatic way. Perhaps he believed or hoped that the rest (i.e. a more indigenous English) would follow, if sufficient attention were paid to prosodic richness and harmony, particularly to metre. As language precedes those who speak it, so phonological structure generally precedes usage and semantics. Joseph's delight in language games, in experimentation, always within quasi-traditional limits, must have disposed him to take risks. When I read his English poetry now, I am aware of a dynamic, aesthetic rationale at work. His classicism resides not so much in adherence to traditional rules of prosody as in the impression conveyed of a transformational, generative symmetry, consistency, pattern, or verbal choreography. He is exceptionally good at improvising, anticipating, like a chess master. Reading his poetry one feels one has been witnessing language itself running through its repertoire.

Maybe his translations are better seen as drafts or guides rather than finished products: "This is the *kind* of thing I'm after. Will the language accept it? Yes? No? Well, we'll see later. Press on! Here's another crux . . ." Certainly, my all too brief first-hand experience – I'll come to it – of translating with Joseph, or rather watching him at work as *he* translated, lends some credence to the above. So, here's another: "New Life".

Well, life can begin at sixty (as I hoped!), but does life "start anew" – in English, I mean? It does, I suppose, when the line goes: "Life starts anew indeed like this – with a painted view", and two lines further down: "With the attendant feeling it's only you / who survey the disaster." Incidentally, the line between, "of a volcanic eruption, of a dinghy high waves beleaguer" is a good example of Joseph's quite Hopkinsian ellipticism ("dinghy [which] high waves beleaguer"). However, while the more natural passive construction "beleaguered by high waves" would not disrupt the basic four-stress sprung rhythm, he needed "beleaguer" at the end of the line, not only for the rhyme but also dynamically. Listen to all four lines: "Life starts anew indeed like this – with a painted view / of a volcanic eruption, of a dinghy high waves beleaguer. / With the attendant feeling it's only you / who survey the disaster. With the feeling that you are eager / to shift your gaze . . ." What follows is a burst of assonances on "ar": *blast / vase* (though I think Joseph pronounced this "vaize"; anyway, it chimes with "gaze" in the first part of the previous line) / *plaster / harbingers of disaster*. Of course, more standard (or less thespian) American pronunciation than Joseph's would flatten the "a's" . . .

The point is that I am surprised, as I read and write, to find that these so-called blemishes do not, in fact, spoil the pleasure these poems give me. At first, they might irritate – because it would surely have been easy enough to fix them? – but finally they are simply absorbed. There is a linguistic openness, an endearing playfulness (in the highest sense) about them. In the title poem ("So Forth"), a translation by the author, the "foreign" accent is particularly marked in the elaborate metaphors or conceits, which are intellectually and harmonically coherent, and yet idiomatically off, sounding rather *ad hoc*, or lexical (i.e. lifted out of a dictionary). Here's one: ". . . when the trees you see / ape fanning-out tracks freed of their wheels' malfunction / and the edge of the forest echoes a rustling junction." Actually, I do not know what "malfunction" is doing – unless, perhaps, it is meant to recall the hiccuppy sound of wheels on a rail-track – apart from rhyming with "junction". The different items seem to have been jammed into place, or as if too few words were being used to tackle too many tasks. There are also numerous small items. For instance: "gaze / fixedly at some point in the distance. And the greater the latter's haze . . .", where "latter", referring to "distance", is too much for me at any rate. Also, does one speak of "haze" as "great"? (But why do I say "one" and put this as a question? A "great haze"? *I personally* might not say it. So what!) Sometimes he will use the apparently full form of a word redundantly, even somewhat incorrectly, if he needs an extra syllable, as with "a bedsheet's linen", instead of "bed linen". Mistake? Possibly. My hypothesis, unprovable, is that perhaps he is saying: "Anyway, this is the *kind of thing* I want. I need two syllables here, and an echo", etc.

A few assonantal rhymes, chosen at random from *So Forth*, that Joseph, when I first knew him, would surely have regarded as dubious, to say the least: *fewer / cruel*; *chirring / chiming*; *finish / fingers*; *plus / class*; *drops / globes*; *death / depth*; *byword / sideward*; *features / future*; *provinces / promises*; *perhaps / impotence* (*-potence / perhaps* are rhythmically analogous, particularly in Joseph's pronunciation; furthermore "perhaps" is preceded in the same line by "snapshot", giving a strong internal rhyme on "ap", the alliterative "p" carrying over into or echoed by the "pot" in "impotence"); *antics / anxious* . . . This last is a typical example of his mimicry, "nx or ngsh" being a kind of slurred reiteration of "nt". The order of some consonants may be identical, or it may be dyslexically reversed, or both at once: *next / architects* [st / ts]. Rhymes may be macaronic: *sorry / memento* . . . *mori*. Often the rhymes are based on slurred consonants as well as strong assonance: *Finite / find it*. Sometimes (e.g. *foreign / fallen*) they seem to depend on the reader either mumbling, or only half listening, as a painter might half shut his eyes to distinguish tonal contrasts. Where, for instance, a consonantal ending might be thought to clash with a vowel ending (*fewer / cruel*) the disparity is minimized. With little effort the "1" can be lost or almost lost: i.e. *fewer / cruer*. Perhaps American English, as suggested earlier, encouraged Brodsky in this regard. But even though he used and obviously relished idiomatic American English, his intonations were rather British – not so surprising, given his regard for Auden, who remained British-sounding but with a hint of New York. To hear Joseph speak American English, as might a Russian who had been subjected to the British public-school system, was itself a macaronic experience. His translations and original English poetry are similarly macaronic. And sometimes, his inventions seem to come straight out of Gilbert: *barometer / Byronic air* or Ogden Nash (the aforementioned *sorry / memento mori*). In short, Joseph's rhymes are often not so much ingenious (although they are) as parodic, which is perhaps only to say that he was learning by example. They are semantically and phonetically inspired approximations. His dexterity or virtuosity can hardly be denied, even if he does not avoid, or apparently even seek to avoid, pratfalls. Again, one is reminded of Nash's exploitation of "bad" poetry.

JOSEPH SEEMS to have been a world-class juggler (rather than a world-class fraud, as Craig Raine styled him). Simultaneity is his stock-in-trade. Should one call this baroque?[53] At any rate, more baroque that classical. He is like the conductor of a large and unruly orchestra, composed entirely of virtuosi. To control them he has to be a martinet.

Pictures of Joseph, at least "official" portraits, often show him that way: chin jutting, basilisk stare, a grim, sometimes scowling expression. Referring to Akhmatova's height, he noted that being with her made you realise why Russia was sometimes ruled by empresses. But actually, there was something quite imperial or imperious about him as well. Both he and his revered Akhmatova were magnified by language, if in rather different ways. However, in less official portraits, he often looks rather rueful, wistful, slightly incredulous or embarrassed to be there, like a street urchin towered over by toffs.

The fact is that I have only begun to explore Joseph's language, *his* English, as it was evolving. There is much that could be done. For instance, one might scrutinize his translations into Russian of other poets, and then compare these translations with his *self-*translations. I made a start, taking his version of Lowell's "For the Union Dead", and found that, while in general he remained semantically close, there was, for instance, far more enjambment than in the original. Mikhail Meilakh, who collaborated with Joseph on the translation of the Metaphysical poets, tells me that the Lowell translation was attempted before Joseph knew English well and that he described it in these terms: "I did it literally with these very hands!" That being so, it is a considerable achievement. Other English poets he translated include, among the moderns, Richard Wilbur and Chaim Plutzik, and of course the aforementioned Metaphysical poets (Andrew Marvell and John Donne). Here is George Kline on Brodsky the translator:

"His usual technique of translation reveals the heightened interest of the young Brodsky in Donne's poetics. At first he read and translated only the first and last lines. Then he put away the original and tried to imagine what Donne had written in between. His five published [in the Soviet Union] translations from Donne [. . .] retain fidelity to the originals, especially as regards metre and the rhyme schemes: to garner exclusively masculine rhymes throughout four whole poems is no mean feat in Russian."[54] Quite true, but it is hard to believe he actually translated that way. On the other hand, did he perhaps feel the need to match himself, imagining what might lie between first and last lines, before embarking on the actual business? Insofar as the end lies in the beginning, insofar as Donne was a "thinking" poet, perhaps Joseph was trying to think his way through, to re-think, to align his thought process with that of Donne, to re-enact, not simply imitate. This could have been a way of honouring Donne, whose poetry itself exemplified thought in action.

But what were the translations like? Take a short poem by Donne, "The Apparition":

When by thy scorn, O murderess, I am dead,
And that thou think'st thee free
From all solicitation from me,
Then shall my ghost come to thy bed,
And thee, feigned vestal, in worse arms shall see;
Then thy sick taper will begin to wink,
And he, whose thou art then, being tired before,
Will, if thou stir, or pinch to wake him, think
    Thou call'st for more,
And in false sleep will from thee shrink,
And then poor aspen wretch, neglected thou
Bathed in a cold quicksilver sweat wilt lie
    A verier ghost than I;
What I will say, I will not tell thee now,
Lest that preserve thee; and since my love is spent,
I had rather thou shouldst painfully repent,
Than by my threatenings rest still innocent.

Now, leaving aside the beauty of Brodsky's Russian version, which is titled *Poseshchenie* or "The Visit", here is a word-for-word, line-by-line back-rendering of it into English:

When your bitter poison shall have killed me,
When suddenly you rid yourself of
The claims and services of my love,
        My shade will come to your bed.
And you, already in the power [*vo vlasti*] of worse hands,
You will give a start. And, greeting the visit,
Your candle will plunge into darkness.
        And you will cling to your partner.
But he, already tired, will imagine
That you are asking for a new caress, and to the wall
Will turn in his feigned sleep.
        Then, o my poor Asp, pale,
In silver sweat, quite alone,
You will not concede to me in illusoriness.

Curses? In them there is much vanity.
Why? I prefer that you
Repent, than that you draw in tears.
        That purity, which is not in the eyes.

The original rhyme-scheme is: *a b b a b/c d c d c/e f f e/g g g*. So, the poem is divided into four parts: two of five lines, one of four lines, and one of three lines. The pattern is quite irregular, as is the metre. The Russian rhymes *a b b a b/c d d c/e e f f e/g g h h*. Donne's poem has seventeen lines (itself rather irregular), whereas Brodsky's has eighteen. Also Brodsky has somewhat regularized the rhyming, retaining the abba pattern, and ending with two couplets rather than with Donne's triplet. Brodsky's basically tetrametric version is more accented, more symmetrical than the source text. While Donne's tone is rather more conversational, Brodsky's language, oddly enough, is simpler, more direct, e.g. the first line: "When by thy scorn, O Murderess, I am dead" (Donne); "When your bitter poison shall have killed me" (Brodsky). Brodsky's rendering of Donne's succinct "A verier ghost than I", however, struggles to hold on to the sense: "You will not concede to me in illusoriness."

But apparently he misunderstood "And then poor aspen wretch", which alludes to the tremulousness of the aspen or poplar, when he rendered it "o my poor Asp" (as though Cleopatra were being invoked). However, this apparent error does return us to the first line: "When your bitter poison shall have killed me", which of course is rather different from "When by thy scorn, O murderess, I am dead". While scorn may be regarded as a poison, it is not specifically characterized as such by Donne. (Bitterness, too, is less specific than scorn.) Furthermore, what it takes Donne six or seven syllables to say, it takes Brodsky eleven. Donne addresses his mistress as "Murderess", whereas Brodsky, later in the poem calls her "Asp", though the Asp is also "poor", as is the "aspen wretch" in the original. It seems to me that if, indeed, he translated first and last lines and imagined what came between, it must have been in the earliest stages of the translation. So, perhaps this exercise or tactic helped to engage his creativity. The translator, suffering from a debilitating sense of unworthiness vis-à-vis the author, is faced with the dilemma of trying to rival him, at least for the purposes of the work in hand, while at the same time regarding himself as unequal to the task. Rehearsing or actively imagining the course or trajectory of the poem might at least boost self-esteem.

The above is an early translation. At first sight, there appears to be little of the flexibility, litheness, *brio* that characterize Joseph's later poetry, either in Russian or English. But when I put the English text away and let the Russian go to work, a quite tragic note is sounded: in particular, the two questions (the second of which goes unanswered, or is answered only obliquely) in the final quatrain – Brodsky turns this into a quatrain, with the most rudimentary of rhyme schemes, *a a b b*; it is not so in the original – which slow, indeed briefly arrest the action, where the source text moves with scarcely a pause towards its conclusion. The greater symmetry of the Brodsky version allows it to accommodate the dramatic pauses, as the narrator steps to the front of the stage. Although the last four lines, in the original, form a semantic unit, they are also effectively integrated into the poem through rhyme: _a_ _b_ _b_ _a_ _c_ _c_ _c._

Joseph's epigraph to _On Grief and Reason_ is by Auden: "Blessed be all metrical rules that forbid automatic responses, / force us to have second thoughts, free us from the fetters of Self." Metaphorical density, the intensely cogitative nature of Donne's poetry, made the expression of difficult and painful emotions possible. Restraint, then, but of the most elaborate kind. And, of course, the labyrinthine intellectualism, intricacy, also commended itself to the young Brodsky, brilliant auto-didact, hungering for world culture. Mental, syntactic, prosodic intensification then? If so, it spilled over between poems, so that firm boundaries were necessary; but the boundaries of Brodsky's poems are somewhat permeable, even if in his performances he stressed last lines, standing amid the applause, staring, as if that which had been so forcefully delivered had somehow rebounded and momentarily stunned the speaker himself!

So far, I have learnt very little about Joseph's English or his methods as a translator into English. On closer examination, his translations of other poets seem to me rather reductive. But, apart from the fact that translation of poetry tends to be reductive anyway, he may be allowing himself greater latitude in which to develop a coherent phonological structure. He strives, after all, not only to render sense, but simultaneously to reproduce the poem's physical shape.

In fact, I've made several forays into _So Forth_ and have already been surprised by Joseph's apparently more tolerant attitude to free verse. Fewer than half the "serious" poems in this, the last collection in English supervised by himself, are rhymed. Does this indicate an increased confidence in his ability to structure poems organically in English, without resorting to set forms? Or was the fact that he was writing more prose having an impact on his poetry as well? Perhaps _not_ to rhyme was for Joseph the ultimate challenge. Auden, of course, in his later poetry also rhymed far less, though the metrics remained regular enough. In Joseph's late poetry, it seems that metre alone is beginning to fulfil the function hitherto performed by metre and rhyme together. Metre and *mind* (thinking) are closely linked, almost synonymous.

Writing and the Man

"ONE'S AFFINITY", said Joseph in a filmed interview,[*] "is for the generation to which one belongs." He was looking at some slides of his friends in Russia. And, of course, chain-smoking. Biting off the filters. His eyes screwed up, as he grimaced, enfolded in smoke. "Well, I'm sorry, well, I'm becoming a bit maudlin . . . [*Would he return?*] Well . . . [*a grin?*] you can't step twice onto the same asphalt . . . [*The new generation?*] I don't really care . . . Well, of course, I'm glad that I'm read . . . But I don't really care what they think." On the other hand: "A reader must grow with a poet . . . I've been cut off, so it doesn't matter where I live from now on." [*How about the sentence, exile? The Arctic Circle, etc?*] "I'm glad of it, really. But for that, I would have ended up a city boy, intellectual, and all that garbage . . ." [*Exile?*] "It's all in the eye of the . . . silly beholder . . . After all, to be on the outside is the core of the whole thing. It is ideal, technically speaking, for the artist."

"Technically speaking." Vintage Joseph! His life is surely one of his finest achievements, at least for us, his contemporaries, those who knew him. He would vehemently disagree. The writing remains and the life is ephemeral. Yes, but the life is subsumed in the writing. Still, it is only the writing that should concern us, or is, in fact, any of our business. OK, but in the writing one sees more than the words; one sees the man himself, and one appreciates or experiences the *example* he set . . . Is there a better word? He'd have loathed "example". Sometimes he compared himself with those he admired (Beckett, Auden, for instance), but never intimating that he considered himself to be in the same league. It was clear that this was not a pose. But nor is it to be taken entirely at face value. And naturally his admirers admired him even more for it! But there is no solution to this, short of becoming a recluse, which for Joseph was no option. As I read his work, as I listen to recordings or stare at videos, I am

164   * Joseph Brodsky, *A Maddening Space*
       (1991 production; 1995 mystic Fire VCR tape)

repeatedly won over by a kind of sophisticated ingenuousness, a tough vulnerability, as though he had no alternative but to remain open, because he found himself, quite rightly, rubbing shoulders with the likes of Auden or Milosz.

This is the lesson that he has been privileged to impart, even if he would never have claimed to be *imparting* anything. He insists that language takes precedence, even over art. Language, in fact, maketh art, as it maketh ethics, and man himself. It is our guide, or perhaps our better, our best part. In his Nobel Lecture he said (in his casual and yet also emphatic way): "On the whole, every new aesthetic reality makes man's ethical reality more precise. For aesthetics is the mother of ethics. The categories of 'good' and 'bad' are, first and foremost, aesthetic ones [. . .]" He continues: "For a man with taste, particularly with literary taste, is less susceptible to the refrains and the rhythmical incantations peculiar to any version of political demagogy."[55] This is defiantly élitist, insofar as it insists on the importance of cultural values that are not instinctual but are instilled through education or apprenticeship. On the other hand, it sets the notion of Art for Art's Sake on its head, and turns Auden's *désabusé* contention (in his poem on the death of Yeats) that "poetry makes nothing happen" into a truism. And, of course, although Joseph never dwelt on what he had endured at the hands of the Soviet bosses, these experiences did lend such comments a certain authority. Nobility or uprightness of character is no guarantee of aesthetic excellence, but Joseph was prodigiously talented and his stamina seemed limitless. He was determined to make full use of his gifts: "until brown clay has been crammed down my larynx, / only gratitude will be gushing from it."

In the post-Communist reality, art has been dethroned – or, rather, it has retreated from the barricades, which in any case seem hardly to exist any more. Art, Good Taste are problematical concepts, and the artist or intellectual is back wherever, on the reservation, if not in the ivory tower, flattering those with money in their pockets, or providing the new bourgeoisie with the fix it needs . . .

The Essayist

Monday, 17 June, 1996

JOSEPH'S ESSAYS are brilliant improvisation. Those in which he takes the reader on a tour of particular poems (Frost, Auden, Hardy) more or less render an account, I am told, of what went on in his classes. Evidently, he would read poems, commenting freely, associatively, as he analysed them line by line, word by word, syllable by syllable. I imagine (and have also been told by some who attended them) that these were inspiring, inspired performances. On the other hand, of course, his teaching "method" did not encourage interaction. But then, whether one likes it or not, it *does* matter who the solo performer is. And, as we know now and as he knew, time was short. Rightly or wrongly, he chose this way of conveying what he wanted to convey. To have done any less would have been to short change his students.

Could it be that the translations, the English verse too, are located somewhere between the complexly or rigorously improvised essays and the poems in Russian, where he gallantly shouldered the burden that it was his fate – or destiny, as some, though probably not Joseph, might call it – to assume? That is, on the one hand, he was committed to his own original, his own source text, but on the other, since it was his own, he was at liberty also to improvise, to invent, to rewrite. All translation can be seen as rewriting, but it is also a question of to what extent. When rewriter and writer are separate individuals, the former may very well feel conscience-bound to keep checking with the latter. Whereas, when they are the same person, even if the rewriter is the writer some time after, there is a greater likelihood that he will allow himself to become the writer again. Indeed, he may feel so obliged if he is to undertake the task at all. Furthermore, as we have seen, Joseph was quite literalistic formally.

166

Joseph in fact encouraged comments from classes, and was immediately appreciative when they were good, and showed frustration when nobody would talk back to him.

The auto-translations and the English poems possess a liveliness that is sometimes missing in his Russian poetry, even if his work in English is not nearly so accomplished. But for readers of Russian whose mother tongue is English, Brodsky's English language performances are revealing. Irony is not lacking, except that he is a brave man and prepared to take his knocks. Or is he, as some apparently think, simply too arrogant to recognize that he is making a fool of himself? One cannot have it both ways.

On Not Saying Goodbye

AS NOTED earlier, what is so bewildering is not being able to make contact with Joseph, to question him – in particular, about his new condition of non-being! The conviction grows rather than diminishes that he is somewhere, that one has only to find the correct formula to raise him. Therefore, if one has not contacted him, it must be because one is not trying hard enough. Which is what I feel about my writing as well – and what he seemed to feel about my translations! Each time I begin to write I must contend with these discouraging feelings. And I am often overcome by fatigue; my mind wanders and has to be redirected. I have to be coaxed, reassured that what I have undertaken is not impossible. But each time is a new beginning.

Joseph, I believe, was able to hold on to what had gone before, so that he was not always starting from scratch. The notion of continuity tallies with that of the primacy of language. A life in language. On the other hand, his fondness for the short form suggests a reluctance to commit himself to a single, long-term project. He particularly recommends the essay, where a claim can be staked without necessarily embarking on a comprehensive programme of scholarly research. The flip explanation would be that he was simply too much of an artist. Apparently his life and work were one, and he avoided getting sidetracked, however significant and attractive the byways. The informal, garrulous essay suited him perfectly, because it came directly out of his life.

And this, is it just an absurdly long drawn out farewell?

"Here I am", says the voice in the poems. "I'm all here, or at least much of me is, much of what I was. Yes, I know, there is the body; I'd be the last to deny it. But in the end, our words are what remains of our worldly presence," *all that is left of a man is a Part of Speech.* I am trying to convince myself that most of that person is in the work, with which one may cohabit, which one may explore, to which the living may turn almost at will. And, finally, that the work is outside time, more durable even than time, as Joseph, echoing pre-reconstructed Auden, kept reiterating.

We shared an obsession, hardly uncommon, with death, and with time and its effects. Of course, Joseph had good reason to concern himself, whereas I had less, even if I did develop cancer a decade after arriving in America. I wrote continually about my father, in particular his death from cancer, nearly thirty, forty years before. Also my mother's death – from a stroke, though at the time she had cancer as well. Neither of them wanted to know what was wrong. She died in 1985, at the age of 85, in London, while I was in the States, this being close to the time when Joseph's mother died in Leningrad.

Translation, on the other hand, is some kind of antidote to such morbid obsessions, positing a kind of optimism. Translation's success, if it is or can be successful, speaks for the longevity of literature, for its spatial and temporal extension. More, it speaks for its immortality. At least, in the short term!

A COUPLE of weeks ago, I read the few letters from Joseph that were in the *MPT* archives at King's College, London. Most of my dealings with him seem to have been in the seventies. I was surprised to find that our discussion of two projects, the second being an anthology of Post-War East European poetry, belongs to that period, approximately a quarter of a century ago.

In a letter to him, in August 1973, back in London but due to return to the States in October to edit an anthology of 20th-century Russian poetry that was to be published by the University of Iowa Press, I mentioned a discussion I had had with a publisher, regarding a bilingual "Russian Poets" series and/or an anthology of nineteenth-century Russian poetry. I asked Joseph for a list of the poets he would include in such an anthology, noting that he had already drawn my attention to several poems by Pushkin's contemporary Evgeny Baratynsky. The bilingual series did not materialize, but the anthology eventually did, in 1989, as *An Age Ago*, translations by Alan Myers, with a foreword and biographical notes by Brodsky. By the time the book appeared, I had long ceased to be involved.

It surprises me that I was talking to Joseph about such a volume as far back as 1973, hardly more than a year after his arrival in the West. I was struck by the paucity of translations, in contrast to the availability of nineteenth-century Russian prose in translation. Presumptuously, I tried to make the case for redressing the balance. Take, for instance, Evgeny Baratynsky (1800–44). Joseph, in his biographical note (in *An Age Ago*) quotes Pushkin: "Baratynsky is unique among us, for he thinks." Thinking, of course, is also what Joseph does. He continues: "The texture of his lines is the strongest evidence for the 'felt thought' thesis, as his argument evolves euphonically and tonally rather than in linear fashion." This is consistent with his conviction that it is language itself that runs the show.

"Baratynsky", he adds with satisfaction, "is an oddity. Even in his earliest elegies [. . .] he is never personal or autobiographical, and leans towards an integrating remark, towards a psychological truth." He might be describing his own work, or at least his own intentions. Brodsky concludes: "It is to his 'psychological' miniatures that the Russian novel of the second half of the nineteenth century owes most, though" (he adds regretfully) "it appears to have failed to inherit his lyrical hero's stoic, clear-eyed posture."

Joseph was not content to limit his participation in this project to that of consultant, but did his utmost to influence the translator, his friend Alan Myers, who was far more responsive than I would have been.

It is true, as Joseph wrote to me, that I had never had to deal with anyone as stubborn as himself. Of course, I was aware of the inadequacy both of my knowledge of the literature and the language – you might think that was enough! – but I suspect that I still believed I could keep the upper hand. I was quite confident about my insightfulness.

In somewhat Nabokovian fashion, I clung to a theory of semantically literalist, almost ad-verbum, inevitably non-formal translation, whereas Joseph, as we know, believed religiously that rhyme and metre must be preserved. But we tried at first not to let this radical difference get in the way of the Russian project. Initially the translators, with Joseph advising, were to be Alan Myers, Bernard Meares and myself. The plan, as it evolved later, must have been Joseph's: the book was to contain selections from his favourite poets, the *essential* poets, represented by their *essential* poems, to the extent that Myers was able to translate these. It was not only on account of his pedagogical or promotional concerns that Joseph wanted to keep such a close eye on this project, but also because it was his baby. What I could contribute, I thought, was a more objective view of the translations, as English poetry. Even if my Russian was still shaky, I had at least been involved in poetry translation for nearly two decades.

So, towards the end of the seventies, the partnership of Meares, Myers and Weissbort was ready to roll, with Joseph

Brodsky riding shotgun. We divided the poets between us, the prize, Baratynsky, going to Myers and myself. Actually, I put in many hours, drafting numerous versions, and experimenting with various approaches, ranging from formal to free verse and even (for my own amusement or edification) parody. But I was frustrated at every turn, producing nothing that gave me the least satisfaction. This seemed to be due to the familiar quandary regarding formal translation. I wrote something about it much later, in a review-essay, also analysing one of Alan Myers's translations of Baratynsky.[56] I tried to show that formal mimesis had necessitated semantic changes, which in their turn brought about changes in tone, in that the English of the translation was less plain, less direct than the Russian of the source text. It was not my intention to denigrate the Myers translation, but it seemed to me that, precisely because it was so deftly carried out, it revealed problems inherent in this approach.

The anthology was Joseph's baby in more senses than one. The selection identifies major figures in his own development, and Joseph's biographical notes are interestingly personal. I have already mentioned Baratynsky in this connection. Joseph concludes his note on Pushkin, whose "rhymes and meters reveal every word's stereoscopic nature", by commenting on the fact that towards the end of his life he turned increasingly to prose, historical novels, or straight history. "It is doubtful that [. . .] Pushkin coveted a career as a fiction writer; it is true, however, that the greatest literary influence of his life was the author of *The History of the Russian State*, and *history is the mother of prose* [my italics]." In this case he might be talking about himself, his interest in Herodotus, for instance, his essay writing, but also in respect to his poetry, with its persistent enjambments, its increasingly accentual rather than syllabic metre.

PS. I had also, as noted, discussed the anthology of East European poetry with Joseph. Here I was more knowledgeable or at least had a track record, in that Ted Hughes and I had begun

Modern Poetry in Translation, in the early sixties, mainly to publish work by the first post-War generation of East European poets, then in their prime. Rivalry between successive generations is not unknown, nor were we immune to it. However, although these poets *were* my older contemporaries, they were unlike their coevals in Britain. Joseph, a little younger than me, had also been drawn to them, especially to the Polish poets – Poland was the Soviet Union's "window on the West"; he had translated some of their work into Russian. But maybe *because* he was, or had been so much closer to them, he was almost wary of them now. At least, it seemed so to me. I had experienced the blitz in London as a child and had uncles, living in France, who survived deportation. However, for the child self, communism was untainted; I did not perceive myself to be threatened by it; it was simply a point on my horizon. For Joseph, a child of the war years, born in 1940, just prior to the blockade of Leningrad, and raised in a political environment, comparable to that of the aforementioned East European poets, the latter probably *did* represent the father generation, having lived out the war as adults, albeit young ones.

By the time I talked to him about an East European anthology, my own plans for one were already quite far advanced. What I had in mind was a collection that brought under one cover some major figures of that generation, rather than aimed comprehensively to represent the Soviet Union's East and Central European empire. That is, my focus was on individuals of a particular generation, who shared certain stylistic and thematic preoccupations, due no doubt to the unprecedentedly gruelling experiences that they had undergone. What concerned me was the survival of the individual, as such, after a calamitous war and in repressive conditions, rather than the survival of nations or cultural traditions. The collection I was planning was similar in scope to the original nineteenth-century collection. Our rôles were, in a way, reversed, in that Joseph was quite enthusiastic about my project, but ended by supporting and advising a colleague of his at Michigan, Emery George, who produced a much larger anthology that did seek to represent the entire region, from Baltic to Black Sea, and did not limit itself to the work of a particular generation.[57]

In the end, as with the nineteenth-century anthology, we parted company, either because our aims diverged, or because of differences with regard to translation . . .

It is instructive to review the correspondence, and not just as a means of reining in one's own mythologizing tendencies. There are so many, often simultaneous beginnings. Proposals from me and from him. Somehow I managed to get two small publishers to bring out a translation series, individual volumes of poetry in translation. Perhaps it was my relative success here that lent our various schemes a certain momentum. Excitement, optimism inform our discussions or reveries. I cannot say whether this tendency had a similar aetiology in both our cases, but it did bring us closer. There was quite a lot of the editor, the talent-spotter and promoter in Joseph. If he *could* be instrumental, for instance, in getting Aleksandr Wat or his own Leningrad contemporary Aleksandr Kushner published, he was happy to do so. He lent his name quite freely and wrote numerous introductions and prefaces to collections of poetry and other books. These short pieces were always interesting and original, though they usually also read as promotional hype. Or maybe not entirely? Maybe they were expressions of enthusiasm, as well as of glee at being in a position to propel works into the public arena . . .

Pasternak: The Joys of English

BORIS LEONIDOVICH, on translating from English:

The possibilities of English metre are inexhaustible. The non-polysyl-labic nature of the English language offers immense scope to English style. The compactness of the English phrase is a pledge of its richness in content, and richness in content is a guarantee of musicality, because the music of a word consists not in its sonority but in the corre-lation between sound and meaning.[58]

(translation by Angela Livingstone)

Two related matters: one concerns Joseph's bringing of English poetry into Russian; the other Pasternak's – and presumably Joseph went along with this – appreciation of English prosody. As a translator of Russian poetry, I am burdened by the mono-syllabic nature of English, the syntactical inflexibility of an uninflected language, and so forth. Principally, I am troubled by what is perceived as a looseness about English. No doubt this is merely an indictment of my own work, so probably I should say *my* English. In any case I am talking about modern translations of Russian, not original work by Hardy, or Yeats, or Frost, let alone Shakespeare.

Free translation seems called for, inspirational, though inspiration is not available on demand. Alternatively, Joseph's radical approach, making use of a purpose-designed Russian-English?

With what did he seek to endow Russian, translating from the English of John Donne, Andrew Marvell, and of his own older contemporaries like Richard Wilbur or Chaim Plutzik? Of course, he would not have used terms like *endow*. Still, what he brought to Russian poetry was, to some extent, gleaned from English. In particular, an intellectual rigorousness. I hypothesize that Brodsky did not so much hide from pain or avoid emotions as *think* his way through them. Baratynsky was perhaps his model. Joseph's rejection of self-pity sustained him, in that it helped to preserve his self-respect, his integrity in the face of the outrages of history. This misled many, including the present writer, supposing him to be detached, cerebral rather than feeling, his poetry a somewhat baffling mixture of wordplay and editorializing.

In an interview with his Swedish friend and translator, Bengt Jangfeldt,[59] he said: "English for me is not merely a cultural language, but an existential language with a specific point of view of the world [. . .] At the core of it is a feeling of responsibility, the ability to look reality in the eye." Later, in the same interview, he remarked: "I find it very satisfying to use English, because it forces one to be more exact. I believe anyone coming from the East has a strong desire for exactitude."

Joseph's poetry is sometimes described in terms that suggest symmetry, balance, harmony, even a certain polish. In fact, his work is often quite rough, almost sketchy. Certainly this is true of the English translations. Here is Pasternak again, the preface to his translation of Shakespeare: "Metaphorism is the natural consequence of the shortness of man's life and the vastness of his tasks, planned for a long time ahead [. . .] The use of metaphor is the stenography of a great personality, the shorthand of its soul."[60] Shorthand for a short life certainly applies to Joseph's work, and intellectually he was always in a hurry, to such an extent that, at least in English, words had a tendency to bottleneck. It is not that he looked for shortcuts or accepted compromise, but metaphorically speaking he did look for metaphors. Pasternak continues: "Impressionism has been characteristic of art since time immemorial. It is the expression of man's spiritual wealth, which pours forth over the edge of his doomed condition." In this connection, he mentions Rembrandt, Michelangelo, Titian, very much to the point when one recalls their late works. D. H. Lawrence spoke of the poetry of the instant, poetry without closure, the rhythm of which came from life itself. There is something improvisatory in this. Improvisation characterizes Joseph's essays, which is why they are so lively. Not that the essays are disorganized, or *un*organized; just that the order comes from within, within the writer and within the writing. Language, thought, appears to be structuring itself.

Pasternak continues: "Verse was Shakespeare's quickest and most direct form of expression. He had recourse to it for the fastest possible recording of ideas. This went so far that in many of his verse episodes one seems to discern *rough drafts for prose* [my italics]. " A poet's prose may be a product of his poetry, especially of poetry as thinking-in-verse. It seems to me that Brodsky's prose is not so much an outgrowth of the poetry, as a parallel medium. One might even put it this way: that he wrote two kinds of prose, the prose of his essays and the prose of his poetry. And while the prose of his English essays might seem more like that of a highly articulate man thinking on his feet, the prose of his poetry is also improvised. Its flow has as much to do with the intellect as it does with language or sound. He insisted on formal constraints, but increasingly thought subsumed these.

Why should the non-polysyllabic nature of English offer, as Pasternak insists, immense scope? What does he mean by compactness? And richness of content as a guarantee of musicality? Is it that the non-polysyllabic nature of English (less kindly put, its implacably monosyllabic nature) sets the writer a problem: how to avoid monotony, without its showing. Or is it that English, being non-agglutinative, non-inflected, is more fluid, more limpid than Russian? I do not think of English as compact. On the contrary. Hopkins, for instance, tries to make it more compact, to energize it, through ellipses and by adjectivizing entire clauses, verb and all. Joseph also manhandles the language. Translating Russian, I, too, try to tighten without denaturing the English, my English. It is only with difficulty that I can conceive of a certain purity or limpidity as being more achievable in a non-polysyllabic, more analytical tongue. This dilemma, again, is alluded to by Joseph in the aforementioned interview with Jangfeldt: "Russian is a multi-syllabic inflected language. Words are therefore more of an acoustical phenomenon than in English. English is really a reductive language, this to say, a language that is always striving to make itself shorter [. . .] So for the Russian ear or eye the word has much greater weight, a denser acoustic mass compared to the same word in English."

Each language has its character or nature, and if we work closely with another language, we tend to prefer it to our own; the translation relationship, unless it is a master-servant one, will favour the original language over that into which it is translated. Translation may be quite demoralizing for the writer, especially if he is insecure. It needn't be though, provided there is reciprocity and one language does not lay down its arms before another, but offers it shelter and entertainment.

And Joseph was a linguistic entertainer, not a linguistic sinner. The rules of hospitality, in fact, suited him down to the ground. Were these rules not akin to those he had adopted for himself, refusing to dramatize or allow others to dramatize his life? What is rather unusual, though, is that he operated in both directions: that is, his Russian entertained his English, and vice versa. There were no conquering armies; it was not a question of unilateral disarmament.

New York: Home

As HE AGED – and in his last years he aged very fast, as if trying to catch up with or even overtake his own end – a kind of world-weariness (mellowness?) seemed to be replacing the earlier acerbity. Even so, the world was still a wonderful place. Joseph's creativity did not desert him.

Talking of wonderful places, what of Joseph and New York City? This was his home for most of his time in the West, even though from 1981 he taught in the spring at Mount Holyoke College and rented a home in South Hadley, Massachusetts. He was also in the habit of spending Christmas in Venice. The Joseph I knew, however, was the New York Joseph, even though I met him first in London and, at least in the seventies, often saw him there, and even though my first visit to him in America was to Ann Arbor, Michigan when he was poet-in-residence at the University of Michigan. I visited him only once in Emily Dickinson country.

New York became his home and he was *at home* in New York. Or that's how it seemed. The City lets (or encourages?) you to be whatever you are, meaning that, wherever you hail from, it is not really possible to continue being a stranger or foreigner there. Everyone is *both* outsider and insider. To live in New York is to become a native New Yorker. If Joseph was going to fit anywhere, it was in New York.

But there is something else. The scale of the city, even if it is now matched by other urban conglomerations, still frees one from the need to measure up to one's environment. It is impossible to measure up to New York. Actually, its scale is still unique.

Perhaps it is the only truly twentieth-century city, which would also means that, among cities, it is the one and only true child of the nineteenth-century. What will it be in the twenty-first century? Joseph did not expect to live into the next century anyway, and perhaps in a way didn't want to. The world is, or appears to be changing radically, while he had sweated blood surviving in it as was. After all, even so brave and virtuoso an improvisers as Joseph has his limits. The price of further change might simply have been too great.

For instance, Russia. There was no longer any impediment to his returning. On the contrary, he would have received a hero's welcome. But he was a world citizen, or rather he was a New Yorker. A hero's welcome might have disturbed the equilibrium he had achieved, at who knows what cost. And besides, as he was fond of saying, being outside was the best situation for the artist. Being a New Yorker allowed him to be outside and at the same time to enjoy the homy comforts it offered.

Perhaps he could have slipped into Russia unannounced, as the fiction writer Tatyana Tolstaya suggests, in a novelistically transcribed interview:[61]

"Do you know, Joseph, if you don't want to come back with a lot of fanfare, no white horses and excited crowds, why don't you just go to Petersburg incognito?" [. . .] Here I was talking, joking, and suddenly I noticed that he wasn't laughing [. . .] He sat quietly, and I felt awkward, as if I were barging in where I wasn't invited. To dispel the feeling, I said in a pathetically hearty voice: "It's a wonderful idea, isn't it?" He looked through me and murmured: "Wonderful . . . Wonderful . . ."

Wonderful, but too late. After all, one of Joseph's great achievements, as George Kline has pointed out, had been to throw himself into the language and literature of his adopted country. He rejected the path of nostalgia, regret, self-pity, lamentation, the fatal choice (if one can call it that) of so many émigré writers, especially poets. And what now, when he was no longer technically an involuntary exile? He had refused to complain about it, just as he refused to complain about his treatment in Russia, or his lack of a formal education. On the contrary, he had valued exile to the arctic region as liberating. And the education in question was a Soviet one, though when he said that the "earlier you get off track the better", he may not have been referring exclusively to the Soviet system.

Furthermore, his own generation, as he acknowledged, was what mattered to him. He kept up, to a remarkable extent, with what was being written by his younger contemporaries, but his real sympathies were with those of his own generation. Although, with the unanticipated collapse or abdication of the Soviet imperial power, he came to see many of his friends again, he had both intellectually and emotionally bade them "farewell" (*proshchaite*), not "good-bye" (*do svidanie*, "see you again"). In a sense, the reunions must have been posthumous affairs. So, when he was shown photos, taken shortly before his departure from the Soviet Union, he suddenly became serious, solemn, grim: "One's affinity is for the generation to which one belongs . . . Theirs is the tragedy . . ." Not of those who emigrated or, like himself, were given little choice other than to leave. And as for himself, well, he had exchanged oppression for freedom and all kinds of material advantage. He had no patience with talk of exile. Perhaps the dissolution of the Soviet State, its transformation, rather than opening the way for his return, simply confirmed his Americanness . . .

Or rather, his New-Yorkerness. New York, as he put it, "reduces you to a size". It is a gigantic impediment to gigantism. And yet, at the same time, it is human. The scale of its monumentality is human. It was also a "Mondrian city". Who, familiar or besotted with New York, does not know what he meant by that? The perpendicularity and horizontality; windows, façades, facets . . .

Anyway, it was his city; that is, he made it his. And he was right about it. In this place, you were not greater than yourself; you were "reduced to a size" (curious that use of the indefinite article), the right size, your own human size. It's not true that you were dwarfed by those canyons; they are clearly the product of human labour, an index to human industry. And strangely heartening, too, even now, nearly a century on . . .

But now I am waxing sentimental. Thinking about the city now, at age sixty-one, it seems to me not a bad place to die in.

I remember being told by Ted Hughes, ten or twenty years ago already, that we had reached the age when the Indian princes abandoned their worldly concerns and retired to the forests. Perhaps New York is the equivalent for urban man? As if one's death there would be less unbearably personal, with that crush of people which somehow leaves you uncrushed, so you feel, even in your isolation, part of a far greater organism, an organism in that it doesn't (quite) self-destruct. There's one positive effect of being "reduced to a size". Joseph, having been deprived of what, as a Jew, he possibly never quite possessed, Russia, having "quit the country that bore and nursed him" and having been forgotten by so many – first you have to be *known* by so many –, having suffered catastrophic loss, however much he insisted that he had left the worse for the better, was now threatened with the early loss of his life. Under these circumstances, New York, perhaps, fitted the bill.

I am waiting for Joseph in Washington Square. It looked like rain before, but it hasn't rained yet. I am watching the skateboarders, the jugglers, the children, the clochards, the mothers, the gangs of youths. Nobody pays any attention to me, and I suddenly feel blissfully unselfconscious. Joseph arrives late. He shuffles over, grinning wryly. He seems in no hurry and doesn't apologize. There is a stillness about him. Suddenly I feel, by contrast, tense, anxious.

We stroll into the Village, towards one of his favourite restaurants. And now it is raining or drizzling. He has to call Maria. He uses a street phone. At the same time, he conveys to me that nothing has changed . . .

A Sour Note

Tuesday, 2 July, 1996

YESTERDAY EVENING, at an art gallery, I ran into an acquaintance, who teaches in New York but spends much time in England. When I mentioned that I was writing about Joseph Brodsky, in particular the English poems, he expressed extreme skepticism. He then vented his irritation, as an American and a professor of literature, at the pedagogical pieces that had appeared in *The New Yorker*. The Frost essay, for instance, was presumptuous; all it did was to state the obvious. That Frost's poetry was "terrifying" was scarcely a revelation. And so on.

From my point of view, though, Joseph's line-by-line, or even word-by-word commentaries are very evocative of the man, his excitement, his sensibility. I love them. If they are also somewhat pedagogical or even pedantic, perhaps this is hardly surprising, but it seems to me that sometimes he may have underestimated his second audience's sophistication; it may be asking for trouble to treat readers of *The New Yorker* like a class of undergraduates, although, of course, the articles were not written, in the first place, for *The New Yorker*. Joseph, evidently, insisted on preserving the classroom character of these pieces, since otherwise he might seem to have been treating Frost himself disrespectfully. You can't win!

On the other hand, as has been pointed out to me, many others were actually drawn to Brodsky's work via his writings in such journals as *Vanity Fair*, where his essay on Auden, "To Please a Shadow", first appeared, in 1983.

A Collective Goodbye?

YESTERDAY I HAD a long telephone conversation with another friend of Joseph's, Jenny Coates. I met her twenty or more years ago, and we met again at a seminar for teachers of translation. We had much to talk about and agreed to contact each other again. So she phoned yesterday, and we continued our conversation. She, like me, found it hard to accept that Joseph was gone, even if his early death was "not unexpected", even if he had, in fact, already lived longer than expected. It was her impression, talking to others who had known him, that the feelings of dismay and disbelief were shared. Furthermore, everyone seemed to have a story to tell, this outpouring being entirely spontaneous. The idea came to her to gather some of these stories in a book; remembering that I had said I was writing about Joseph, she had decided to ask me what I thought. Of course, this is not going to happen. Even with the best intentions in the world, it could hardly fail to be maudlin.[62]

It occurs to me, somewhat speciously perhaps, that a collective goodbye may be a little like translation. To share your feelings is to translate them. Yet they remain your own, just as the source text, translated, remains at the same time inviolably itself. But once a translation *also* exists, it is as if this inviolable source text can settle even more resolutely *into* itself. Like a coming of age, the necessary loss of a primary innocence . . .

If I hesitate, it is because I do not, cannot know what Joseph himself would have made of this writing of mine, although I have a pretty good idea! I suppose it would have surprised him, as it has me. He loathed biography, and perhaps he would have regarded this as a covert memoir. Is it? I do not know what he thought of the many essays and even books, literary studies, written about him. Maybe he was pleased, flattered. Perhaps it was easier for him to deal with the less good ones. Those which were truly insightful might have been troubling, insofar as his thought was in flux and here it was already being evaluated, interpreted. When he himself wrote, it was in a speculative, almost casual manner, even if the tone was assertive.

We discussed translation, Jenny too being a translator. I tried unconvincingly to explain why I thought Joseph's English translations were seminal. The trouble is that I am not really convinced, however much I wish I were. The prolixity of this journal is the product of my uncertainties! Hardly surprising then that in conversation – with Jenny, for instance – I should have sounded not so sure of myself.

For instance, I began by describing how, in his translations of his own work, when faced by some knotty problem, Joseph tended to take evasive action, to invent his way out of the predicament. I wanted to add that, paradoxically, this helpless-ness, if one can call it that, impelled him to create a coherent artefact . . . Or something of the sort. Jenny, misunderstanding me, or perhaps understanding me only too well, responded at once: "It's what talented people do when they do not know a foreign language well enough." They invent, that is they try to paraphrase, the ultimate paraphrase being gesture or mime, after words and even sounds or noises have failed to get the message across. So, were Joseph's translations, his improvisations, a kind of charade? If so, then the same may be said of any translation. To translate, after all, is to become (often) agonizingly aware of the limitations of the target language. With reluctance, but ineluctably, we surrender pieces of territory, settle for less than the whole. But the territory we surrender, the compromises we accept, concern the source as much as they do the target language. Unless we mobilize our forces, we are in danger of throwing in the towel even before we've climbed into the ring. But once one does assume an aggressive stance, one is almost on one's own, almost free to do as one wishes, insofar as that is possible with one's hands tied behind one's back! Though the restraints are symbolic, not real . . .

"It's what talented people do when they do not know a foreign language well enough." Quite so, but ... Not just a matter of grammatical infringements then, of imperfectly assimilated idioms, etc. Rather, Brodsky is forced to paraphrase, to start inventing before it is strictly necessary, if it ever is. I might have added, though, that perhaps none of this really mattered, since he was virtually rewriting the poem in English anyway, his purpose at the same time being pedagogical, to demonstrate that a formal rather than semantic copy of the original was achievable. And after all, if he, a non-native, could transplant the form, then surely a native could do even better, with fewer semantic compromises. Was his aim so modest, or did he actually believe that he might be on his way to writing the "definitive" English translation? A little of both? And perhaps he *was* on his way. I don't see how we can ever know, translation not being an exact science. He did not, at this time, claim to be able to write a good English poem. He simply wanted, he said, "to give an approximation of what it's like in Russian". This might be taken to mean that he wanted it to sound like a poem, except that he went on to specify: "I'd rather sound cumbersome and accurate than smooth and different." In a review of *To Urania* Derek Walcott remarks:[63] "one is grateful that the knots are there, that the rough nap of the lines is not smoothed by the flatiron of an even English diction ... The kind of translation that turns Doctor Zhivago into Omar Sharif." But other reviewers, as we have seen, were not so generous or understanding. They were not even prepared to give Brodsky the benefit of the doubt. For them, there was no doubt.

However, when I say that he avoided difficulties, it sounds as though I'm not giving him the benefit of the doubt either. I regarded such liberty-taking as irresponsible, reckless, even when the translator was the author himself. But, as noted earlier, this is an absurd position. Still, his cavalier ways astonished me at the time; it had been such an agony working with or rather under him. On the other hand, he rarely if ever criticized my translations for having got the meaning wrong. It is as if this did not really bother him, since it could easily be fixed at some time in the future. My versions probably did not even get to the starting post!

Most likely it was as much the experience of my last meeting with him as the shock of his death that made me look more closely at Joseph's writing – or, to be honest, look at it closely for the first time, insofar as I was no longer locked in an unequal struggle with him.

Zabolotsky in Brooklyn Heights

EN ROUTE TO ENGLAND, in December 1995, I stayed in New York for three days (15–17 December). I intended to spend as much time as possible with Joseph, so that he could show me what he thought needed to be done with my translations of Nikolay Zabolotsky. We had talked on the phone, and I had sent him a selection of poems from the manuscript, for him to forward to Farrar, Straus & Giroux, with his recommendation. He had offered to do this, although he did not hold out great hopes; nevertheless, he was prepared to use what influence he had, since Zabolotsky was for him, it seemed, among the four or five major poets of the century, to be ranked alongside (or perhaps just a little below?) Akhmatova, Mandelstam, Tsvetayeva and Pasternak. Zabolotsky was possibly the only poet, wholly of the Soviet era (chronologically), who belonged in this company.

I was not sure why Joseph so admired him. In fact, it surprised me, perhaps because he rarely referred to Zabolotsky.[64] So, was it perhaps because there was no need to insist on Zabolotsky's excellence that Joseph had not included him among the Russian poets, living or dead, whose work he tried stubbornly to promote? Promotion of Russian poetry, linked inevitably and closely to translation, he took very seriously. Even his own work was not allowed to stand in its way. He was pleased with his own successes, or what he took to be his successes, but almost as a child who had struck lucky. Or perhaps – almost certainly – he understood the "American scene" better than I did. I do not know what he really thought of my translations. But at least I was not turning Zabolotsky into a *vers-librist*. Still, he also made it clear that it was not because he thought the translations particularly good that he was supporting my endeavours. He encouraged me, to the extent that he did, more because I happened to be the one translating Zabolotsky, there being no one else who had invested so much in the project, even if Joseph considered that there was still a good deal more to be invested.

I phoned him after I had checked into my hotel on the Upper West side. But as tended to happen, all we did was agree to speak again later – in a vain attempt, I suppose, to preserve the illusion of freedom! He said he would like to spend two days with me, as he had a lot to say about Zabolotsky. Finally, on the Friday, when I called him from the office of a friend, he told me to come on over to Pierrepont Street, in Brooklyn Heights, in a couple of hours, as he was looking after Anna, his daughter, until his wife Maria got home.

He greeted me as enthusiastically as ever and then explained that we would have to wait before getting down to business, as Maria had not yet returned. He was reading to Anna – translating actually, he told me ruefully – from a Russian children's book. The apartment was a duplex, his study being at the top of a flight of stairs. The high-ceilinged living room was lined with bookshelves, covering all the available wall space. Joseph took some time out to make us tea and meanwhile I read to Anna, who seemed very adaptable. Maria returned. Next to the staircase was a pile of books, Joseph's latest collection of essays, *On Grief and Reason*. It had just arrived from FSG, he told me, presenting me with a copy. We went up to Joseph's work room, accompanied by Anna whom Joseph carried on his shoulders. This caused me some concern, on his account, but did not seem to bother him. I had studied him covertly, because Irina Muravyov had told me he was not well; that is, that he was *particularly* unwell. I saw no sign of anything amiss and he did not mention his health.

Did my visit recall for him his early days in the West, when his health was still relatively robust? I slipped easily enough into a domestic rhythm with him. After a while Joseph tenderly sent Anna off and we set to work on the opening lines of *Torzhestvo Zemledeliya,* "The Triumph of Agriculture", as it is usually called in English. Joseph preferred "Agriculture Triumphant". *Torzhestvo* can mean "Triumph", "Celebration", "Exultation"; so, "Celebration of Agriculture" is another feasible title. The

Russian word for a Roman Triumph is *Triumf.* Since *Torzhestvo* is a noun and not a participle, Joseph was "taking liberties" from the very start. He had come up with this idea during one of our phone conversations, triggered, I think, by my concern that the title "The Triumph of Agriculture" seemed to take itself too seriously.

Torzhestvo is a kind of verse play or dramatic poem, the location a village about to be collectivized, the protagonists a soldier, representing "progressive" views, various peasants, animals, and a plough. There is also, in effect, a narrator, though he is not identified as such. With "The Triumph of Agriculture" Zabolotsky hoped to placate the Party ideologists, although he did not abjure his beliefs in a revolution that would include all living things, not only humans. His visionary poem met with an unfavourable reception, not only because the Party's notion of the Revolution was quite different. "The Triumph" was, in fact, read as a kind of slander on collectivization. Later, in 1936, at a speech before a plenary session of the Leningrad branch of the Union of Writers, during a discussion on Formalism, Zabolotsky tried to defend himself, but was not prepared to renounce his own early work.

Close as his idealistic vision might be to the ecological thinking of our days, it was far removed from the official optimism of the time. In the speech, Zabolotsky said he understood now that the "concept was at fault in that it mixed realistic and utopian elements", this leading to a certain blurring of "the depiction of the class struggle". He further admitted that formalist devices were still present and had led to interpretation of his poem as ironic or parodistic. However, against the advice of friends, he objected to the crude and insulting attacks that had been made on him.

I did not think that either the subject of "Agriculture Triumphant", however unorthodox the treatment and the ruralist or ecological vision of a comprehensive revolution, or the poet's attempts to placate the régime were likely to appeal to Joseph, even if he admired Zabolotsky's technical mastery and appreciated his independent stance. But I never discussed the political aspect of Zabolotsky's poetry with him. And clearly it did not put him off. I suppose that what particularly appealed to Joseph was the fact that Zabolotsky was one of the thinking poets (like Baratynsky in that respect). He thought in verse that parodied a great variety of modes, historic and contemporary. The late poems, also vehicles for Zabolotsky's Goethean nature philosophy, decried by some as evidence of the poet's retreat from bold experimentation, were as far as they could be from the anodyne Party-approved lyrics extolling the Russian countryside.

What we worked on together – all that we worked on – in the four or five hours we had, was the first twenty-four lines, the "Prologue". I had despaired of ever rendering these lines convincingly. Whatever approach I took, the English remained unviable. My last version, the one I had sent to Joseph, resorted to a kind of impacted diction, which I hoped would at least hold the reader's attention, not lose him right from the outset.

The rhyming of the original is energetic, the pace brisk, with two primary stresses per line. The line is basically octosyllabic, alternating eight and seven syllables (feminine / masculine rhymes). This is maintained until the last four lines when it comes to a stumbling halt. The effect, then, is of an abrupt lapse into prose.

The large number of feminine rhyming words poses a problem in English, of course. The Russian recalls children's rhymes or fairy tales, especially if one reads the poem, as it is possible to do, in a jog-trotting trochaic manner. As Joseph pointed out, Zabolotsky uses classical or traditional metres only to subvert them. The metrical instability reflects the uncertainties in the opening passage, contradicting the optimism conveyed by the poem's title. This macaronic tendency might also have appealed to Joseph, whose own poetry is modernist in its sometimes radical juxtapositions. The playfulness is also typical of the OBERIU poets,[65] whose verse is both object-centred and absurdist. They created a kind of theatre of the absurd in twenties Leningrad, and "Agriculture Triumphant" contains elements of absurdist drama.

Here are the first few lines of my pre-Brodsky version:

> Not well-meaning and yet handsome,
> who is this, his eyes upon us?
> It's a peasant in no hurry,
> peering through his spectacles.
> In the distance, granaries rise,
> slabs of white against the skies,
> through the window corn is gazing . . .

I was contemplating this in despair when I visited Joseph. There are other equally or more inept versions, the considerable variation between them showing how desperate I was. I simply could not get a grip on this particular passage, even from a literalist point of view, and so I kept changing the version more or less arbitrarily in the hope that perseverance would be rewarded, that I might stumble on something more acceptable. The very first line, *Nekhoroshii, no krasivyi* (literally: "Bad / sinister, but handsome") flummoxed me. Clearly ambivalence is being expressed, but as a start even to a *mock* epic poem, however absurdist, it is impossibly flat.

The following is an attempt to get around this, changing the order of the first two lines. The version is even more awkward than the one above, though perhaps less jarring metrically. My dissatisfaction with it was due, I suppose, to my having had to have recourse to padding and passive constructions ("through his spectacles we're seen", etc.) in an attempt to regularize the rhythm and secure a few rhymes, or assonances. Still, there did seem to be a little more flow and follow-through to it.

> Who is this, his eye upon us –
> a handsome-looking man, but mean?
> It's a peasant, in no hurry,
> through his spectacles we're seen.
> In the distance, granaries rise,
> slabs of white against the skies,
> through the window corn is gazing . . .

Another, earlier version is less developed. The metre is imitated at the beginning, after which the line shrinks. Actually, when I now compare this version with the original, I am struck – perhaps, because it is itself more metrically variable than other versions – by the trochaic and variable accentual character of the latter. While some of the prologue goes with a paeonic swing (the first four lines, for instance), line five is partly trochaic and more emphatic. There is a more even alternation between two- and three-stress lines than I had earlier observed, perhaps influenced by my own rollicking rendition.

> Who is this that looks straight at us,
> a handsome man, but also ugly?
> Staring through his spectacles –
> a peasant in no kind of hurry.
> Sections of white grain-stores stand
> in relief against the background,
> through the widow corn is gazing . . .

Joseph sat on the floor, with my translation. When I made to squat down too, he said there was no need; it was just that for him it was more comfortable. So, I hovered, as it were, in an armchair, while he sprawled, rather like a child, with its toys, more or less at my feet. In fact Anna sat with him for a while. But first he asked me to give him the copy of *On Grief and Reason*, opened it, thought for a moment, and then wrote the inscription referred to earlier. This seemed to put him in a good mood, almost the right frame of mind.

Joseph was plainly disposed to treat my version as no more than a rough draft, if even that. Actually he pretty well discarded it altogether, starting from scratch: "There's a lot to be changed here!" For instance? "It is not *sprightly* enough", he let me know. The teeming infelicities of the version appeared not to concern him nearly as much as this, the failure to sense or to render the metrical jauntiness of Zabolotsky's Russian. By sprightly, he evidently also meant lively, playful and (perhaps?) a little cocky or cheeky; but what he had his eye or ear on, in particular, was the rhythm.

Actually, Joseph did not directly criticize my version. He sought to show by example, rather than by pointing out faults. Valentina Polukhina, in a paper on Brodsky's views on translation, quotes him as saying: "It is nice to have had so many collaborators, but it also has its disadvantages, because when you change what they have done you run into ego-storms. I had several and quite heavy ones. I nearly broke with several people over it. I was accused of all kinds of things, including plagiarism."[66] This was shortly after the publication of *A Part of Speech* (1980) and presumably I was one of the people he had in mind. He did plagiarize, in that he treated as working drafts what some translators regarded as finished or near-finished products. Joseph respected translation as such, but was quite casual in his attitude to translators. He was casual, too, about his own translations, driven to produce them only because versions by others were too far from what he wanted and was convinced was achievable.

At any rate, whether he had modified his views or not – I suspect he had not – he was now more circumspect or diplomatic than before. Besides, I had indicated that I had come round to his way of thinking, at least with Zabolotsky. Actually, I may not have been entirely persuaded that he was right, but still there was a basis now for collaboration between us. Nevertheless, I was disappointed at his comment about my translation lacking the sprightliness which was so characteristic of Zabolotsky, which was indeed of the essence. Still, he had identified one of its principal inadequacies. And he came up with an extremely useful piece of advice. "With Zabolotsky", he said, "if in doubt always go for the more absurd." So, while Joseph was a hard task-master, he also believed in semantic or interpretive freedom – that is, once the basic "aesthetic balance" had been taken care of. "What you're trying to do," he insisted, "is to sustain a certain aesthetic balance, which does exist in the original, and if it does exist you simply try, by different means, to resurrect that balance."[67]

So, we – or rather Joseph – started over again. I scribbled notes, as he improvised, trying somehow to English the bounce of the original, not bothering much about the niceties, but as he went producing rhymes that pleased him. His way with English, at least at this stage, was uninhibited. He seemed to have instantaneous access to all of it, that is everything that he knew about it and in it. The entire process was bold, even joyous, certainly liberating, like his advice to plump for the most absurd solutions, and it made little of the agony that, for the most part, translation had become for me. In fact, he grew quite animated, rising to his feet and walking around the room. As his mind engaged with the poem, so did his body.

What was apparent was that the original poem had been safely internalized and all he now had to do was cast around in English. There was a rather touching confidence that the English poem was there, somewhere, to be found. He was trying, not to get it all down in detail, but to catch its likeness, to establish at least the "aesthetic balance".

From his point of view, the resistance he encountered in his English language colleagues must have seemed perverse. My contention, and that of others, was that he was trying to Russianize English, not respecting the genius of the English language, that he wanted the transfer between languages to take place without drastic changes, this being achievable only if English itself was changed. The question is, what did he mean by "accurate" or "different"? In his lexicon "accuracy" and "difference" referred to form rather than sense, meaning the whole body, the feel, movement, as well as shape of the poem. Form for him came first: "It is the vessel in which meaning is cast." Form ensured memorability; rhyme and metre, as well as being mnemonic, imparted a sense of inevitability. His criticism of my rhymes, for instance, was that they were too oblique, more a matter perhaps of wishful thinking than of fact. One might almost go so far as to say that for Joseph, in principle at least, form determined content. This is not to say that it does, but to approach through form rather than through sense is to keep the ego from shouldering everything else out of the way. Joseph could afford to indulge his ego, because in the main he was a servant of the Muse. Not that his poetry was semantically weak. Rather the contrary.

As dinner approached, Joseph told me to type out the result of
"our" deliberations. I did so on his portable Hermes typewriter,
with him watching and waiting, as I tried to read what I had
scribbled.

> Not so good and yet so lovely,
> who is this that looks at us –
> that's a peasant rather gravely
> through his specs directs his gaze.
> Granaries were showing whiteness,
> in the distance full of brightness,
> rye was staring through the slats . . .

Last Conversation with Joseph

JOSEPH STOOD with me outside his house, in Pierrepont Street, waiting for the taxi. It was late and there was scarcely any traffic. We chatted. That was our last time together.

Back in the hotel, I opened the copy of *On Grief and Reason*, read the inscription: "May what's behind be at least matched by what's ahead." Then I turned to the last piece in the book: "In Memory of Stephen Spender". It recalled that occasion, the London Poetry International of 1972, when I had met Joseph and when he met Stephen Spender for the first time. In fact, he and Auden stayed with Stephen and Natasha Spender in Loudoun Road. Spender died on 16 July 1995. Joseph wrote his little memoir between August 5th and 10th, six months before he himself died. Spender was eighty-six. Joseph recalls Spender saying, with his familiar grin: "The nineties is a good time to die." He describes how Auden, Spender, and Natasha Spender looked after him, like parents. He recalls, the beauty of Spender's voice that first evening of his arrival in London: it "felt as if all the nobility, civility, grace and detachment [*sic*!] of the English language suddenly filled the room." He recalls how important MacNeice (I do not, however recall his ever mentioning MacNeice or for that matter Cecil Day Lewis), Auden, Spender were to him in London: their poetry "unshackled me – above all metrically and stanzaically." It was not so much their moral vision, the generational differences being too great. Furthermore: "What I was aware of then, am now, and will be to my dying day is their extraordinary intelligence . . ." (not unnatural that death should be mentioned so often in this piece, and yet one wants retrospectively to warn him: "Don't say it!") Above all, though, it is the affinity he talks of ("Call this influence; I'll call it affinity") to which this tribute testifies. It is filled with the "gentleness and civility" that he sees as Spender's prevailing qualities. It is composed of the snapshots (accompanied by reflections) that he speaks of as all that remain of a person. Photos, in particular, bring him as close to nostalgia as he ever gets. With regard to a photograph of Auden and Spender laughing ("This unbearable snapshot laughter!"): "That's what one is left with – with these arrested instants stolen from life without any anticipation of the far greater theft ahead that will render your hoard the source of utter despair. A hundred years ago we would be spared at least that." Later he returns to the theme: "People are what we remember about them. What we call life is in the end a patchwork of someone else's recollections. With death it gets unstitched, and one ends up with random, disjointed fragments, with shards, or, if you will, with snapshots." At the reception after the funeral, people keep talking about the "end of an era". Joseph objects to this. As he leaves, in response to someone arriving who says this to him: "I muster a broad cheerful, Stephen-like grin and say, 'I don't think so', and walk away."

I closed the book and sat for a while. Then I called Joseph. I told him that I had read the piece on Stephen Spender first: "I just wanted to tell you how much it has moved me, how wonderfully it evokes him." Joseph: "I am so glad you said that. It is music to my ears!" Then I contributed one or two memories of Spender of my own, his diffidence, tentativeness, the apologetic smile, so well described by Joseph – and the beauty of his voice. In January 1989, Stephen Spender and Natasha came to an international poetry festival in Bhopal, India, where I happened to be, as the guest of an arts centre located in that tragic city. I had previously seen Spender in Iowa, where he was giving a series of lectures on the writers of the thirties, at a small liberal arts college, in Mt. Vernon, a tiny town, close to Iowa City. (This excellent institution is called Cornell College, and it occurred to me that perhaps Spender thought he was going to Cornell University.) He was held more or less prisoner there, and one day, with the Irish poet Richard Murphy (teaching that semester in the University of Iowa's Writers Workshop), we "rescued" him and drove him to a park and then to Cedar Rapids, a mid-sized industrial town close by for a pretty indifferent Chinese meal. Spender was touchingly grateful. Later, Paul Engle had Spender over for dinner. Paul began to reminisce about thirties Germany, which he visited when he was a Rhodes scholar in Oxford: "There was blood everywhere, bodies lying in the gutter", he roared. Spender raised his eyebrows. "Oh", he interjected mildly, "I don't remember seeing any bodies." In Bhopal, Spender read with his usual shuffling and squirming around, as he loomed over the microphone, before the huge and rapt audience. In the question-and-answer period, he was asked, rather aggressively: "Would you tell us, Sir Stephen, who were your influences." Spender peered in the general direction of the questioner, moved around a bit, at last raised the microphone to his level, and said apologetically: "Well, I tend to think that one writes one's own poetry." There was an appreciative burst of applause at that, and Spender grinned doubtfully. The "tend to" still tickles me. Joseph laughed out loud as I recounted this. We talked a little more and agreed to meet soon, in the New Year, to continue working together on Zabolotsky's poetry.

In his tribute to Spender, Joseph again claimed that he wrote English prose in order to close the language gap between himself and Spender and Auden. The age gap could not be closed, the intelligence gap, he dared to think, was occasionally narrowed when he was at his best.

For me, to return to Joseph's remark about photography, it is his taped voice that is even more evocative than pictures. When I listen to him, to it, I am shocked by his insouciance, his casualness and at the same time directness. I recall how, after coming out with some brilliant comment, gazing around as if the words had simply been snatched out of the air and he was as surprised as everybody else, he would suddenly swivel his head in your direction, his chin would shoot forward, and he would fix you with as intense, challenging or measuring a look as you are ever likely to experience. As I listen to his voice, I find myself also waiting for what he might have to say about the present situation, including his own absence.

Defending the Bard

I SPENT THREE days in New York, visiting Ann Kjellberg, Joseph's former assistant, and attending a memorial service for Joseph. Joseph was naturally the subject of conversation with a number of people. One such was Adam Szyper, a Polish Jew, who lives in the US, writes in Polish, translates his own verse into English, and spends some months of each year in Poland; another was David Curzon; and then there was Mike Braziller; and various others at the Samovari Restaurant whose owner Roman Kaplan held a reception after the service.

David Curzon, as he had done on other occasions, told me that he thought Brodsky's poetry (in English) "went nowhere". Some of the short poems seemed to have a point; the long ones were superficially busy but in the end "lost you". What was clear was that the translations, for whatever reason, failed to convey to Curzon the wholeness of the originals. On the other hand, it is arguable that Joseph was writing a single poem throughout his life. That is, the individual poems are really components of a single large one. In translation, of necessity, only a selection is available – and a somewhat fortuitous or arbitrary one at that, even with Joseph supervising the process. So, not only are there the problems of translating such allusive and intricate verse, but the context is lacking. I believe that Joseph was only too aware of this. He would rather desperately or despairingly mark three or four poems for me in the various collections of his poems in English, not, I think, because these seemed to him the most successful translations, but more because they were keys to the larger vision. And though he was flattered and impressed by the skilful translations of his work by the likes of Hecht or Wilbur, he in fact wanted something more, or something different. In his note to *A Part of Speech*, he wrote: "a good number of poems included in this collection belong, chronologically, in *Selected Poems*, published in 1973. The reason for my putting them into this book, however, is not so much a desire to provide the reader with the complete picture as an attempt to supply this book with a semblance of context [. . .]" And with regard to his revisions, of course, comes his disarming: "I have taken the liberty of reworking some of the translations to bring them closer to the original, though perhaps at the expense of their smoothness." In an interview, also cited above, he is more outspoken: "I'd rather sound cumbersome and accurate than smooth and different." He is not being easy on his English reader, but the stakes could not be higher.

My attempts to defend Joseph's poetry have been rather unsuccessful. Part of the trouble is that he is often attacked from positions occupied at various times also by myself. And it seems, I am still undecided. So, when these negative opinions are stated – with conviction, as they invariably are – I begin to vacillate.

I met Adam Szyper at the Kiev Restaurant; we were to appear together on an arts channel. At one point, the filming being done with, Adam asked me about Brodsky, saying that although he respected him, he found his poetry cold, overloaded with allusions, and so forth. What he appeared to be saying was that Joseph was an élitist writer, an intellectual snob even. I tried to convince him that, on the contrary, Joseph was a man of humility and deeply, if eccentrically, cultured. When Adam pointed out that he was talking about the poetry and not necessarily the man, whom in any case he did not know, I insisted that the man and the writing were one and the same. So, the question was: Can one be humble in human, yet arrogant in literary terms? Can you separate the two? Why shouldn't it be possible to be humble, modest and also to write in an élitist manner?

Joseph was a servant of language. No particular credit for what was achieved through his agency was claimed by him. His gift was just that, a gift. But I was unable to get this across. Still worse, I felt there was something else going on, as though I were sneakily implying the opposite of what I was saying, in effect agreeing with Adam.

That my feelings about Joseph were so ambivalent was disturbing, and in my confusion I made a hash of "defending" him. "With friends like me . . .", I thought. I might have repeated some of what I had written over the last year and, in fact, I think I tried to do that. Nevertheless, my words seemed to lack conviction.

Sunday, 9 February, 1997

But before this – wasn't it the main reason for coming to New York? – I went to see Ann Kjellberg, not far from Morton Street, in the Village, where Joseph had lived. We went on to a Vietnamese restaurant, apparently one of Joseph's favourite eating places. Mostly we talked about him. Ann gave me a copy of the notorious *Financial Times* review by Craig Raine. She wondered why Raine had not spoken out when Joseph was alive and could have responded. I indicated to Ann that it was usually hopeless to defend oneself or for others to defend one against attacks of this sort, if only because for the refutation to be decisive, it was necessary to elaborate in a way that bored people or that was hard going. Perhaps, if any response was called for, it was a response in kind: this would result in a slanging match.

Later I read the actual review.[68] It did not seem to me as insulting as Ann had intimated, although it was certainly less polite than Christopher Reid's *London Review of Books* piece. Joseph, Raine writes, could be "strangely nervous – the obverse of his more characteristic dogmatic panache". The reason for this diffidence, he suggests, "may have been connected with the well-nigh inaudible but consistent under-current of skepticism that accompanied the noisier acclaim." A negative spin had been put on a quality that others, myself included, saw as having more to do with Joseph's humility. Many of Raine's comments or observations are also inaccurate, for instance the claim that Akhmatova merely said that Joseph was "interesting". In any case, Brodsky is not short of illustrious admirers of his Russian poetry.

Raine congratulates himself on being among the few with the courage to blow the whistle on Brodsky as a poet in English. In the same year that Christopher Reid wrote his "devastating indictment", he (Raine) "delivered a lecture in which I marvelled at the incompetence of Brodsky's poems in English". Brodsky, according to Raine, is himself to blame for "recklessly re-working the translations of Anglophone poets like Anthony Hecht and Richard Wilbur". A briskly unsentimental reference to Brodsky's heart condition, "exacerbated by a suicidal smoking habit" allows Raine immediately to refer to the line in "May 24, 1980", already discussed by Reid: "thrice let knives rake my nitty-gritty." Raine takes it by now as given that the line is simply absurd. Michael Hofmann, on the other hand, in his laudatory *TLS* review,[69] describes the line as written "with Byronic swagger [. . .], not there just as a bit of misuse or obscurantism [. . .]" Hofmann does the best he can, but is on the defensive. Later, he returns to the theme somewhat more combatively: "for all his modesty and clutter, Brodsky isn't an empirical English type of poet. [. . .] His metaphors tend not to be visually accurate – or visually exhaustible [. . .]" Hofmann permits himself only one shot – at least I think it is a shot – across the bows of his Martian friends: "Martianism affects to enrich the world, adding a clever self to whatever's in view. Brodsky [. . .] does the opposite: he subtracts himself." I think Joseph would have liked that.

However, quite understandably, Michael Hofmann discusses the relationship between Russian and English in rather general terms. What *was* grasped by Joseph's critics, was that his English was non-standard. By permitting the occasional anomalous usages to remain, Joseph perhaps left himself more open to attack than he need have done. Predictably, his attackers took advantage of this, and would not acknowledge that he might be attempting to deal with larger issues of prosody and phonology. Or if they did, they played it down, in view of the preposterousness, as they saw it, of his English. Hofmann goes so far as to claim that "we read it [Brodsky's English poetry], as it were, both with the English and Russian parts of our English minds." Raine might object that there is no "Russian part" of the English mind, or at least of most English minds, that to talk of such a thing was disingenuous. So, what is Hofmann advocating or excusing? Linguistic adulteration, hybridization? In his 1988 piece Christopher Reid, as we have seen, had already anticipated this kind of claim: "It is necessary [. . .] to counter the notion that something fresh, healthy, rich in artistic potential and urgently needed is being introduced into the poetic repertoire through this exotic treatment of the language . . ."

MORE AGREEABLY, I find myself remembering what the publisher Mike Braziller[70] said over lunch. Mike had accompanied us to the memorial service for Joseph in St. John the Divine. He liked Joseph personally, although he was among those who found his poetry, in English translation, baffling. Just before meeting Mike, I had visited an Israeli writer who had told me that she once took a poetry course at New York University (NYU) and struck lucky, getting Joseph Brodsky. Evidently, Joseph tended to talk *at* the students. She, being used to the Israeli or European system, was not put off by this, but was simply grateful to have so brilliant and inspiring a teacher, in her very first semester. I mentioned this to Mike who remarked that he, too, had been lucky enough to have classes with Joseph at NYU. I asked him if there was much interaction between Joseph and the students. He said that Joseph was interested only in the nuts-and-bolts of the poetry, in the words, indeed, the very syllables. He had never had so illuminating a teacher when it came to discussion of prosody. On the other hand, Joseph was not much concerned about more general aspects of the work, and if students strayed from the verbal material, he would grow impatient and could be quite dismissive, sometimes scathingly so. But if a student asked him a question to do with sound, movement, form, he was enormously attentive. He spoke, Mike said, as a poet. His classes were unprecedented, in that they took you *inside* poems . . . And one should not forget that the poems Mike, a native born American, was talking about, the poems with which Joseph was so inward, were English poems!

This does not tally with Craig Raine's scorn for Brodsky, who he alleges is incapable of scanning English poems. Actually, the example Raine gives does not, it seems to me, prove his point. "Hardy's two lines 'In a full-hearted evensong / Of joy illimited' are straightforward iambs . . .", he says. "There is no sign of

undercutting detected by Brodsky in 'evensong' and 'illimited'." Really? Does Raine hear the words thus: "evensong",
"illimited"? [71]

Listening

I HAVE been experimenting with "phonemic" or "homophonic" translation, i.e. imitating the sound of the original text and paying minimal attention to the sense. An absurd procedure, except that it makes one listen closely. Predictably, the resulting text is elliptical, discontinuous, whatever the original may be like; in this case, the original was a poem by Baudelaire. I have invited students in two classes (at King's and at Warwick) to experiment with the technique, listening only, or in the first place, to the sound of the poem and attempting to "translate" that.

Does this have any bearing on what Joseph was doing? Up to a point. But, of course, although he might be prepared to adjust the meaning, so as to preserve more of the form, he never lets go of the poem's content, in a futile attempt to produce a phonological replica. Actually, it seems to me that homophonic literalism is out of the question with Russian, whereas it might yield some marginal benefits with languages more closely related to English, such as French or German. The phonemic translation of Baudelaire's "La Cloche fêlée" was, it is true, absurd, but there were some amusing moments. Here is the first stanza:

> Il est amer et doux, pendant les nuits d'hiver,
> D'écouter, près du feu qui palpite et qui fume,
> Les souvenirs lointains lentement s'élever
> Au bruit des carillons qui chantent dans la brume.

Phonemic version:

> Elate, armoured and douce pond; ah, the needy veer.
> Day cooter, pray differ, key-pal, bitter, achey fumes,

> The souvenirs' longtime lent-mint, say *Levée!* –
> Oh, bluey day-carillons which chant . . . Darn lab-room!

It is inevitable that whatever one "translates" in this way will sound like some wacky experiment. Still I am tickled by such oddities, quite uncharacteristic of my own style, as: "The souvenirs' longtime lent-mint", etc. Mostly, though, what interested me was the fact that this exercise, as noted above, obliged me to *listen* closely to the French poem, to hear it only *as* sound.

I have just spent an afternoon experimenting with "May 24, 1980". The results are even more unpromising. This may be because it is by now so familiar that I cannot separate sound and sense in so artificial a manner? But I think there's more to it than that. Hard as it is to imitate French, it seems harder to imitate Russian. Particularly noticeable is the absence of certain sounds in English: "*kh*" (as in the Scottish loch); the soft "*e*" as in "yes"; "*zh*" as in French "je". The frequently occurring inflections, like the "*oo*" of the feminine accusative, cannot be matched in English. There are far more "*v*'s" in Russian than in English . . .

A fundamental problem, as we know, is the monosyllabic nature of English, so that for metrical reasons it is often necessary to find combinations of English words to represent a single Russian word. I spent almost an entire afternoon searching various lexicons and came up with very little. Here, with abject apologies to Joseph's shade, are the first few lines of my phonemic version:

> Yah, huddle Mr Dick's sphere, let's
> go, fusing all voice, rock and clique. Was John in
>   the barracks?
> Jill humoured him, he growls in roulette.
> A beedle chortles nigh it, skim in fracas.
> Swiss suttee led nicker, I zeroed in on Palmira [. . .]

Not impressive even by the pretty abysmal standards of my Baudelaire. Also I cheated! Practically no sense survives, and even so there are still lacunae. Nor do I even feel – as I did with the French poem – that I now know more about the phonetic structure of the original.

Joseph would probably not have been particularly amused; still less would he have been tempted to try it himself. But had he been tempted, I am sure he would have made a much better job of it. Note the number of proper names, for instance: Mr Dick, Jill, Palmira (?). Is "barracks / fracas", for instance, a useful half-rhyme? Even if I allow myself greater latitude, substituting "I" for the Russian "*Ya*" (I), rather than "Yah!" or some such. And even if I allow myself to translate (i.e. not imitate the sound of) recurring prepositions, it seems that Russian does not lend itself happily to this exercise!

The Shape of "May 24, 1980": Compensation

Friday, 14 February, 1997

ONE DOESN'T have to be a genius to realize that phonological literalism is just a game – and rather a silly one. But what of Joseph's own brand of literalism? I'll turn again to "May 24, 1980":

Strong rhyming, strong even by Brodsky's standards, is needed, in order to sustain the mock-heroic stance or tone, the mock pathos. In his reading, as we have seen, Joseph builds to a climax with parallel stressed and resonating lines: "What should I say about life?*[Shto skazat' mne o zhizni?]* / That it's long and abhors transparence / *[Shto okazalas' dlinnoi].*" And yet ... What *is* the Russian text saying about life? Simply, that it is long. There is nothing about abhorring transparence. That life is long – or rather, *seems* long – is not, on the face of it, a startling proposition, except that Joseph's life was not long, nor did he expect it to be. And yet it *was* long, not in years, but in other ways. (He spoke of his life in Russia as his "previous incarnation", and indeed it was, even if it set the stage for his subsequent "incarnation". It was a complete life in itself, though he lived it as a young man.) But, more generally, the intensity here – his voice, at this point in the poem, rises almost to a wail (the repeated "*ee*" sound in *zhizni* and *dlinnoi*) – contrasts with the almost banal content. In the English, striving for memorability in the last four lines, Joseph throws caution to the winds and starts re-inventing the poem: hence "abhors transparence", and the arguably disastrous, entirely new departure: "Broken eggs make me grieve; the omelette, though, makes me vomit." What was quite direct becomes oblique, even given the shock effect of such words as "vomit" and "gushing". There is perhaps a danger of hyperbole, melodrama, in overcompensating for loss. But above all there is a danger of losing touch with the original poem, of introducing into it something that does not consort with the rest, that is not cut from the same cloth. Concentration has been replaced by ingenuity. This can happen when a poem has passed beyond revision, as it were, and is actually being rewritten. Bits of the "new" poem attach themselves to the old and the writer may try to integrate them, either because he doesn't see them, or because he doesn't want to see them for what they are. That is, he may lack objectivity, and once the deed is done he may be blind to the effect.

A priority for Joseph was to obtain, almost at any cost, strong rhymes to match the Russian. Does he indeed go too far here, beginning to drop out of one poem and into an inevitably less satisfactory alternative one? In fact, in English, the rhymes are even stronger, and not only because rhyme tends to draw more attention to itself in English. The Russian has feminine rhymes throughout, as with one exception does the English, the feminine rhymes in the last four lines being particularly Gilbert-like: *transparence / vomit / larynx / from it.*

Another way of looking at this. Even where one presumes he was at his wit's end, for instance with the "broken eggs" metaphor, it turns out that he wasn't really (or maybe his ingenuity or boldness gets him out of a tough spot). It could be said that the original line, "Only with grief do I feel solidarity", is untranslatable. It can hardly be paraphrased, since it is itself parodying bureaucratic (Party) jargon (*solidarnost'*). With the more familiar "broken eggs" metaphor, Brodsky keeps the politics in, although the metaphor is also quite jejune. However, the procedure is risky.

So, even when trying to preserve the form, Brodsky is as attentive to sense – even if not strictly *the* sense; he is prepared, for whatever reasons, to deviate from the latter. The point is that in English the form has semantic implications. In this instance, in the Russian text, the protagonist feels "solidarity" for (i.e. identifies with) those who are suffering, sorrowing, grieving. The term "solidarity", however, unless it is simply an antiheroic gesture, transforms an uncontroversial, positive statement into a problematical one, with negative overtones. But the negativity associated with the term *solidarnost'* is undercut by the last word of the poem which rhymes with it: *blagodarnost'*, or "gratitude". In the English, Brodsky appears to be saying that the human suffering entailed, say, by a political revolution distresses him, whereas the revolution itself, or its outcome, simply produces revulsion. This does not mean that he is a reactionary; only that he dislikes being told what to do, certainly by politicians. Still less does he like being told what to think. In spite of this concern, the import being that human history is filled with suffering, he will continue to voice his gratitude for the gift of life until death muzzles him. The Russian is more concise, but the sense is less changed than it at first seems to be: he feels "solidarity" only with sorrow, human suffering, meaning that he does *not* feel solidarity with the Party, or any party for that matter.

There is a tendency in translation to hyperbolize, and clearly Joseph is not immune. As he said: "You may lose, in the case of this or that rhyme, but while you've lost it here, you try to make it up in another line [. . .]" That is, the translation was a continuation of the source text in and into English, as well as being a re-presentation of that text. This had to happen, if the translation was to live, if the poem was to be made new. However, as we have seem, Joseph tries to combine it with a formal literalism.

If form is reproducible – i.e. if the same form has identical or largely identical effects in both source and target languages – then "foreignizing" is not the issue here. It's not at all certain that Joseph saw it as an issue – he'd probably not have put it that way in any case – but in practice (objectively speaking!) he *did* make foreign.

Brodsky into Brodsky

THOUGH, WE should not look for identity of _sound_ in Joseph's translations of his own poetry. We can begin to look for a kind of identity of movement.

Take the opening lines of his translation of "May 24, 1980":

> I have braved, for want of wild beasts, steel cages,
> carved my term and nickname on bunks and rafters,
> lived by the sea, flashed aces in an oasis,
> dined with the-devil-knows-whom, in tails, on truffles . . .

The movement is energetic, the alliteration and assonance crisp. The "d's" and "t's" in line 4, for instance, are aligned accentually as well as symmetrically balancing one another. Actually, the natural stress is not on "devil" but on "whom" [_sic_]; the alliteration, therefore, enhances the secondary or perhaps alternative stress on "devil", drawing one's attention to that word. The pairing of "in tails" and "on truffles" balances the preceding agglomeration ("the-devil-knows-whom") and is semantically as well as rhythmically pleasing. Line 2: "carved my term and nickname on bunks and rafters" is a series of little peaks (_term / name / bunks / rafter_), in contrast to line 3: "lived by the sea, flashed aces in an oasis", which, with its strong caesura, proceeds along a horizontal axis (as distinct from the succeeding line, with its two pauses, after "whom" and "tails"). The variation of semantic units is dynamic: line 1 – a single semantic unit; line 2, four units (actually two pairs); line 3, two; line 4, three, the second and third being paired.

Of course, it is hard for me to dissociate my reading of the poem in English from Joseph's own rendering. He phrased English, as though it were Russian, reciting Auden in this manner, which was very different to the way Auden himself read. At a Columbia University panel discussion in October

1996, Tatyana Tolstaya, the novelist (the other panellists were Susan Sontag, Mark Strand and Derek Walcott) started from the rather commonplace premise that poetry cannot be translated: "I tend to read [the poems translated into English by Joseph himself] in a Russian way, with Russian accentuation, with the accents that find themselves in the same places and coming in the same order as a Russian person speaking English would find . . . You as Americans are not aware of that, it's Russian English." One would be tempted to ask: In that case, what readership did the translator have in mind? Surely not Russians, who could read the poems in the original. Tolstaya then gave a demonstration, trying also to explain the importance, indeed indispensability of rhyme in the Russian tradition. Mark Strand, who admittedly does not know Russian, also took up the question of Joseph's rhymes, about which there have been so many complaints: "they're not really rhymes. Imagine somebody speaking with Brodsky's heavy Russian accent; he never heard those rhymes the way we hear them, so I think his choice to write slant rhymes accommodated the mispronunciation, often. [. . .] Joseph had any number of alternatives before him; he hadn't grown up in the language. His choice, his range of options, was greater than that of a native speaker [. . .]"

Strand concludes: "We usually say someone is translated into English, or into Russian, and it's very unfair, because you don't translate a poet into a language, you translate him into the idiom of the translator [. . .] *The fact is that Brodsky translated Brodsky into Brodsky* [my italics]." Which, I suppose, brings one close to Ted Hughes's ideal, expressed in an editorial to *MPT*: "The very oddity and struggling dumbness of a word for word version is what makes our own imagination jump." Hughes was certainly not envisaging a self-translator with the command and authority of Brodsky. Russian speakers who also have a high regard for Brodsky's Russian poetry are, of course, more inclined to look closely at Brodsky translated into Brodsky, to take it very seriously indeed, although not for the same reasons, perhaps, as well-disposed native English speakers might take it. More than just a self-commentary, the English text represents a reaching across by the author himself from one language and literary tradition to another. The author is enabling the languages themselves to communicate, as well as bringing two parts of his own linguistic self into communion with one another.

But maybe this is a special case? Is his example likely to catch on? Will Joseph's engagement with English have the kind of lasting effect I appear to be trying to convince myself it will? Or will it, rather, be looked upon as an anomaly, an interesting but one off, or perhaps even finally misguided experiment? Who can say? I do believe, though, that his work in English at least suggests new standards for translation of Russian poetry, and perhaps for the translation of poetry in general. Rather than ducking them, he has met seemingly intractable problems head on. It is true that he was in a privileged position, being the author. Still, to do what he did required courage as well as foolhardiness, although it is, I suppose, arguable that he had no alternative than to write "Russian English". His "impatience" comes, I think, from a growing realization that translators have their limitations and that it is both unfair, as well as impractical to lean so heavily on them. He alone is in a position to apply the radical procedures noted above. But reckless it was, because in so doing he laid himself open to criticism, the English he had mastered being so idiosyncratic. It is hardly surprising that he was impatient, having such a full linguistic agenda and so restricted a life expectation. His critics might respond that however understandable his behaviour, these matters cannot be hurried. It takes time to gain control of a language and it also takes a less impulsive nature. Finally, he must be judged by the product itself . . .

Although it is too soon to do that, it's what I have been trying to do!

Tidying Up JB

ON MONDAY and Tuesday of this week I talked to a translation seminar at the Manchester Institute of Science and Technology (UMIST) about Joseph Brodsky's "self-translations". I had dinner with Michael Schmidt[72] on the Monday, after the seminar, and we discussed Craig Raine's review. Joseph's writing in English was not simply an act of hubris, I insisted. Michael, though he probably didn't agree, invited me to contribute an essay on the subject to *PN Review*. I thought that perhaps I would. Am I hoping that this invitation to write will help me to focus, to translate into more accessible, more succinct terms my thoughts about Joseph's English? In my particular circles of writer-friends, there was little enthusiasm for Joseph's English poetry or translations into English of his own poetry. I make a strange advocate, in that I shared these sentiments. He never commented on anything I wrote about him, so perhaps he never even saw it. On the other hand, did he *ever* directly confront his critics? Perhaps, as Craig Raine alleges, he was more unsure of himself than he appeared to be. At the same time, he made no concessions either, although it seems that he did take account of what was said about him. For instance, his tolerance of slant rhymes increased (although that may well have been simply because they became more audible to him) and his translations grew more accentual and less accentual-syllabic. All of this gave him greater room for manoeuvre and helped him to normalize his English syntax, although his eccentric ways had, to some extent, become a habit or fixed style (as Christopher Reid maintained they had).

Mark Strand was quoted as saying that Joseph's rhymes were "not really rhymes", that the slant rhymes "accommodated the mispronunciation". Joseph, he suggested, heard English, as he pronounced it, heavily accented. Due to the stronger stress, unstressed sounds tend to coalesce more in Russian than they do in English, so that what we call slant rhyme is a commoner feature of Russian poetry, especially post-classical poetry. Is it arguable that the increasing exploitation of slant rhyme in Russian poetry parallels the rise of free verse and the actual abandonment of rhyme in English? I dare say Joseph would have disagreed; nevertheless, he *was* more willing to accept slant rhymes. And naturally the more clearly he heard these rhymes, the less insistent they had to be. However ingenious his rhyming, maybe he was also adding another string to his bow: absence of rhyme. True, Joseph's Russian accent, his own renditions, enhanced the sound patterns, but they were in any case becoming more distinct. I would recommend only that when reading him a moderate, generic American accent be adopted, certainly a flatter "a", and a more slurred "r".

It is encouraging that an American poet of Mark Strand's distinction should defend Joseph Brodsky's English poetry *as poetry*. Michael Hofmann does the same, as does Lachlan Mackinnon, in that obituary; Derek Walcott too. Peter Viereck, the eminent American poet, translator and political thinker, who taught with Brodsky at Mount Holyoke College, told me that he felt "Joseph's technically 'incorrect' self-translations . . . give a better, newer understanding of our own language. As if English were a prism suddenly turned to a new angle." Still, by and large, the impact, at least on the English side of the waters, was negative. Joseph did not help matters, although one knows what prompted him to translate his own work. One is tempted to tidy up around him, even if the ethics of this are dubious.

I am bothered by the thought that it might have been possible to render his work less vulnerable to attack by the guardians of law and order, those driven by their outrage into a kind of grammarians' pedantry?

So, back to "the Poem". I have made a line-by-line analysis of it. Below finds me struggling with the first line.

"I, not some wild beast, entered the cage." Or, more literally, "instead of some wild beast . . ." "I, in place of [more literally] some wild beast entered the cage."

My first version seems more able to convey the sense of someone being treated not just like an animal, but like a savage beast, as though he were dangerous. So, why not: "I, not some wild beast, entered / went into the cage"? First, because I am then concentrating again almost exclusively on sense. Even if I am able to keep the basic four-accent line, the metre gets fudged. And second, because how, if the semantic thrust of the Russian is my main concern, can the feminine rhymes be preserved? In Joseph's version of the line, "cage" becomes "cages", which gives him the stress on the penultimate syllable. The Russian line contains more syllables than the English, but the anapaestic or rising movement has been kept, although the English does so in an abbreviated manner: Russian: $uu/ |\ uu/ |\ uu/ |\ uu/ |\ u$; English: $uu/ |\ uuu/ |\ // |\ /u$. I suppose that the anapaest makes the reader less likely to emphasize the first syllable, the word "Ya" (I). "I have braved for want of wild beasts, steel cage" puts the emphases where they should be semantically. The plural "cages" is quite acceptable, since the cage, in this context, is any cell. Why the emotive, hyperbolical "braved", other than because of the alliteration with "beasts" and the need for an accented monosyllabic word at this point, to establish the anapaestic metre? And why the addition of "steel", semantically redundant (the cages *would* have metal, probably steel bars) other than that it echoes "beasts", just as "cages" phonetically recalls "braved"?

If I try to forget the Russian, I am still uneasy. The wild beasts, after all, have no choice in the matter, so does the metaphor hold up? Indeed, had they a choice they would not chose to be locked up in a cage, although it might be argued that once in the cage, they display their customary fortitude. In that case, Joseph's use of the verb "braved" is off, since what he must mean is, "I am being brave": "In the absence of wild beasts to be

brave about their captivity, I am being brave about my captivity."
But that certainly won't do! The difficulty remains unresolved.

So how about: "I am brave, for want of wild beasts, in cages"?
Or if we are talking about bravado rather than bravery, then:
"For want of wild beasts, I pose as brave/brave it out in the
cage." No, he is making a simple comparison, indicating that he
has been shut up in a cage, as though he were some wild beast.
This is the way opponents of the régime, however non-political,
are treated. In other words, they are not treated as human beings.

Already Joseph's own strategies are not looking so far-
fetched! Starting the line with "Instead of a wild beast", which
English syntax might urge, places too much emphasis on "wild
beasts". If we invert, as I did in one of my versions, and begin,
"It was I, not some wild beast", then the "I" receives even more
emphasis than it does when it comes first. The Russian (literally,
"I entered instead of a wild beast the cage") is sayable in a single
breath, rather than breaking down, as does the English, which-
ever way you chose to translate. I am tempted to leave Joseph's
translation as is, or to substitute something very like it. In which
case, better to leave it unchanged. *I have braved, for want of wild
beasts, steel cages.*

What is apparent is that, as I move through the poem, trying to
make as few changes as possible, increasingly I feel the pull of
the original Russian, his first writing of the poem in Russian.
The sense exerts more and more influence over me. And yet,
I can also see that in Joseph's own re-writing of the poem, even
if nuances have been lost, somehow the drama, insofar as the
music embodies it, survives. This I cannot match, as I try to take
my lead from him. The formal mimesis demanded by Joseph
necessitates such changes in the literal meaning of the text as
most translators would be unwilling to make. And his idiolect
cannot be copied. Exclusively for his own use?

Even so, maybe Joseph was led astray by his own renditions
of "May 24, 1980". That is, he heard what he wanted to hear:
the Russian through the English. And so, I suppose, that is how
one should read his versions. What I have been attempting

experimentally to do, is follow him, learn from his literalistic attention to the sound structure. In principle, this should be possible, but the translator cannot be expected to adopt or parody Joseph's idiolect, or deliberately to pronounce (mispronounce) words as Joseph did. The dilemma is obvious.

"May 24, 1980": Into the Lions' Den

Sunday, March 2, 1997

LAST WEDNESDAY, I talked to a translation class at the University of East Anglia (UEA) about Joseph, and then again tried to present "May 24, 1980", reading the Russian, Joseph's version, and excerpts from the critical reviews. I tried also to convey my own thoughts and findings, such as they are, on the relationship between Joseph's Russian and his English. Finally, I read my own revision, in which I had attempted to remove the blemishes and had discovered that they were not so easily removed, since Joseph had worked them into that self-consistent whole Lachlan Mackinnon speaks of in his Brodsky obituary. Eventually, I asked students what they thought of Joseph's self-translation. I expected them to be dismissive, but they were not. It seems that I need not brace myself so much, at least when addressing young people. Evidently, they were not plagued by the kinds of doubts that troubled me, but accepted Joseph's English for what it was, *his* English. Whether my mumble about idiolects predisposed them in his favour, I don't know. I doubt it. For instance, I was pleased with myself for altering "Huns in saddles" to "Huns in the saddle", it being so minimal a change and so clearly an improvement, I thought. But the workshop, on the whole, did not mind "in saddles". "That [life is] long and abhors transparence" didn't bother them either. After all, "nature abhors a vacuum" it was pointed out to me.

In short, the students in the workshop (admittedly accustomed to reading and thinking about translations) were quite open-minded, indeed considerably more so than myself, though it is true that it was not their own translations that were in the line of fire. "Worn the clothes nowadays back in fashion in every quarter", however, *was* felt to be distinctly flabby. One person objected to "waded" the steppes. For me this conveyed the notion of someone making his way through breast-high grass, but it was pointed out that the steppes were not like the American prairies and that the grass was, in fact, short. The Russian word *slonyalsya* means "wandered about aimlessly", "loitered", etc. I had imagined that what he had in mind was an arduous, but directionless progress, by foot, in contrast to the Huns' thunderous gallop through. After a short discussion, it was agreed that "waded" should stay. In general, the Brodsky version went down very well. It was remarked that he used language "in a creative way", that he "brought together two parts of himself" and that this was altogether "fascinating". Indignation was expressed at critics taking it upon themselves to "correct" him. (I hoped that they did not regard me as such an interfering busybody, presumptuous though my experiments must seem.) Anthony Vivis, a well known translator of plays, who teaches at UEA, suggested that another term should be used for what was happening here. It was misleading to call these English versions by Brodsky "translations"; he suggested "trans-energizings".

After this surprisingly affirmative discussion, I was even more reluctant than usual to read my revision of a revision. But the class insisted. To my surprise, it was received with polite interest and even approval, not necessarily as an improvement on Brodsky's version, but as a viable enough alternative. An advantage in talking to translation students is that they are prepared to consider multiple versions of a text and do not assume that there must be one *correct* translation. Also, they tend to be less attached to standard or conventional usage and prepared to take a chance or two. It was felt (I have not always seen it this way) that Joseph's English, whatever else it might or might not be, is energetic. His ear for idiom might occasionally have let him down, but he *heard* what he was writing, was sensitive to movement, balance, the specific gravity of words, etc. "That it's long and abhors transparence" balances "What should I say about life?" phonologically as well as semantically, whereas "It was longer than a day", with or without a question mark, does not. Agreed!

As was noted by Jean Boase-Beier, who directs the MA Translation Programme at UEA, it would be instructive to try out Joseph's translations on a group, without giving the author's name or explaining that these were translations. People would be asked to pay attention to diction, prosody, syntax, rhymes and so forth.[73] Rather along the lines of the trials, I suppose, conducted and described by I. A. Richards in *Practical Criticism*.

Revising *"A Part of Speech"*

IT IS PROBABLY wrong to draw any general conclusions from examination of a single poem, even though that poem has been picked upon by critics and even though my attention was directed to it by the author himself. Since I was responsible for a translation of the sequence "A Part of Speech", the title poem of Joseph's 1980 collection, extensively revised or re-written by him, perhaps I should take a look at that, with an eye both on Joseph's translation, as published in the book, and my version, as published in the magazine *Poetry*. Michael Hofmann, in his *TLS* review, describes Joseph's version of "A Part of Speech" as being "as good as anything produced by the roster of American poets working with him in the rest of the book." He continues: "he always had the final say himself anyway; and while [. . .] it is obvious that 'Exeter Revisited' had to be written in English by the poet, I think one would continually make mistakes elsewhere in any 'blind tasting' of translations." Yes, except that, as noted earlier, "A Part of Speech" was not one of the poems translated by Joseph himself from scratch. He had wanted it to be published under our joint names but, firmly seated on my high horse, I rejected this proposal, insisting that he take full responsibility for it! What would have happened to that translation had I, instead, insisted on collaborating with Joseph? Would I have got my own way from time to time?

I cannot resist continuing to quote Michael Hofmann's elegant review at greater length. He seems to hit the nail on the head again and again:

I think Brodsky was good enough to play by two sets of rules. Even in English, his poems have irresistible verbal authority [. . .] I think he wrote in such a way as to draw on American and Russian at the same

time. There is something binaural or bipolar about the writing, an
uncomplicated and perfectly natural contract with the reader [. . .]
the reader continues to endow it with the status of an original, fully
intended and supervised in every detail.

Hofmann is open-minded enough to give Joseph's English a hearing, even while he does not conceal his bemusement and even bewilderment.

"A Part of Speech." Joseph changed the order of the poems in his own English, and dropped five of them.

In this sequence, as it was more personal or autobiographical than many of his other poems, Joseph particularly wanted to maintain the form – even if he was already moving away from syllabo-tonic towards more accentual verse. My rhymes were intermittent and at best assonantal, with only the occasional full rhyme. Under the circumstances, Joseph felt compelled to rewrite my versions. Occasionally he found a line or two which he liked enough to work around. Otherwise, he either clipped or lengthened, or simply re-did what I had done.

With the second poem of the sequence, our versions are relatively close. Mine:

The north crushes metal but leaves glass intact,
teaches the throat to utter: Let me in!
The cold raised me and placed in my hand
a pen to warm my clenched fist.

Freezing, I see the sun going down
over the sea, and no one about.
Either the heel slips on ice, or the earth itself
arches underneath the foot.

And in my throat, where laughter, or speech,
or hot tea is the norm,
the falling snow rings clear and your "Farewell"
is dark as Scott wrapped in a polar storm.

Joseph's:

The North buckles metal, glass it won't harm;
teaches the throat to say, "Let me in."
I was raised by the cold that, to warm my palm,
gathered my fingers around a pen.

Freezing, I see the red sun that sets
behind oceans, and there is no soul
in sight. Either my heel slips on ice, or the globe itself
arches sharply under my sole.

And in my throat, where a boring tale
or tea, or laughter should be the norm,

snow grows all the louder and "Farewell!"
darkens like Scott wrapped in a polar storm.

With all its imperfections, Joseph's version is patently superior.
It is also truer to the original, except insofar as his determination
to come up with stronger rhymes has led him to permit or intro-
duce enjambments: "sets / behind" "no soul / in sight". On the
other hand, he does confine these to a single stanza, the middle
one, this variation on the form producing a symmetry of its own.
Still, that middle stanza seems to me rather laboured. And the
homophonic rhyme "soul / sole" is dubious. Glancing again at
my translation, only now (!) do I see that I too have an enjambment in that middle stanza. Anyway, he has retained enough of
my wording and word choices for there to be a family resemblance between the two versions.

Another poem, quite often quoted, is number 7 in the Russian.
Joseph understandably promotes it to number 1 in the English.
First, Joseph's version:

I was born and grew up in the Baltic marshland
by zinc-gray breakers that always marched on
in twos. Hence all rhymes, hence that wan flat voice

that ripples between them like hair still moist,
if it ripples at all. Propped on a pallid elbow,
the helix picks out of them no sea rumble
but a clap of canvas, of shutters, of hands, a kettle
on the burner, boiling – lastly, the seagull's metal
cry. What keeps hearts from falseness in this flat region
is that there is nowhere to hide and plenty of room
        for vision.
Only sound needs echo and dreads its lack.
A glance is accustomed to no glance back.

This is a brilliantly close translation, with some intensifiers (e.g. *pallid* elbow; wan *flat* voice; seagull's *metal*/cry). The rhymes are all strong, with only "voice / moist" somewhat less so, particularly since Joseph has had to resort to inversion, "like hair still moist". The "elbow / rumble" rhyme, which is not even assonantal, the Russian pair (*lokot'* [elbow]/*rokot* [rumble or roar]) being almost homonymous, is a good example of Joseph's feel for the shape of words; "rumble" rumblingly echoes "elbow", especially with "but a clap of canvas . . ." following hard on it. Even the improbable enjambment, "metal/cry [full stop]", is purposeful. The exact feminine rhyme ("kettle / mettle") makes the reader pause before "cry". Then there is another pause and a fresh start: "What keeps hearts from falseness . . ." Form and content synchronize. The poem turns on itself, like a helix. The final couplet has been metrically regularized, made less circuitous, more concrete, more "English", even though it is *so* elliptical, as to be somewhat un-English too.

So, perhaps, translation into English gave him an opportunity, motivated or occasionally encouraged him pragmatically to revise the original, although the *actual* original remains unrevised. I dare say that, at a deeper level, the changes occasioned by or during translation did not trouble him, since the original did remain and was not itself changed by the process, unless he himself decided to change it; he seemed not much to mind what appeared in magazines, so long as he had control of the books, the books representing his serious experiments in English self-presentation, and in some sense a homage to his English masters, from Donne to Auden. It would not be surprising if in the translations, or in the translating, he became aware of certain blemishes and attempted to correct these in the English. My supposition is that he saw these as problems of English, not of the Russian; the onus here was on English to measure up to Russian. My contention has been that Joseph was trying to resolve or reconcile something larger than the differences between individual poems in Russian and English translation: namely, the incompatibilities of English and Russian syntax, prosody as such. But there must have been a limit even to his powers of compromise. As his English drew closer to the native norm, so his translations into it also moved towards a norm, but bringing along or incorporating certain discoveries that he had made along the way. So, in those last two lines ("It is only for sound that space is always an obstacle: the eye does not complain of the lack of an echo") space is an obstacle only to sound, but the eye does not complain about the lack of sound. Here the poet seems, among other things, to be exalting silence, and the vision generated by silence. Joseph's English version, in its concentration, its introspectiveness, conveys a more metaphysical sense of the desolate, the isolated; at the same time, the pairing of "glance . . . no glance" startles us with its idiom-defying concreteness.

By way of anti-climax, then, here is my version!

I was born and grew up in the Baltic marshes, by the edge of
zinc-grey breakers, always coursing in twosome up the
 ledge of
the shore, and from here all rhymes derive, that wan voice
 as well,
winding between them, if it does at all,
like moist hair. Propped on a crooked elbow,
the helix will unwind from them not a rumble only,
but the clap of canvas, of shutters, of hands, a kettle
boiling on the oil-stove, at most – the cries of seagulls.

In these flat lands, what keeps the heart
from falseness is there's nowhere to hide, you stand out,
and it's only sound space puts a check on:
the eye does not regret the lack of an echo.

We start off similarly (or he alters little in my first line?) but then
diverge, with only the occasional word choice recalling my earlier
version. A characteristic weakness is my willingness to grasp at
almost anything construable as rhyme, even if it amounts only to
a consonant ("heart / stand out"). As a result, I am led into
meaningless or misleading enjambments: "what keeps the heart /
from falseness . . ." Joseph's is a tighter, more energetic, more
dramatic piece of writing. My translation is looser, with considerably less *chiaroscuro*. If I was prepared to ignore or modify the
beat, encouraged by the more accentual nature of this sequence,
and also to exploit chance assonances, I was not prepared or able
to grasp the poem in both hands, as it were, and re-shape it.
While Joseph takes charge from the start, I more or less allow it
to shape *itself*. Occasionally I get lucky, in which case, Joseph
tries to retain what I've chanced upon . . .

New Versions for Old

SHOULD I continue? It seems, after all, that contrary to what I thought when Joseph sprung it on me, his "revision" of my translation of "A Part of Speech" is actually a new version. I am the last person to read it without prejudice, since I can hear echoes of my own words and phrases, and as indicated, occasionally fragments of my version do survive. It was generous of him to offer to let the poem go out under my name, but I was surely right not to accept. My motives were no doubt mixed: I did not want to get credit for something I had not done, but neither did I want to take the rap for Joseph's un-English English. Having for so long regarded myself as the injured party, I am reluctant to face the possibility that Joseph simply took my much deliberated translation and used it more or less as raw material, as he might have used a far less polished version, or even a plain crib. That he seemed not to distinguish between cribs, or working drafts, and actual versions was, of course, disconcerting.

I am looking at number 10. Joseph's version is almost entirely different from mine, not just lexically, but in the concreteness of its imagery. This surprises me. After all, I'm the Englishman; it's I who am supposed to be the pragmatist! It seems he'd learnt his English lesson well. Maybe, when he commended "A Part of Speech" to me and proposed that I translate it, this was because he suspected that it would lend itself to the kind of treatment, in English, that he (far more than I) had now given it. Perhaps – this is sheer speculation – my versions disappointed him, because I had not risen to the occasion, helping these already quite "English" poems further into English. Instead, like a "faithful translator", I had clung to the original, doing the best I could with the rhymes, without distorting the literal sense.

Listen to Joseph's condensed, energized English, as the items are listed . . . (As Michael Hofmann wrote: "the poems are basically sums, great lists of like or unlike items – the apples and pears of arithmetic – converted to their particular emotional-ontological valency.")

> Near the ocean, by candlelight. Scattered farms,
> fields overrun with sorrel, lucerne, and clover.
> Towards nightfall, the body, like Shiva, grows extra arms
> reaching out yearningly to a lover.
> A mouse rustles through grass. An owl drops down.
> Suddenly creaking rafters expand a second.
> One sleeps more soundly in a wooden town,
> since you dream these days only of things that happened.
> There's a smell of fresh fish. An armchair's profile
> is glued to the wall. The gauze is too limp to bulk at
> the slightest breeze. And a ray of the moon, meanwhile,
> draws up the tide like a slipping blanket.

I doubt whether any reader, accustomed to the ellipses of modern poetry – not to mention of American as against British English – would conclude that this was a translation, or would find it particularly "foreign". Joseph's version follows the original wording as closely as mine, and he has even managed to repeat the alternating masculine and feminine rhymes.

How much more abstract, almost romantic is my version:

> "Near the ocean",[74] by candlelight, all around –
> a field, lush with clover, sorrel and alfalfa.
> In the evening, like Siva, the body grows arms
> that yearn to reach out and touch the beloved.
> An owl drops into the grass, onto a mouse,
> and rafters creak for no reason,
> in a wooden city you sleep more sound,
> because these days dreams contain only what has happened.
> There's a smell of fresh fish. The silhouette
> of a chair is sticking to the wall.

> Limp gauze stirs in the window, and in the bay the moon's
> beam
> pulls up the tide, like a blanket that has slipped.

I note that I, too, made an effort to alternate masculine and feminine line endings, although it broke down completely in the last four lines. I am embarrassed to find that I was prepared to write "sleep more sound [rather than soundly]", for the sake of the unsatisfactory assonantal rhyme with "mouse" (this is surely more egregious than Joseph's rather American informality, "since you dream these days only of *things that happened*", instead of "that have happened").

I said that Joseph remains semantically close, but actually he takes the usual, or more than the usual interpretive liberties. Thus, "scattered farms" is added; a mouse "rustles through grass", whereas in the original, the owl simply drops onto the mouse. In a more explanatory mode, at the risk, perhaps, of sounding somewhat pedantic, he rewords the penultimate image: the gauze is too limp to fill out (bulk) at the breeze coming through the window, whereas in the original, more is left to the imagination, the fine gauze stirring limply in the window. The last line, on the other hand, is a good example of the objectifying tendency observable in this version: "slipping blanket" rather than my "a blanket that has slipped".

I have not spoken of the sound structure of Joseph's version, as compared with the original, or with my very different version. His version is firmer, more businesslike, more confident – meaning also *linguistically* confident. It is brisk, as befits a catalogue, whereas mine is almost dreamy, sentimental or romantic. The tone is wrong. Compare, for instance: "a field, lush with clover" to "fields overrun [it *is* overrun / overgrown, *not* lush!] with sorrel"; "arms that yearn to reach out and touch the beloved" to "arms reaching out yearningly to a lover"; and "An armchair's profile is glued to the wall" to "The silhouette of a chair is sticking to the wall".

Leftover Comments on "May 24, 1980"

Sunday, 9 March, 1997

ON FRIDAY, I talked to a group at University College, London about Joseph, in particular "May 24, 1980". There were some interesting comments. For instance, Alex Stillmark, a Heine scholar, observed about the famous or infamous line, "twice drowned, thrice let knives . . .", that it at once reminded him of the well-known song, which he had learnt in the joint services school: *Zhil odnazhdy kapitan / On ob'ezdil mnogo stran / Raz pyatnadtsat' on tonyl / Pogibal sredi akul*, ending: *I ne razu dazhe glazom ne morgnul.* (There once lived a captain / He travelled to many countries / Fifteen times he drowned / And he perished among sharks . . . And not once did he even bat an eyelid.) The hero is a kind of Baron Munchausen character. Dr Stillmark also caught echoes of late Heine in the poem, particularly in the last lines about the mouth being crammed with clay. On the other hand, the Akhmatova of "Poem Without a Hero", I am assured, is probably more in evidence here than Heine. Remember that it is "the devil-knows-whom, in tails . . ." In her "Prose About the Poem"[75] Akhmatova notes: "Most of all I will be asked who the 'Prince of Darkness' is . . . ; he is, very simply, the devil. He is also in 'Tails': 'That most elegant Satan.'" I find the "captain" reference persuasive, since it is in keeping with the mock-heroic *tone* of this poem. One need hardly continue to puzzle over the change from thrice to twice drowned, etc. This too is quite Munchausenish. Or maybe, as suggested above, it didn't really matter how many times you drowned, since once was usually enough.

But was Joseph also intimating that he had indeed drowned, or rather died, since being anaesthetized, going *under*, was also a kind of dying, and had been reborn twice (two operations), unstitched three times (actually, it would be twice, since the first time they would have had to *make* an actual incision rather than unpick it). The English version, assuming no knowledge on the reader's part of these details of Joseph's medical history, lends itself more easily to an interpretation, an explanation . . . I can distinctly hear Joseph chortling! It is just as likely, is it not, that he actually did nearly drown several times? After all he started smoking again as soon as he possibly could. That, despite his efforts, he did not take the best care of himself is putting it mildly.

After my lecture, a man came up to assure me that the more he thought about "let knives rake my nitty-gritty" the more he liked "nitty-gritty". After all, that's what it means, he said: "The heart of things." In my talk at UEA I had mentioned that when I looked up "nitty-gritty" in my *Random House Dictionary*, one of the definitions I had found was: "heart of the matter". The reason I hadn't repeated this in my UCL talk was that it hadn't gone down too well at UEA. Chicken! But students, both at UEA and at UCL, found it much easier to come to terms with Joseph's English than I, its would-be defender.

Against Formal Translation

Wednesday, 26 March, 1997

INTERESTINGLY I keep coming across more or less authoritative, or at least self-assured comments on formal mimesis, and how inappropriate it generally is: e.g. an essay by Harry Levin, "The War of Words in English Poetry" (*Contexts of Criticism*, Harvard, 1957). I found the reference to Levin in a book by Vilas Sarang, *The Stylistics of Literary Translation: A Study with Reference to English and Marathi*, which the author gave me when I visited him in Bombay. When I finally started turning its pages, some years later, I discovered that it was a most lucid work. It is peculiarly relevant in the present context. About the English-Marathi poet Arun Kolatkar (with whom, incidentally, I spent two enjoyable days bumbling around Bombay) Professor Sarang writes:

Modern translation practice generally seems to disregard rhyme, and probably wisely so, for rhyme can force the translator into making distortions of sense or syntax. A self-translator, however, may use his special position to exploit rhyme to good effect, as Arun Kolatkar does in some of his self-translated poems. What is interesting is that Kolatkar has achieved more subtle and sophisticated rhyme arrangements in the English versions than in the original Marathi. [. . .] In Marathi off-rhymes do not seem to work well: they have never been deliberately and systematically attempted by poets as they have been in English. On the other hand, multisyllabic rhyme can be effectively made in Marathi, whereas in English it could only suit comic verse [. . .]

So, Sarang claims that the use of slant-rhymes or off-rhymes in the English translation produces a more subtle effect that the straightforward Marathi rhymes. Off-rhymes "do not seem to work well" in Marathi, whereas they do in English (as in Russian) poetry. Multisyllabic rhymes, on the other hand, do work in Marathi, whereas in English their use is generally limited to comic verse. With the Kolatkar poems, the off-rhyme in English suits the content rather *better* than the straight rhymes in Marathi: a translational gain. But apart from that, Sarang concedes that it is inadvisable to imitate rhyme in English translation.

One difficulty, of course, is that rhyming in English can become monotonous, whereas slant-rhyming expands the semantic and acoustic opportunities. So, here is Harry Levin on the monosyllabic nature of English:

This preponderance [of monosyllabic words]*, by putting a limitation on the number of rhymes most available, has specifically increased the problems of writing poetry in English. Its positive lesson, for poetic technique, has been to encourage the development of unrhymed or blank verse. Negatively, the "sure returns of still expected rhymes" have made such banalities as breeze and trees hard to avoid, and therefore to be avoided by all serious poets. With the exhaustion of obvious combinations, the search for others leads farther and farther afield, culminating perhaps in the farthest-fetched periphrastics of Ogden Nash. Rhyme itself, we must stop to remember, was an importation in England; and doggerel – the desperate endeavour to rhyme, if need be, at the expense of every other consideration – has been a periodic symptom of the need for readjustment.*

Exploring the reasons for this situation, he continues:

During Skelton's time, around 1500, the phonetic transition to modern English took place; and its decisive consequence for prosody was the disappearance of the final e. This reinforced the iambic impetus of the language which has favoured the end-beat more and more [. . .] Another reason for the dearth of unaccented terminal syllables is that English has fewer suffixes than the more inflected languages; nor has it that inclination toward diminutives which helps to make Italian or Russian so fertile in rhyme. Hence it cannot afford to alternate masculine and feminine endings, as continental poetry so

consistently does. Not only is it deficient in rhymes, but any attempt
at a <u>rhyme of two or more syllables has a weakening, a relaxing, or</u>
<u>else an explicitly facetious effect</u>. [. . .] Notice too how the condensa-
tion of the English language forces [the translator] *to insert extraneous*
<u>matter,</u> if he is working line by line, in order to <u>compensate for the</u>
<u>surplus of syllables</u> [in the source <u>text</u>]. *In view of these difficulties*
[. . .] it was quite natural for English and American poets to practice
free verse [. . .] Meanwhile Anglo-American poets have been reviving
the strictest of the old forms; but they have eased their task and
enlarged their verbal repertory by utilizing off-beat stress and allow-
ing assonance to serve for rhyme.

But I now find this persuasively eloquent statement somewhat
limited, even dogmatic: "and therefore to be avoided by all serious poets"; "cannot afford to alternate masculine and feminine
endings". In any case, isn't the argument undercut, if not
contradicted, by the last comment on the revival of strict form;
Levin seems to miss the implications here. So, perhaps, it is a
matter of degree, or rather of that and what the language and
language users can tolerate at any particular time. Kolatkar may
use slant-rhymes in his self-translations, but he is, in any case,
a bilingual writer (he won the Commonwealth Poetry Prize for
a collection of poems written in English). Joseph's English,
accomplished as it was, was not that of a native or bilingual
speaker. A Russian woman to whom I showed Joseph's translation of "May 24, 1980" – admittedly, she was not particularly
interested in poetry! – commented that <u>his English</u> was at once
<u>identifiable as "Russian English"</u>. That is too dismissive, but
whether it be "Russian English" or not, it is perhaps less of an
authenticated "English" than is Kolatkar's, given the long
history of English on the subcontinent.

I am setting off for Israel in an hour. A very troubled Israel. But I'm not going to be allowed to forget about Brodsky! Richard McKane[76] just phoned and mentioned that he had bought *So Forth*. He wonders just how English the cadences are. My rather facetious response was that the cadences were "Joseph", rather than "English". He half agreed. As he reads it, he said, he can hear Joseph. But what will it be like in twenty years? I observed that the self-translations will be of interest, as long as the originals are, since they are commentaries on the latter by their author. It is rare – though it may become less so – for authors to write their poems twice, that is to produce two reciprocal, "definitive" versions.

Last But Not Least

Saturday / Sunday, 17 and 18 May, 1997

THERE IS A curious interview with Joseph by Michael Scammell in *Index on Censorship*,[77] which had been established shortly before this, on the initiative of Stephen Spender among others, as the organ of the Writers & Scholars International, the aims of which were "to promote the study of the suppression of freedom of expression". Again, it is surprising to find Joseph so insistent, this early in his life in the West, on his right to be judged solely as a writer, a poet, and not categorized as a dissident or a victim of oppression. He sensed the direction of the interview almost from the start, answering some factual questions briefly, but as soon as Scammell, innocuously enough, begins to lead: "When did it become clear to you that your poems were not going to be published generally in the Soviet Union and what was the effect of this realization upon you?" Joseph shoots back: "I must say that it was never really clear to me. I always thought that they would be published one day and so this idea has had no effect on me at all [. . .]"

And more of the like follows. Joseph answers non-committally whenever he can, but as soon as the questioner begins to probe, he reacts. "Why do you think they sent you to prison?" "I don't really know. In any case that seems to me, if you don't mind my saying so, a typically western approach to the problem; every event has to have a cause and every phenomenon has to have something standing behind it. It is very complex. Sometimes there is a cause, perhaps. But as to why they put me in prison, all I can do is repeat to you the items in the indictment. My own answer perhaps won't satisfy you, but it is very simple. A man who sets out to create his own independent world within himself is bound sooner or later to become a foreign body in society and then he becomes subject to all the physical laws of pressure, compression and extrusion." Joseph refuses, time after time, to don the mantle of the tragic exile, the martyr, the victim. "How did trial and prison affect your work?" "You know, I think it was even good for me, because the two years I spent in the country were from my point of view one of the best times of my life. I did more work then than at any other time. During the day I had to do physical work, but since it was agricultural labour, it wasn't like in a factory and there were lots of period of rest when we had nothing to do."

Scammell, perhaps growing a little exasperated with all this, finally says: "What is your attitude to people who take a stand and why have you personally never done so yourself?" Joseph, rejecting both mantle of freedom-fighter and that of feeble aesthete (despite the remarks about boredom), responds rather defiantly, provocatively, and perhaps equally exasperatedly: "It is all very simple, really. The point is that the person who seriously devotes himself to some sort of work – and in my case *belles lettres* – has in any case plenty of problems and difficulties that arise from the work itself, for instance doubts, fears and worries, and this in itself taxes the brain pretty powerfully. And then again I must say that any kind of civic activity simply bores me to death. While the brain is thinking in political terms and thinks of itself as getting somewhere, it is all very interesting, attractive and exciting, and everything seems fine. But when these thoughts reach their logical conclusion, that is when they result in some sort of action, then they give rise to a terrible sense of disillusionment, and then the whole thing is boring."

He develops this: "I think that for the writer who first of all concerns himself with his own work, the deeper he plunges into it, the greater will be the consequences – literary, aesthetic and of course political as well." Joseph is unconvinced of the effectiveness of efforts in the West to help "unorthodox" Russian writers, casting doubt even on the publication of such writers in the West: "[. . .] All you can do is to help people get published. But I am not sure how helpful this is. I suppose it gives one a pleasant sensation, a sense of not being without hope: up or down, you still exist and you still haven't perished. It gives a certain psychological relief to a man living in rather uncomfortable circumstances. But here again you get all sorts of problems arising, because all forms of comfort are in a way a sort of escapism." This is interestingly reminiscent of remarks made by concentration-camp prisoners about the possibly deadly effect of hope. It also sheds a little light on Brodsky's natural stoicism, the need to live with reality and not with pipe dreams. Scammell pointedly suggests that the publication of Brodsky's poetry might have helped him maintain his position of independence, influenced his writing. He denies all this: "Maybe it did help in some way, but I must confess that I doubt it very much. You see, I am not representative in any way, I cannot stand for anything or anybody except myself."

So, Joseph establishes the parameters, right from the start. He refuses to play. He was an individual in the Soviet Union and he's damned if he's going to give up being one now that he is in the West. It seems that he knew exactly what he wanted. This was, to say the least, a different kind of exile. An exile rather ahead of his time, almost post-Soviet. He frequently puzzled those awaiting him with friendly intentions. In some cases, Joseph seems too dismissive of liberal opinion. But he is self-consistent. Paradoxically enough, his rejection of the part of hero was itself heroic. He covered all the bases. The media which was not to be deterred by his ironical comments continued to describe him as a victim of the totalitarian state, while those who knew him better began to develop a more nuanced understanding of the East-West dichotomy. His belief in art, his elevation of it (and language) over politics, was distinctly sinewy and non-escapist.

Postface

WHEN I BEGAN this writing almost a year and a half ago, I intended . . .

Well, I intended *nothing*. Rather, I was dealing, as best I could, with a persistent grief. And that led me to revisit our various times together. And that, in its turn, led me back to his writing, or one might say led me to it for the first time, because – as he put it: "all that is left of a man is a part of speech." I tried to separate the strands of our understandings and misunderstandings. The journal became as much a self-interrogation as an interrogation of our friendship. I found myself moving, quite confusingly, between private and public, between affinities, issues of friendship, and problems of translation. Of course, the journal is also about translation. It is a confession, too, although I have tried to limit that aspect of it, and not only because I know how much Joseph disliked confessionalism.

While writing, I have talked to others. I have been made aware of many different points of view, which not surprisingly are often conflicting. From these I have taken what seemed to illuminate my own perceptions and ignored, or left for others to explore or not explore, those which it seemed impertinent to work with. It has not been hard for me to steer clear of his "private life", since I was hardly privy to it. Quite a few of my remarks are speculative. But I have tried, in general, not to overindulge myself in what at worst is simply fiction-making.

As I looked at one or two of Joseph's translations and, again, at many of his Russian poems, I was once more brought up against my ignorance, my over-dependency on intuition, my inability to pick up allusions. I also became aware – as I hardly was before – of the scale of the Russian tragedy, the truly heroic grandeur of the life, say, of Akhmatova. And Brodsky.

I have been listening to Purcell's *Dido and Aeneas*. And were I not convinced that it would come across as sentimental, I would re-name this manuscript "Remember Me". Dido cries: "Remember me, but ah! forget my fate!" In a letter to Brodsky (probably 10 July 1965; for an English translation, see Anna Akhmatova, *My Half Century, Selected Prose*, 1992) Akhmatova writes: "I'm at the hut. The well creaks, the ravens caw. I'm listening to the Purcell (*Dido and Aeneas*) that was brought on your recommen-dation. It is so powerful that it's impossible to talk about it." In an earlier letter (20 October 1964) she had written: "Promise me one thing – that you will stay perfectly healthy, there's nothing on earth worse than hot-water bottles, shots, and high blood pressure – and the worse thing is that it's irreversible. And if you are healthy, golden paths, happiness, and that divine communion with nature, which so captivates all those who read your poetry, may await you." Alas, he was unable to heed her advice, but the reciprocal nature of their relationship, in spite of the age difference, is evident. One understands, he observed, walking beside Akhmatova, why Russia was sometimes ruled by empresses. But he did walk beside her.

NOTES

1   Charles Osborne, *The Life of a Poet*, London, 1980, p. 325.

2   Yefim Etkind, *Protsess Iosifa Brodskogo*, London, Overseas Publ., 1983, p. 61.

3   *Iosif Brodskii, Bol'shaya kniga intervyu* [Joseph Brodsky, The Big Book of Interviews], ed. V. Polukhina, Zakharov, Moscow, 2000, p. 48.

4   Roger Garfitt, "Near and Far East", *London Magazine*, June–July 1974, pp. 104–6.

5   Stephen Spender, "Bread of Affliction", *New Statesman*, 14 December 1973.

6   *Iosif Brodskii, Bol'shaya kniga intervyu*, note 32, pp. 44–50.

7   See Volume II of *Sochineniya Iosifa Brodskogo*, St. Petersburg, 1992.

8   *Watermark*, pp. 102–3.

9   This volume eventually appeared, in a somewhat expanded form, over twenty years after Max Hayward and I began work on it and thirteen years after Max's death, as *20th Century Russian Poetry: Silver and Steel*, edited by Albert C. Todd and Max Hayward (with Daniel Weissbort), New York, Doubleday, 1993.

10 See V. Polukhina's interview with Derek Walcott in her book *Joseph Brodsky Through the Eyes of his Contemporaries*, Macmillan, 1992, p. 316.

11 Yves Bonnefoy, "On the Translation of Form in Poetry", *World Literature Today*, 52–53 (Summer 1979), pp. 374–9.

12 Joseph Brodsky, "Beyond Consolation", *New York Review of Books*, 7 February 1974, pp. 13–16.

13 Lachlan Mackinnon, "Joseph Brodsky", *The Independent*, 30 January 1996, p. 12.

14 Michael Hofmann, "On Absenting Oneself", *Times Literary Supplement*, 10 January 1997, pp. 6–8.

15 Charles Simic, "Working for the Dictionary", *New York Review of Books*, 19 October 2000, pp. 9-12.

16 George Steiner, "Poetry from the Shadow-Zone", *The Sunday Times*, 11 September 1988.

17 Michael Schmidt, "Time of Cold", *New Statesman*, 17 October 1980.

18 Vladimir Nabokov, "Problems of Translating 'Onegin' in English", *Partisan Review*, 22 (1955), pp. 496–512.

19   *The Iowa Review*, Vol. 9 No. 4, Fall 1978.

20   Yefim Etkind, *Zapiski nezagovorshchika*, 1977, pp. 146–7. *Notes of a Non-Conspirator*, London, 1978.

21   Ian Hamilton, "A Russian in Venice", *The Sunday Telegraph*, 21 June 1992, p. viii.

22   See the rather odd interview, entitled "Esthetics is the Mother of Ethics", which is to be found in *Periplus: Poetry in Translation*, eds. Daniel Weissbort and Arvind Krishna Mehrotra, Oxford University Press, New Delhi, 1993.

23   V. Polukhina, *Joseph Brodsky Through the Eyes of his Contemporaries*, London, 1992, p. 306.

24   V. Polukhina, *Joseph Brodsky Through the Eyes of his Contemporaries*, London, 1992, p. 315.

25   Osip Mandelstam, *The Complete Critical Prose and Letters*, 1979, pp. 397–442.

26   Joseph Brodsky, *Less than One*, London, 1986, p. 150.

27   Christopher Reid, "Great American Disaster", *London Review of Books*, 8 December 1988, pp. 17–18.

28   Peter Porter, "Satire with a Heart", *The Observer*, 14 December 1980, p. 28.

29   Donald Davie, "The Saturated Line", *Times Literary Supplement*, 23–29 December 1988, p. 1415.

30   It's a relief to find I'm not on my own. I recently came across a remark by Seamus Heaney (in an interview with Valentina Polukhina, 1 February, 1997): "My feeling is that in English, a poet like Gerard Manley Hopkins is close to the kind of phonetic and intellectual combination I imagine happens in Mandelstam and, I think, perhaps in Brodsky." See *Iosif Brodskii, trudy i dni* [Joseph Brodsky, Works and Days], eds. L. Loseff and P. Vail, Moscow, *Nezavisimaya gazeta*, 1998, p. 264.

31   But see *Joseph Brodsky: The Art of a Poem*, eds. L. Loseff and V. Polukhina, London 1999, pp. 68– 91: V. Polukhina's essay on this poem, which explores its complexity from many angles.

32   See Russian version of this interview in V. Polukhina's collection of Brodsky's interviews, *Iosif Brodskii, Bol'shaya kniga intervyu*, Moscow, 2000, pp. 109–121.

33   See V. Polukhina's interview with N. Gorbanevskaya and L. Loseff, in *Joseph Brodsky Through the Eyes of his Contemporaries*, London, 1992, p. 79 and p. 121.

34   *Watermark*, p. 5.

35   For more on Brodsky's own interpretation of the poem, see the interview with George Kline in V. Polukhina's collection, *Iosif Brodskii, Bol'shaya kniga intervyu*, Moscow, 2000, pp. 13–16.

36 In Russia, a poet's fortieth birthday has something momentous about it, Pushkin having died at 37. Mandelstam of course did live to 45. But 40 plus was not doing too badly!

37 *Modern Poetry in Translation* is a journal, founded by Ted Hughes and myself in 1965, and co-edited by us for 10 issues. It continued after this and, indeed, still exists. It was edited by myself until 2003, and is now edited by David Constantine.

38 Joseph Brodsky, "Beyond Consolation", *New York Review of Books*, Vol. 21 No. 1, 7 February 1974, pp. 13–16.

39 Paul Engle, American (Iowan) poet, teacher, father of the first Writers Workshop (at the University of Iowa), with his wife Hualing Nieh founder of the International Writing Program (at Iowa), inventor of the Translation Workshop, also the first of its kind. It was Paul Engle who invited me to Iowa in 1972.

40 *Modern Poetry in Translation: 1980*, interview with Stanley Kunitz.

41 Rosette C. Lamont, "Joseph Brodsky: A Poet's Classroom", *The Massachusetts Review*, Vol. XV No. 4, pp. 553–577, Autumn 1974.

42 Interview with N. Gorbanevskaya, *Iosif Brodskii, Bol'shaya kniga inter-vyu*, Moscow, 2000, pp 230–237.

43 *Ibid.*, p. 195.

44 *Post-War Polish Poetry: An Anthology*, edited by Czeslaw Milosz (3rd edition), 1983.

45 "D.H. Lawrence" in *The Dyer's Hand and Other Essays*, by W.H. Auden, 1968, p. 287.

46 Joseph Brodsky, "Beyond Consolation", *New York Review of Books*, Vol. 21 No. 1, 7 February 1974, pp. 13–16.

47 Christopher Reid, "Great American Disaster", *London Review of Books*, 8 December 1988, pp. 17–18.

48 To describe Auden as "the greatest mind of the twentieth century" has always seemed to me a bit odd. Gratitude, one imagines, is partly responsible. I am reminded of the late Peter Levi's response to a question put to him in a questionnaire sent to a number of writers by Valentina Polukhina: "Why was Auden so appealing to Brodsky?" "He liked Auden's sophistication, his metrical mastery and his minor Atlantic Goethe persona."

49 The poem had appeared in the *Times Literary Supplement*, 9 February 1996.

50 See G.S. Smith on Brodsky's versification. Prof. Smith has written exhaustively on this subject: e.g. *SEER*, Vol. 80. No. 3, 2002; *Modern Language Review*, 97, 3 (2002).

51 George Steiner described Brodsky as the most "Latinate" of poets. Joseph was indeed obsessed with the Classical world, especially Rome. His English, too, tended to the polysyllabic Latin rather than the

monosyllabic Anglo-Saxon. So, perhaps the distance between Russian and English also encouraged his Classicistic leanings?

52 Joseph Brodsky, *So Forth*, New York, 1996, p. 10.

53 There is a book by David MacFadyen, which I have not read, titled *Joseph Brodsky and the Baroque*, 1998.

54 *Modern Poetry in Translation*, new series No. 10, Winter 1996.

55 "Uncommon Visage" in Joseph Brodsky, *On Grief and Reason*, 1995, pp. 44–58.

56 *An Age Ago: A Selection of Nineteenth-Century Russian Poetry*, selected and translated by Alan Myers, with a foreword and biographical notes by Joseph Brodsky, Penguin, 1989. And see "An Age Ago: The Maturing Ego", *PN Review*, September–October 1990, pp. 48–54.

57 Emery George, ed., *Contemporary East European Poetry*, 1977. The hardback edition of the anthology edited by myself, *The Poetry of Survival: Post-War Poets of Central and Eastern Europe*, did not appear until 1991, although it was completed by the time of *perestroika*, in 1989.

58 *Pasternak on Art and Creativity*, ed. Angela Livingstone, CUP, 1985.

59 *Attbehaga en Skugga* [To Please a Shadow], Stockholm, 1988, pp. 439–452, unpublished translation by Tatiana Schenk.

60 "Notes on Translation", *Pasternak on Art and Creativity*, edited by Angela Livingstone, 1985, pp. 187–191.

61 T. Tolstaya, "On Joseph Brodsky (1940–1996)", *New York Review of Books*, 29 February 1996.

62 It is worth pointing out that something similar (alluded to above) was compiled in Russia, edited by L. Loseff and P. Vail: *Iosif Brodskii, trudy i dni* [Joseph Brodsky, Works and Days], Moscow, 1998.

63 Derek Walcott, "Magic Industry", *New York Review of Books*, 24 November 1988, pp. 35–39.

64 But see Solomon Volkov, *Conversations with Joseph Brodsky*, New York, 1998.

65 OBERIU, short for "Obshchestvo Real'novo Iskusstva" [Society of Real Art], an important post-Revolution literary grouping to which Zabolotsky belonged for a while.

66 Valentina Polukhina, "Brodsky's Views on Translation", *Modern Poetry in Translation*, new series No. 10, Winter 1996, pp. 26–31. She is quoting D. M. Thomas, "Interview with Brodsky", *Quarto*, December 1981, p. 11.

67 *Ibid*. Here Valentina Polukhina is quoting from Tom Vitale, "A Conversation with Joseph Brodsky", *Ontario Review*, 23, 1985–6, p. 9.

68 Craig Raine, "A reputation subject to inflation", *Financial Times*, 16–17 November 1996, p. xix.

69 Michael Hofmann, "On Absenting Oneself", *Times Literary Supplement*, 10 January 1997, pp. 6-9.

70 Son of the publisher George Braziller and publisher of Persea Books, with which for a while I edited a poetry translation series.

71 I have written a piece on Brodsky's analysis of some poems of Hardy (see his long essay, "Wooing the Inanimate", in *On Grief and Reason*) in which I attempt to show how inward he could be with these English poems ("Staying Afloat: Thomas Hardy and Joseph Brodsky", in *Russian Literature*, Vol. XLVI Nos. III–IV, 1 April–15 May 2000, pp. 251–260, Special Issue: Brodsky as a Critic, guest editor Valentina Polukhina).

72 Poet, critic, translator, teacher, founder-director of the Carcanet Press, editor of *PN Review*.

73 V. Polukhina has discussed "May 24, 1980" from every conceivable point of view, except that of Brodsky's English. See her and L. Loseff's collection *Joseph Brodsky: The Art of a Poem*, London, 1999, pp. 68–91.

74 I thought the reference might be to the Robert Lowell collection, and so put it in quotation marks.

75 Anna Akhmatova, *My Half Century: Selected Prose*, edited by Ronald Meyer, 1992.

76 Prolific translator of Russian (and Turkish) poetry, including Akhmatova, Gumilyov, Hikmet and Mandelstam.

77 This appeared in *Index on Censorship*, Vol. I Nos. 3–4, autumn–winter 1972, at the time of the London Poetry International.

ACKNOWLEDGEMENTS

Extracts from the work of Joseph Brodsky are reprinted by permission of Farrar, Straus and Giroux, LLC:

Collected Poems in English by Joseph Brodsky. Copyright © 2000 by the Estate of Joseph Brodsky. Also by permission of Carcanet Press Ltd, Manchester.
Joseph Brodsky: Selected Poems by Joseph Brodsky. English translation Copyright © 1973 by George L. Kline.
Watermark by Joseph Brodsky. Copyright © 1992 by Joseph Brodsky.

The following poems are reproduced in whole or in part in Daniel Weissbort's own translations: "May 24, 1980", "On Love" and "A Part of Speech." These translations are made for the critical purposes of this book and are not for reproduction without the permission of the Estate of Joseph Brodsky and Farrar, Straus and Giroux, LLC. Readers are referred to the *Collected Poems in English* by Joseph Brodsky for authorized translations of most of these poems. "The Jewish Cemetery in Leningrad" was not published by Brodsky in his lifetime.

For permission to quote other copyright material we thank the authors and publishers as listed in the Notes. We would be glad to rectify any oversights in a future edition.

INDEX